Cooperative Learning
in Context

SUNY series, The Social Context of Education
Christine E. Sleeter, Editor

Cooperative Learning in Context

An Educational Innovation in Everyday Classrooms

Evelyn Jacob

State University of New York Press

Published by
State University of New York Press, Albany

© 1999 State University of New York

Portions of text from chapter six are reprinted from "Cooperative Learning:
Context and Opportunities for Acquiring Academic English," from *TESOL
Quarterly*, *30(2)*. Reprinted by permission from the publisher.

For information, address State University of New York Press,
State University Plaza, Albany, N.Y., 12246

Production by Diane Ganeles
Marketing by Patrick Durocher

Library of Congress Cataloging-in-Publication Data
Jacob, Evelyn.
    Cooperative learning in context : an educational innovation in
everyday classrooms / Evelyn Jacob.
        p.   cm. — (SUNY series, the social context of education)
    Includes bibliographical references and index.
    ISBN 0–7914–4241–1 (hc. : alk. paper). —ISBN 0-7914-4242-X (pbk.
: alk. paper)
    1. Group work in education—United States—Case studies.   2. Team
learning approach in education—United States—Case studies.
    3. Effective teaching—United States—Case studies.   4. Educational
change—United States—Case studies.   I. Title.   II. Series: SUNY
series, social context of education.
    LB1032.J33   1999
371.14`8—dc21   98-47344
                                                                 CIP

10 9 8 7 6 5 4 3 2 1

To Bruce

Contents

Tables

Preface

I became interested in cooperative learning because of its potential benefits for culturally diverse classrooms. A considerable body of research in experimental settings indicated that cooperative learning improved students' academic achievement, self-esteem, attitudes toward school, and relationships with peers. Theory and research in the area of second language acquisition suggested that cooperative learning should also help second language learners acquire English. My initial goal in conducting this study was to observe and understand the processes that contributed to cooperative learning's success in everyday classrooms.

I expected this book to be a success story of how and why the teachers' uses of cooperative learning resulted in improved teaching and learning in their classes. However, this book presents a mixed picture of successes, failures, and missed opportunities. The story is more complex and less conclusive than I had expected. Context became my focus as I tried to understand this complexity.

I still think that cooperative learning is a powerful instructional strategy. However, I now understand that cooperative learning, like other educational innovations, requires careful attention to contextual influences to reach its full potential. Cooperative learning is not a "magic bullet" in everyday classrooms; but it does not deserve the fate of innovations that are tossed out when they do not seem to work.

I hope that this book will prove useful to educators in several ways. First, I hope that the experiences reported in the study will help educators consider context in deciding when and how to use cooperative learning in their own schools and classrooms. Second, I hope that this study will encourage developers and disseminators of *all* educational innovations to recognize the importance of context and to anticipate how context may affect the ultimate success or failure of their innovations in everyday classrooms. Third, I hope that this study will help educators pay more attention to context as they use the wide variety of educational innovations available to them.

Acknowledgments

I am deeply indebted to the principal, teachers, other staff, and students at Maplewood Elementary School (a pseudonym). Without their help and willingness to participate, this book would never have happened.

At George Mason University, Dean Larry Bowen supported the project through several faculty research grants, and Dean Gustavo Mellander provided support for producing the index. George Mason University also provided research assistants. Two grants from Virginia's Commonwealth Center for Teacher Education supported my analyses of the teachers' uses of cooperative learning.

Numerous individuals helped in various stages of the project. Donna Christian was instrumental in bringing this study from the realm of ideas to a specific research proposal. Carolyn Adger put me in touch with Maplewood School's principal. Betty Smallwood, an ESL specialist, administered and scored English proficiency tests of second language learners; Taejung Welsh, another ESL specialist, did reliability scoring on these tests. Julia Lara collected data on the local community. Transcription, especially transcription of videotapes of the cooperative learning groups, was a long process. Betty Smallwood, Julia Lara, Sandy Nelson, Margaret Couture, and Edyth Wheeler produced preliminary transcriptions of subsets of the data. Lan-Jane Wang, Shu-lin Tung, and Sondra Patrick entered quantitative data into a computer, checked it, and wrote the SPSS programs needed for the quantitative analyses. Mittie Quinn provided useful bibliographic searches.

Several people helped with the qualitative data analyses. Edyth Wheeler helped identify and code the participant structures in the cooperative learning groups. Sondra Patrick did preliminary bracketing of some of the videotape transcripts. Lori Rottenberg's expertise in second language acquisition was instrumental in the analysis of second language learners' opportunities for acquiring academic English; Sondra Patrick and Edyth Wheeler also participated in these analyses.

Donna Christian, Virginia Collier, and Deborah Short provided helpful comments on early versions of our work on students' second language acquisition in cooperative learning groups. Two colleagues, Sharon Gerow and Gail Matthews-DeNatale, commented on the first complete version of the book manuscript. Their editorial and substantive comments helped me take the next major step in constructing the book. Martin Ford and Art Chickering offered useful counsel as I sought a publisher for the book. I appreciate reviewers' suggestions, Christine Sleeter's interest in the book, and Priscilla Ross's support at SUNY Press.

My husband, Bruce Davis, read and commented on the entire manuscript several times, from its early through its later versions. This book has definitely benefited from his unrelenting commitment to clarity and his "outsider" perspective. But his contributions to the book extend far beyond his editorial comments. Although I cannot thank him for typing the manuscript or handling all the household chores, I can and do appreciate his interest, encouragement, humor, and support throughout this project.

Transcription Conventions

Convention	Explanation
(( ))	Something was said but it is unintelligible
((word))	Probably what was said but not clear
sit down	Emphasis or stress
I'm rea-	Break in a word
I don't like—	Break in a phrase
(pause)	Longer than "normal" pause
Uh huh	Positive
Un un	Negative
(looks at paper)	Description of participant's action
[seems pleased]	Interpretive or explanatory comment
//	Co-occurring statements or actions
. . . .	Segment of transcript deleted

One

Studying the Contexts of Cooperative Learning

This is a study of how two teachers and their students used a particular educational innovation, cooperative learning, in everyday classrooms in a culturally diverse, suburban elementary school.[1] I studied the use of the Teams-Games-Tournaments (TGT) method of cooperative learning in a fourth grade mathematics class and the use of Learning Together (LT) method in a sixth grade social studies class.

Cooperative learning is a powerful instructional innovation, with an impressive body of theory and experimental research to support it. Yet, although there were some indicators of success in both classrooms, in neither classroom did cooperative learning reach its full potential.

In the fourth grade mathematics class, TGT had mixed results. Students had opportunities to learn procedural mathematics, aided one another in getting correct answers, and enjoyed TGT practice sessions. The teacher said she would give TGT an 8 on a scale of 1 to 10, and the class met the school's district's criterion number of objectives to be passed. Although the frequency with which students gave help and gave explanations increased during the school year, less than half of the peer help given involved explanations, and students missed opportunities to help one another almost as frequently as they offered help. Also, the principal and director of the school's mathematics lab were concerned that this "high math" class had not passed as many objectives as the previous year's class.

In the sixth grade social studies class, LT also had mixed results. LT afforded students opportunities to learn comprehension-level social studies, to help one another and to cooperate on joint assignments. It gave the teacher opportunities to observe students' work

1

and to help them as needed. Students enjoyed working in LT, and the teacher was generally pleased, viewing LT as helping her students to learn social studies and to work well together. However, the way the students enacted LT minimized the amount of help they offered one another and often involved students giving answers rather than explanations. In about half the tasks in which the teacher asked the students to cooperate, the students either did not work together cooperatively or stopped working cooperatively.

In this book I show how contextual influences help explain why this happened. This emphasis on contextual influences is not meant to diminish the importance of teachers' and students' actions. In the classes I studied, teachers and students were active in creating, acquiring, challenging, and resisting contextual influences. The book emphasizes contextual influences because paying attention to these influences can help maximize cooperative learning's chances of reaching its full potential in everyday classrooms.

The patterns in these case studies probably are similar in many ways to the experiences of other teachers and students who have used cooperative learning and other educational innovations. Contextual influences were so pervasive in these two classes that it would be difficult for me to imagine that the context in which an innovation is used does not affect its results in significant ways.

Patterns of mixed results, like those exhibited in the two classrooms studied, have happened frequently with other educational innovations. Later chapters suggest that greater attention to the importance of context could help developers, researchers, instructors and users of educational innovations to improve the success of those innovations in everyday classrooms.

Prior Studies of Context and Educational Innovations

The conventional approach to studying the use of educational innovations in everyday settings is acontextual (Snyder, Bolin & Zumwalt, 1992). Typically, researchers compare how teachers use an innovation to a list of "fidelity criteria" that developers or researchers have determined are important to fulfillment of the developers' goals.

However, many studies have shown that a wide array of educational innovations have been influenced by their context (e.g., Cochran-Smith, Paris & Kahn, 1992; *Educational Evaluation and Policy Analysis,* 1990; Elmore & McLaughlin, 1988; Grant, Peterson & Shojgreen-Downer, 1996; Hamilton & Richardson, 1995; Huberman & Miles, 1984; Little & McLaughlin, 1993; Michaels, 1990; Pace, 1992; Smith & Keith, 1971; Smith et al., 1988; Staessens, 1993; Sturtevant, 1996; Talbert, McLaughlin & Rowan, 1993).[2] Anthropological studies of a wide range of innovations abroad indicate the importance of taking the local context into account if an innovation is to be effective and sustainable (see Foster, 1969, for a classic review).

Cuban's (1984; 1993) study of teaching practices in the United States between 1890 and 1990 lends a historical dimension to the analysis of context and educational innovations. In the second edition of his study, he evaluated six explanations from the literature on educational stability and change. Cuban found each explanation insufficient to explain the major historical patterns he found. His synthesis from these various arguments, which he called "situationally constrained choice," emphasized contextual influences. In explaining the dominance of teacher-centered instruction Cuban (1993) stated:

> Teacher-centered instruction over the past century has been largely shaped by two overlapping contexts. Long-term cultural beliefs about the nature of knowledge, what teaching and learning should be, and the social setting (the ethnic, racial, and social backgrounds of the children attending school) established the outer context. The school and classroom organizational structures formed the inner context within which individual teacher beliefs and an occupational ethos worked their influences in shaping a durable practical pedagogy called teacher-centered instruction. Intertwined as these situational influences are, disentangling them and assigning a relative weight to the influence of each is impossible (p.260).[3]

In studies of contemporary innovations, some scholars have argued that adaptation to the local context is *necessary* for successful implementation (Berman & McLaughlin, 1978, cited in Elmore & McLaughlin, 1988; Guskey, 1986; Hall & Hord, 1987; McLaughlin, 1990). In a review of research on curriculum innovations, Snyder, Bolin and Zumwalt (1992) acknowledged the growing attention to contextual influences on educational innovations by identifying interest in contextual influences as a distinct perspective (termed "mutual adaptation" by the authors) within the study of educational innovations. McLaughlin (1990) referred to a similar perspective as the "implementation perspective" in policy research.

Methods and Conceptual Framework of this Study

The overall purpose of this book is to understand contextual influences on teachers and students using cooperative learning in two culturally diverse, suburban elementary classrooms. To address this overall goal I constructed a case study of each class. Each case study has two components: a naturalistic component and a comparative component. This chapter describes the basic methods of each component. The Appendix presents the details of my research methods and describes the context of the study.

Naturalistic Component

The naturalistic component is the core of each case study. For each classroom I examined its setting, how the teachers and students used cooperative learning, what and how students learned in the class, and contextual influences on the teachers and students.

I collected most of the data during the 1988–89 academic year. I spent 3 to 4 days a week at the school, observing in the school and classrooms, interviewing the teachers and students, and videotaping cooperative learning groups. A pilot study preceded the main period of research.

Several aspects of this study's conceptual framework merit discussion here. Drawing upon educational anthropology for the overall approach, the study presents the teachers' and students perspectives. Thus, the case studies use terms such as cooperative learning as the teachers and students used them.[4]

In analyzing the data, I used concepts from the cultural-historical tradition, a multidisciplinary approach to the study of context and cognition started by Lev Vygotsky and his colleagues Luria and Leont'ev in the Soviet Union during the early twentieth century.[5] I will identify these concepts later in the chapter and explain how I use them.

Teachers and Students as Learners

Both teachers and students in these classes were learners.[6] I view learning as an active process. Learners do not automatically learn what is available to them or is presented to them. Learners are active agents in the process of learning.[7]

Teachers' Learning. In discussing teaching and learning, Brown, Collins and Duguid (1989) distinguished between learning about something and learning how to do it. Teachers in the classrooms learned not only about cooperative learning, but also how to use it. More specifically, they learned how to use particular methods of cooperative learning in particular classrooms.

I found work within the cultural-historical tradition helpful in conceptualizing this part of the study because some research in the cultural-historical tradition has studied adults learning on the job in contexts that do not involve intentional instruction. Much of what the teachers learned was the result of learning on the job.

A considerable body of research on "everyday cognition" (e.g., Rogoff & Lave, 1984) has used the cultural-historical approach to study the everyday lives of adults. In their everyday lives, adults engage in work and nonwork related social practices that involve cognition and learning. A social practice is "a recurrent, goal-directed sequence of activities using a particular technology and particular systems of knowledge" (Scribner & Cole, 1981, p. 236).

> All practices involve interrelated tasks that share common tools, knowledge base, and skills. . . . practice always refers to socially developed and patterned ways of using technology and knowledge to accomplish tasks (p. 236).

Lave and Wenger (1991) have elaborated on the practice approach. They see all learning as both an integral part and dimension of social practice. Learning often derives from participating in a social practice without intentional instruction. "Participation involving technology is especially significant because the artifacts used within a cultural practice carry a substantial portion of that practice's heritage" (p. 101).

Learning, in Lave and Wenger's (1991) view, primarily involves becoming a member of a community of practice, with newcomers moving from the periphery of the community to the center.[8] Newcomers to a practice not only continue aspects of previous practice but also may contribute new features to the community of practice.

Students' Learning.   The practice approach was also useful in conceptualizing the study of students' learning. This study views cooperative learning itself as a social practice and as part of the larger social practice of "doing mathematics" and "doing social studies."[9]

Conventional researchers generally view students' interactions as processes contributing to outcomes, the outcomes representing what students learned as measured on various tests. However, interactions can be examined directly for evidence of students' thinking and learning, and are so viewed here. This is consistent with the cultural-historical approach's focus on processes rather than static outcomes. For example, Forman and Cazden (1985) argued for focusing on interactions because "one can observe the process of cognitive growth directly, rather than having to infer it from pretest-posttest performance" (p. 331).

To analyze students' learning in the cooperative learning groups, I drew on Leont'ev's (1978, 1981) tri-level concept of "activity" from the cultural-historical tradition. The first level, that of "activity," is tied to a socially constructed motive (e.g., getting food). The second level, that of "actions," is tied to goals that are instrumental to achieving a motive (e.g., going shopping may be instrumental to the motive of getting food). The third level, that of "operations," involves how an action is carried out (e.g., writing a grocery list prior to going shopping).

In this study the "activity" level involved "doing mathematics" and "doing social studies." "Actions" comprised students' efforts to complete worksheets or to answer individual questions. "Operations" referred to the processes occurring within "actions." Within this framework, my basic unit of analysis for studying students' learning, termed "episodes," was students' "actions" in answering individual questions.

To analyze students' peer interaction in the cooperative learning groups I used the concept of "participant structure" from educational anthropology. Participant structures refer to "patterns in the allocation of interactional rights and obligations among all the members who [are] enacting a social occasion together" (Shultz, Florio & Erickson, 1982, p. 94).

Some of the students in each class were learning English as a second language. Learning to talk as a member of the community of practice becomes important from a social practice perspective because it is necessary for full participation in the practice (Lave & Wenger, 1991). In the classes students needed to use both basic, face-to-face conversational proficiency and "academic language" (see Cummins, 1984, for a discussion of this distinction). Moreover, it is important that instruction in content classes support second language learners' acquisition of English even after they have left ESL or other special language programs (Collier, 1987, 1989, 1995; Cummins, 1981). Second language learners' opportunities were examined for acquiring English in cooperative learning groups.

Context

The concept of context is central to my data analyses.[10] In examining contextual influences I focus on those specifically related to cooperative learning. This contrasts with a focus on contextual features that influence innovation and teacher development in general (see Sparks & Loucks-Horsley, 1990, for a discussion of the latter).

The concept of context has been used to examine a wide range of human behavior in a variety of settings through the perspectives of many disciplines. It broadly indicates phenomena needed to understand or interpret some focal event. However, the concept of context seems to escape precise definition (Goodwin & Duranti, 1992).

One approach views context as the circumstances in which a particular event occurs, "the set of circumstances or facts that surround a particular event, situation, etc." (Stein, 1967). Studies using this approach to context usually provide an introductory chapter, like chapter 3 of this book, that describes the overall setting of a study. Context in this approach can be used to help determine the generalizability of a study. The underlying assumption is that if another context is similar to the one of a study, then the reader can feel comfortable generalizing to the new context.

Another approach, more relevant to the core analyses, views context as more directly involved in what happens in the focus of study. Context in this sense influences what happens and helps one understand participants' behaviors.

As reported above, the approach to context in this study draws on work in the cultural-historical tradition, originally developed by Vygotsky and his colleagues, and extended in more recent work.[11,12] Vygotsky saw context as a broad influence on children's development of "higher mental functions" (e.g., thinking, reasoning, and problem solving) (Minick, 1989). Publication of Vygotsky's work in English has called attention among English-speaking scholars to two kinds of contextual influences: "tools" provided by society for cognitive activity, and face-to-face social interaction.[13] Tools comprise technical tools (e.g., pens, text books, computers) and psychological tools (e.g., language, number systems, writing). These tools transform the structure and processes of the activity being performed and thereby influence what is learned (Vygotsky, 1981). For example, editing with a word processor is a different activity than editing with a pen or pencil.

Vygotsky also asserted that higher mental functions have their origins in face-to-face interactions: "Every function in the child's cultural development appears twice: first, on the social level, and later, on the individual level" (Vygotsky, 1978, p. 57). Thus, features of social interactions directly influence cognitive learning. Contemporary cultural-historical scholars added these contextual features to the prevalent cognitivist view that saw task structure and knowledge domains as the only relevant contexts for cognitive activity (Engestrom, 1993).

However, Vygotsky's view of contextual influences extended beyond the influence of tools provided by society and of social interaction. His broader view "emphasizes the organized system of social practices that constitute the world into which the child is born. It is the child's progressively broader participation in this social system . . . that underlies his psychological development" (Minick, 1989, p. 163). In this view, features of social relationships also become an important part of the context for learning. Erickson and Shultz (1992) made a similar point from an anthropological point of view, arguing that academic tasks involve a social component as well as a subject matter component.

Recent work in the cultural-historical tradition (e.g., Chaiklin & Lave, 1993; Forman, Minick & Stone, 1993) elaborated on Vygotsky's ideas, adding other contextual dimensions and expanding the concept of context in relation to cognitive activity. Scholars have shown the importance of understanding the social meanings and goals of the activities in which cognitive activity takes place; the local cultures, patterns, and institutions; and the larger culture and social institutions. The "larger culture and social institutions" in the contemporary United States comprises many cultures—for example, ethnic cultures; religious, occupational, and gender subcultures; and groups that contest these cultures.

Lave and her colleagues (Lave, Murtaugh & de la Rocha, 1984) described two basic approaches to local context. One approach views context as "an identifiable, durable framework for activity, with properties that transcend the experience of individuals, exist prior to them, and are entirely beyond their control" (p. 71).[14] Thus, one might examine the physical, economic, political, or social context of human behavior.

The second approach to local context discussed by Lave, Murtaugh and de la Rocha (1984), prevalent today in many traditions studying human interaction, sees context as something created by humans through their interactions (see also Goodwin & Duranti,

1992; Erickson & Shultz, 1981). Individuals signal to each other and negotiate verbally and nonverbally their interpretations of the context and meanings of their interactions. This approach stresses the importance of understanding the context as the participants interpret it during a given activity at a given point in time rather than from the researcher's perspective. For example, students and their teacher mutually create different contexts within the same classroom as they engage in various activities. Morning announcements constitutes a different context than mathematics class, reading groups, computer time, or snack time.

I view context as both stable and as created by individuals through their interactions. Therefore, understanding how the teachers and students define their contexts is central to understanding their behavior.

My main focus is on contextual features within the school. Unlike many studies that draw on the cultural-historical tradition, I do not take an exclusively "micro" view that focuses only on the processes of interpersonal interactions. Nor do I take primarily a "macro" view. Although I discuss some influences of the school district and larger cultures, political influences and the influences of gender, ethnic, class and peer cultures are beyond the scope of this study.[15]

I examine six categories of contextual influences that previous cultural-historical work has identified as having potentially significant influences on learning (see Jacob, 1997, for a discussion of the categories). These comprise: (1) task structure and knowledge domains, (2) psychological and technical "tools," (3) interpersonal interactions and social relationships, (4) individual and social meanings, (5) local cultures and institutions, and (6) larger cultures and institutions.

Contextual features that involve meanings often can be placed in more than one category. When a choice was necessary, I selected the category that had the most "saliency" for the contextual feature. For example, the meaning of mathematics as a procedural activity could be discussed at the national/international level, the school district level, the school level, or the teacher and student levels. I elected to discuss it primarily at the school district level because the school district mandated that its teachers use a particular procedural mathematics approach. How such multi-level meanings are embraced, transformed, contested or rejected at different levels is an important part of how context influences learning.

Within my school-level focus, the study of interpersonal interactions becomes important in two different ways: the interactions not only form part of the context in which learning takes place but also constitute part of the evidence for learning processes. But looking at the task and interactions does not tell the whole story.

I look at school-level contextual influences beyond interpersonal interactions for several reasons, the primary one being that other contextual influences were important in understanding what happened in the classrooms. Second, a school-level view is useful because the school is the level at which most educational practitioners operate and can have influence (see chapter 8). Third, a broader perspective toward context lays a strong foundation for examining contextual influences on educational innovations in general (see chapter 9).

Comparative Component

The comparative component of the study addressed two questions: How did the academic performance, attitudes, and language proficiency of students who experienced cooperative learning compare to the academic performance, attitudes, and language proficiency of other students? How did context influence these matters?

To obtain data for the comparative component, tests were administered at the beginning and end of the focus year to assess students' content learning and attitudes and to measure second language learners' English proficiency. I compared students in the focus classes to similar content classes in which the students did not participate in cooperative learning. Because some students in the focus classes also used cooperative learning in some of their other classes, I compared students who had the most cooperative learning overall to those who had the least.

Organization of the Book

Chapter 2 examines cooperative learning, with a special focus on the two methods used in the classrooms. Chapter 3 describes the larger setting of the two case studies. Chapters 4 and 5 present the two case studies, showing the influence of context on how teachers learned to use cooperative learning and on how students learned within cooperative learning groups. Chapter 6 examines the opportunities second language learners had for acquiring English during cooperative learning in the two classes. Chapter 7 compares the case studies and their contributions to the understanding of contextual influences on learning and cognition. Chapters 8 and 9 suggest implications for cooperative learning and for educational innovations generally.

The body of the book focuses on telling the stories of the teachers and students, highlighting their perspectives. Some qualitative researchers would have included more of themselves in the body of the book (see, for example, Van Maanen's, 1988, discussion of impressionist tales in which the stories of the researcher and the participants are merged). I chose not to do this because I did not wish to detract from the book's main focus. "My story" appears in the Appendix, which discusses my background, the history and methods of this study, and the contextual features that influenced how I conducted the study.

Regarding my use of terms, the literature on educational innovations typically discusses teachers as implementing innovations. "Implement" means "to put into effect according to or by means of a definite plan or procedure" (Stein, 1967).

I chose to speak of the teachers' activity as using cooperative learning. "Use" means "to employ for some purpose, . . . to apply to one's own purposes" (Stein, 1967) and is more consistent with the contextual approach taken here.

In terms of the tense I use to discuss the study, I consciously chose the past tense because in many ways the setting of this study no longer exists. The school building remains but the principal and focus teachers are no longer there. The mathematics curriculum has changed, and many other aspects discussed in the study may also have changed. What I discuss is presented at a point in time, from my point of view. But the study offers insights about context and educational innovations that have wider implications.

Two

Cooperative Learning

Cooperative learning is a diverse group of instructional methods in which small groups of students work together and aid each other in completing academic tasks.[1] An impressive body of experimental research has found cooperative learning to be an effective instructional method (D. W. Johnson, Maruyama, R. T. Johnson, Nelson & Skon 1981; Sharan, 1980; Slavin, 1990, 1996). Cooperative learning is widely used in current programs for educational reform.

Although some widely available methods of cooperative learning have been developed by teachers,[2] major methods of cooperative learning promoted in the literature have been developed by scholars from social science theories. For example, Slavin and his colleagues developed the Student Team Learning methods from motivational theory in psychology (Slavin, 1983; Slavin, 1990). David and Roger Johnson developed the Learning Together method from social psychological theories of Morton Deutsch and Kurt Lewin (D. W. Johnson & R. T. Johnson, 1989). Cohen developed the Complex Instruction approach to groupwork from sociological theory, primarily expectation states theory (Cohen, 1993, 1994).

The considerable body of research associated with the development of cooperative learning methods is primarily experimental, having been conducted in laboratory or field experiments. (See D. W. Johnson, Maruyama, R. T. Johnson, Nelson, & Skon, 1981; Sharan, 1980; and Slavin, 1990 and 1996 for reviews.) These studies usually compared one or more methods of cooperative learning to teacher-led classes, or compared cooperative learning to individualized and competitive approaches. This research documented cooperative learning's effectiveness in raising academic achievement and self-esteem,

13

improving students' attitudes toward their peers and toward school, and improving relations among diverse groups of students.

In attempting to explain cooperative learning's success in these studies, developers of the major approaches have drawn on the theories that motivated their work, and have identified features of cooperative learning that correlate with academic achievement or some other explicit goal. Slavin (1990, 1994), for example, stressed motivational issues and argued that the features of individual accountability, team recognition, and equal opportunities for success are central to Student Team Learning's success in improving academic achievement.

Scholars have also focused on processes within cooperative learning groups that seem to be related to academic success. Webb (e.g., 1982, 1983, 1985) conducted a series of influential studies that examined relationships between aspects of peer interaction and achievement. Webb's (1989, 1991) reviews of these and similar studies indicated that giving explanations was positively associated with achievement. However, the effect of receiving help varied. "Receiving explanations is sometimes helpful, receiving information has mixed effects (or no effect), and receiving only the answer is harmful" (Webb, 1989, p. 26). Receiving a lower level of help than is requested is also harmful (Webb, 1991). D. W. Johnson and R. T. Johnson (1985) concluded from a meta-analysis of their studies that the process of elaborative rehearsal of the material, support from team members, and "constructive controversy" among students increase the achievement benefits of cooperative learning.

Cognitive theories (e.g., Piaget, 1926; Vygotsky, 1978) pointed to qualities of students' peer interactions that may contribute to students' learning within cooperative learning groups. Vygotsky's work stressed benefits of collaborating with a more expert peer because what a student carries out jointly with another could be incorporated into his or her individual repertoire. Piaget's work stressed the benefits of cognitive conflicts among students that expose students' misconceptions and lead to higher-quality understandings. Both the Johnsons (D. W. Johnson, R. T. Johnson, & Holubec, 1993a) and Slavin (1987b) have developed frameworks that combine their motivational approaches with cognitive theories.

However, even though theory and research predict that cooperative learning will improve students' education in everyday classrooms, cooperative learning may be developing a track record typical of many educational innovations. Although cooperative learning has a strong record of success in *experimental settings,* it has not always fared as well in the few studies of cooperative learning in *everyday classrooms* when teachers have not received strong external support (Castle & Arends, 1992; Cohen, Lotan & Catanzarite, 1990; Meloth & Deering, 1994; Perrenet & Terwel, 1997). These research studies suggest that positive outcomes for cooperative learning are not automatic in everyday classrooms. Certainly, they were not automatic in the everyday classrooms involved in this study.

Methods of Cooperative Learning Studied

This study examines cooperative learning in two classrooms in Maplewood Elementary School.[3] The first classroom was Miss Grant's fourth grade mathematics class, which used the Teams-Games-Tournaments (TGT) method of cooperative learning. The second classroom was Mrs. Parker's sixth grade social studies class, which used the Learning Together (LT) method of cooperative learning.

Because much research and development in cooperative learning has happened since I studied Miss Grant's and Mrs. Parker's classrooms, I will discuss recent work as well as work available to the teachers.

Teams-Games-Tournaments

TGT is one method of cooperative learning within the highly structured Student Team Learning group of methods developed and researched at Johns Hopkins University. TGT was originally developed by David DeVries and Keith Edwards (Slavin, 1986, 1994), but is now widely associated with Robert Slavin. Slavin and his associates developed the Student Team Learning "family" of cooperative learning methods. The impetus for these methods was motivational theory from social psychology. "Teamwork works because it creates a social and motivational environment that expects and assists maximum effort" (Slavin, 1986, p.5).

After developing STL methods, the Johns Hopkins team extended their work by integrating curriculum with STL methods. Cooperative Integrated Reading and Composition (CIRC) is a program for teaching reading and writing in grades 2–8, while Team Accelerated Instruction (TAI) is a program that combines cooperative learning with individualized instruction in mathematics for grades 3–6 (Slavin, 1994).

More recently, the Johns Hopkins team developed two comprehensive restructuring programs that include cooperative learning as a central feature. Success for All is a reading, writing, and language arts program for grades pre-K to 6 that includes: an integrated curriculum and instruction package; reading tutors; half-day preschool, full-day kindergarten or both for eligible students; a family support team; a program facilitator; initial staff training and follow-up with coaching; and an advisory committee (Slavin, Madden, Dolan, & Wasik, 1996). Building on Success for All, the Johns Hopkins team created a design for a comprehensive elementary schools for the twenty-first century, called Roots and Wings. To the basic features of Success for All, they added new programs for grades 1–5: a program in constructivist mathematics (MathWings) and an integrated social studies and science program (WorldLab) (Slavin, Madden, Dolan, & Wasik, 1996).

Even though the Johns Hopkins team has developed programs beyond the original STL methods, the basic STL methods are still being used and taught independent of the recent Success for All and Roots and Wings programs (e.g., Slavin, 1994). The basic features of TGT and the other STL methods remain the same, although the current training manual (Slavin, 1994) presented a more detailed discussion of some features than the manual (Slavin, 1986) available to Miss Grant.

TGT has four basic components: teacher presentation, team study, tournaments, and team recognition (Slavin, 1986; 1994).[4] The teacher begins a cycle of TGT with direct instruction. In the current manual Slavin (1994) added that teachers should take an active learning stance in their teaching by initially arousing students' interest, actively demonstrating concepts or skills, and involving students in guided practice.

After receiving direct instruction from the teacher, students then study the material in four-member teams, comprising students of heterogeneous past performance. "Most often, [team] study takes the form of students discussing problems together, comparing answers, and correcting any misconceptions if teammates make mistakes" (Slavin, 1986, p. 15). The current manual (Slavin, 1994) added a discussion of the importance of team-building activities and the need for the teacher to stress that the teams should practice active listening, encourage each other, and explain answers to one another so all teammates will do well in the tournaments.

After completing the team study, students compete against members of other teams at three-member tournament tables, where students are grouped so they are similar in previous performance. At each tournament table students are given a sheet with numbered questions, the corresponding answer sheet, and a set of numbered cards placed face down on the table. Students take turns being the "reader," who selects a card and tries to answer the corresponding question. Others at the table may "challenge" the reader by offering a different answer to the question. The student with the correct answer keeps the card. If the reader is wrong, there is no penalty. If a challenger is wrong, he or she must return a card (if he or she has one) to the deck. If no student gives the correct answer, the reader returns the card to the deck.

Students take turns as reader until all the questions have been answered or the teacher announces the end of the tournament. At the end of each tournament, students count the number of cards they earned during that tournament. The individual scores are then converted to "tournament points:" 60 points for the highest scorer at each tournament table, 40 points for the next scorer, and 20 points for the lowest scorer. Team averages are calculated by adding the number of tournament points each team member earned, and then dividing by the number of team members. Because students at each tournament table have similar records of past achievement, all students have an equal opportunity to earn points for their teams.

The teacher then recognizes or rewards the winning team or teams. Each team can earn a certificate or other team reward if the team's average score meets or exceeds a criterion score. Suggested criterion scores are slightly lower in the current manual than in the one Miss Grant used. Teams earn "super team" if the average is 45 or above (50 or above in the previous manual), "great team" if 40–45 (45 or above previously), and "good team" if 30–40 (40 or above previously).

To maintain equality at each tournament table, Slavin (1986, 1994) stated that a bumping system should be followed. After each tournament, students should be reassigned to tournament tables (highest scorer going to a higher ability-level tournament table and lowest scorer going to a lower ability-level tournament table) to assure that competitors at each table are equitably matched against one another.

The manuals for Student Team Learning methods (Slavin, 1986 1994) presented detailed instructions for assigning students t teams and tournament tables, and for the bumping system. The ma uals also provided samples of team study worksheets, tourname sheets, tournament scores sheets, team summary sheets, and te award certificates.

Both manuals (Slavin, 1986, 1994) presented three features central to Student Team Learning methods of cooperative learn team recognition or rewards, individual accountability, and equal opportunity for success. These features may be considered the "fidelity criteria" for TGT.

The goal of team recognition or rewards, such as certificates or special privileges, is to motivate teams to succeed. Team rewards are based on team scores that result from points students earn while competing at tournament tables. Because team rewards are given when teams achieve at or above a designated criterion, all teams may achieve a particular criterion in a given week and be equally rewarded.

Individual accountability means that a team's success depends on the learning of individual team members. In TGT, team study helps students prepare for individual assessments at the tournament tables, where each student's performance contributes to his or her team's score. Slavin argued that individual accountability motivates students to help one another learn since their team score depends on the performance of each team member.

TGT provides equal opportunity for success by having students compete at tournament tables against students who have demonstrated similar levels of past achievement. The developers assume that this will result in all students being challenged to do their best. The bumping system is designed to maintain equality at each tournament table.

Learning Together

Like the Student Team Learning methods, the Learning Together method is rooted in motivational theory. The developers of LT, David Johnson and Roger Johnson, based their work on that of Morton Deutsch, who built on Kurt Lewin's motivational theory (D. W. Johnson & R. T. Johnson, 1989).

Although the Johnsons' early work focused on developing and researching the Learning Together method of cooperative learning, in recent years the Johnsons have expanded their work by adding "informal cooperative learning," consisting of students working together in temporary, ad hoc groups and "cooperative base groups," comprising long-term support groups (D. W. Johnson, R. T. Johnson & Holubec, 1993a, 1994a). In addition, the Johnsons have developed procedures to foster constructive academic controversy (D. W. Johnson & R. T. Johnson, 1992) and peaceful resolution of student conflicts (D. W. Johnson & R. T. Johnson, 1991a, 1991b). They also have done extensive work on "the cooperative school," which focuses on changing school culture to create a setting in which cooperative learning in classrooms will flourish (D. W. Johnson & R. T. Johnson, 1994). Notwithstanding these extensions, Learning Together continues to provide the core of the Johnsons' work and they continue to refine Learning Together and update the manuals (e.g., Johnson, Johnson, & Holubec 1992, 1993b) for their own workshops on cooperative learning.

LT is not a structured process like the Student Team Learning methods. Instead, LT involves five principles that teachers can apply in various ways, in a wide range of situations, and with existing curriculum and materials.

The Johnsons' (D. W. Johnson, R. T. Johnson, & Holubec, 1986, 1993a, 1994a) five requirements for LT are: (1) positive interdependence; (2) face-to-face promotive interaction; (3) individual accountability; (4) interpersonal and small group skills; and (5) group processing. These may be considered the fidelity criteria for the LT method. Because LT is based on principles rather than procedures, the Johnsons discuss alternative ways that teachers can achieve the basic requirements (see D. W. Johnson, R. T. Johnson, & Holubec, 1986, 1993a). Over time, the Johnsons have refined and elaborated their ideas of how best to achieve these requirements.

Positive interdependence means that students' success is linked to the success of the others in their group, and that students perceive that they "sink or swim together." In *Circles of Learning,* the book used by Mrs. Parker, the Johnsons indicated that positive interdependence could be achieved through mutual goals, division of labor, division of resources, differing roles, or joint rewards. Later editions (i.e., D. W. Johnson, R. T. Johnson, & Holubec, 1993a, 1994a) indicated that, based on recent research, goal interdependence is central (i.e., students must perceive that they can achieve their learning goals only if all group members attain their goals), and that combining goal and reward interdependence is better than using goal interdependence alone. Other forms of interdependence can be added to these "core" forms of interdependence.

In discussing face-to-face promotive interaction, the Johnsons now stress both the motivational and cognitive components of such interactions.

> Promotive interaction is characterized by individuals providing each other with efficient and effective help and assistance, exchanging needed resources such as information and materials and processing information more efficiently and

effectively, providing each other with feedback in order to improve subsequent performance, challenging each other's conclusions and reasoning in order to promote higher-quality decision making and greater insight into the problems being considered, advocating the exertion of effort to achieve mutual goals, influencing each other's efforts to achieve the group's goals, acting in trusting and trustworthy ways, being motivated to strive for mutual benefit, and a moderate level of arousal characterized by low anxiety and stress (D. W. Johnson, R. T. Johnson, & Holubec, 1993a, p. 3:20).

Individual accountability means that each student is held accountable for learning the material. Although the students learn together, each must perform alone to show that he or she has learned the focus skills or knowledge. In a more recent statement (D. W. Johnson, R. T. Johnson, & Holubec, 1993a), the Johnsons added that individual accountability also involves holding each student accountable for contributing his or her fair share to the group's efforts.

Use of interpersonal and small group skills means that students must learn appropriate skills for being a productive group member. Students must be taught such skills if they do not already have them, and they must be motivated to use them.

Group processing means that groups must regularly examine their functioning and the use of appropriate social skills. The teaching of small group skills and regular group processing are hallmarks of the LT method. In their later work (D. W. Johnson, R. T. Johnson, & Holubec, 1993a), the Johnsons presented five steps involved in group processing: (1) the teacher or students assess the quality of students' interactions; (2) each learning group receives feedback; (3) groups set goals for improving their effectiveness; (4) the whole class processes how it is functioning; and (5) groups and the whole class celebrate their successes.

In the book Mrs. Parker used, the Johnsons (D. W. Johnson, R. T. Johnson, & Holubec, 1986) offered the following example of an LT class:

Linda Scott, in her Moundsview, Minnesota 5th-grade classroom, assigns her students a set of math story problems to solve. She assigns her students to groups of three, ensuring that there are high-, medium-, and low-performing math students and both male and female students in each group. The instructional task is to solve each story problem correctly and to understand the correct process for doing so. Each group is given a set of story problems (one copy for each student) and a set of three "role" cards. Each group member is assigned one of the roles. The **reader** reads the problem aloud to the group. The **checker** makes sure that all members can explain how to solve each problem correctly. The **encourager** in a friendly way encourages all members of the group to participate in the discussion, sharing their ideas and feelings (p. 13).

The Johnsons also discussed how the teacher met the five requirements of Learning Together. The teacher achieved positive interdependence by requiring each group to agree on the answer and the process for solving each problem (goal interdependence) and by assigning students different roles. Supportive face-to-face interaction occurred as students enacted their roles and reached agreement on how to solve each problem and on their joint answer. The teacher held each student accountable by selecting one answer sheet from each group to score and asking one student from each group to explain how to solve a problem. The teacher emphasized small group skills by assigning the roles of checker and encourager. At the end of the class each group was expected to process their functioning by identifying something helpful that each group member had done and something that each member could do to make the group even better the next time.

Three

The Larger Setting

Several localities (county, school district, local community and school) help situate the two focus classrooms.

The county in which the classrooms were located is a suburb of a mid-Atlantic city in the United States. Traditionally a European American suburb, the county has become increasingly diverse in the past 20 years. The 1990 census indicated that 77% of the population was European American, 12% African American, 8% Asian American, and 3% "other." Across these categories, 7% were Hispanic American.

The median household income was approximately $55,000. Eighty percent of those employed held a white collar job. Ninety percent of persons 25 or older had at least a high school degree, and 50% had a bachelor's degree or higher.

The school district had a reputation for providing high quality public education to approximately 100,000 students. SAT scores routinely have exceeded the national averages.

Paralleling changes in the county's demographics, during the 1980s diversity increased in the school district, with minorities increasing from 13% to 30% of the student population between 1975 and 1985. Much of this rise was due to an influx of Vietnamese and Salvadoran refugees. In 1988–89, the school district classified 32% of its students as minority.

During the 1987–88 school year the school district began to focus on hiring more minority teachers and on improving minority achievement on standardized tests, which lagged behind European American achievement. One study showed that African American and Hispanic American students tended to fall behind other students in math performance as early as the third grade. Another study showed that African Americans and Hispanic Americans

lagged behind their European American and Asian American counterparts on the California Achievement Test. In 1988 African Americans in grades 3, 5, and 8 scored 23 to 40 points lower than European
American students, while Hispanic Americans in grades 3, 5, and 8
scored 17 to 27 points behind European American students. During
this period parents and a citizen's committee assailed the school district for its poor performance, and local papers discussed the disparity in numerous articles.

Maplewood Elementary School, the site of the two focus classrooms, was located in a diverse working-class neighborhood in a mature suburb. However, its students came from two different areas in
two different census tracts. One census tract was less diverse and
more affluent than the other. In the 1990 census 82% of the first census tract were European American, compared to 63% in the second
census tract. In the first census tract, the median household income
was approximately $70,000; in the second, the median household income was approximately $40,000.

Although the local community was diverse, there were no enclaves comprising predominantly a single ethnic group. A nearby
commercial area included restaurants and shops reflecting the diversity of the community: Asian, Mexican, Salvadoran, Italian and
kosher restaurants; Asian, Latin American, Greek, Middle Eastern,
Italian and kosher grocery stores.

Maplewood Elementary School comprised grades K–6. Of its approximately 625 students, 50% were European American, 18%
African American, 16% Asian American, 15% Hispanic American,
and 1% Native American. Over a third of the students received free
or reduced price lunch and breakfast. The school received federal
Chapter 1 funds to support instructional and enrichment activities
for students in grades K–4 who were below the 40th percentile on the
California Achievement Test.

The school building was shaped like a large E, with three parallel wings housing the classrooms. The "top" wing was for grades K–2;
the middle wing was for grades 3 and 4, a resource room, the primary
special education self-contained room, and the math lab; and the
"bottom" wing housed grades 5 and 6, resource rooms, the intermediate special education self-contained room, and the gym. The media
center was between the K–2 and 3–4 wings. The "side" of the E included the all-purpose room/cafeteria, kitchen, staff lounge, entrance
lobby, school office, guidance room, and art room.

Mr. Harris, the principal at Maplewood Elementary School, had
been at the school in that role for three years. He was European

American and had grown up in the community near the school. He seemed to thoroughly enjoy being principal. He was very visible around the school. An active participant in whatever was happening, he brought energy and enthusiasm to whatever he did. For example, on Halloween, when many staff and students wore costumes to school, he did not participate halfheartedly but donned a professional-looking clown costume with makeup and wig.

In January of the focus year Mr. Harris announced that he had been appointed the principal of a new elementary school that would open the next September. In February he assumed this new position. In an interview for a local newspaper, Mr. Harris said that starting a new school was exciting because it allowed him to hire staff for the new school who have a similar philosophy about educating children and the mission of elementary schools. In Mr. Harris' absence, the assistant principal, Mr. Kogan, became acting principal.

The school district reported that 79% of the professional staff at the school were women and 7% were minorities. The teachers generally liked the principal and seemed committed to providing a quality education for the students. His departure in February upset many of the teachers, and forced them to decide whether they wanted to be interviewed for Mr. Harris' new school, stay at Maplewood, or transfer to another school.

The students liked the atmosphere at Maplewood. When I asked students what they would tell a new student about the school, their responses were generally positive. Thep, a sixth grader, said: "There's a lot of work involved here. (pause) The teachers are great." Doria, another sixth grader, said: "There's a lot of teachers that she would probably like. When Mr. Harris was here, everyone liked him and now that he's gone it's still nice, but a lot of us miss him."

When school started at 8:45 A.M. students went to their homerooms. Between the time that they arrived and morning announcements, a period of approximately fifteen minutes, all students in the school did "bellwork," which involved review questions in math or language arts. Mornings were generally devoted to "core" subject of math, reading, and language arts/English. Social studies and science were taught in the afternoon.

In addition to regular classes, all students had "specials," such as art, music, and physical education. Some students were "pulled out" for special support activities such as English as a Second Language (ESL), reading, or counselling. Various programs and assemblies caused further interruptions to the normal schedule from time to time. The curriculum, the daily schedule, and its "interruptions" formed a fairly stable pattern in which teachers worked and students learned.

The ESL program was part of the school context for second language learners in the focus classrooms. When second language learners entered a district school, they were given an English language test to determine whether they needed ESL classes. Students were also tested upon request of the ESL teacher, at least once a year, to see if they qualified to be "exited" from the ESL program. The school district provided a curriculum that the ESL teachers were expected to follow.

Mrs. Archer was the ESL teacher at Maplewood. She had become an ESL teacher after being a teacher's aide for many years. She was European American, and she expected to retire from the school district in a few years. She clearly cared about the ESL students she taught, and she related to them in a warm, accepting, "grandmotherly" way.

Mrs. Archer had the following objectives displayed on a chart in her classroom: 1) to help students increase their understanding of spoken and written English, 2) to help students produce complete sentences with ever increasing accuracy, 3) to help students learn to write words and sentences using the structures taught, and 4) to help students learn to communicate with growing accuracy and fluency. She said in a discussion with me that the school district stressed structure and grammar, and that she tried to expose the students to the vocabulary used in their academic classes.

ESL students usually were "pulled out" from their language arts class for ESL class, usually for 40–50 minutes. ESL classes were based on students' grade level placement rather than their English language performance, resulting in ESL classes with students at many different levels of English proficiency. During the focus year, students from two grades usually were in one ESL class, with an average class size between 6–10 students. Beginners also had another class in the afternoon, and some teachers would send beginning students to the ESL classroom at other times when they felt that the students would not benefit from the regular class.

Mrs. Archer seemed to follow a general pattern in her classes. She would begin the class with a review or introduce new material. Students then did some kind of individual written work on worksheets, working alone but asking help from their classmates or the teacher as needed. Mrs. Archer did not assign grades but filled out a quarterly ESL progress report on which she evaluated students' progress in listening comprehension, speaking, reading, writing, vocabulary, and spelling. She and an aide also ran an after-school homework club two afternoons a week, when there was a late bus available to take students home.

The ESL class also had an important para-academic role for the second language learners—it was a "safe" place for them, a "home base" and "community" to which they regularly returned. Mrs. Archer said, "The best [thing about ESL class] is that they can interact with one another here. When they go back [to their regular classes], they're just one [ESL student among many native speakers], lost."

Homerooms in the school were heterogeneous in both "ability" and ethnicity. The principal wanted all subjects taught in mixed-ability groups—i.e., he did not want any "tracking" in the classes. However, the principal's intent was not always realized, and teachers sometimes grouped their students by past academic achievement.

There were three fourth-grade teachers at Maplewood Elementary School. Miss Grant, the teacher in one of the focus classes, was young, European American, and energetic. She had a very full life outside of Maplewood School: she was taking classes for a Master's degree in education, and was preparing to get married at the end of the school year. She and another fourth-grade teacher coordinated most of their teaching. They grouped students by achievement across their two homerooms for spelling and reading, but not for language arts, social studies or science. Miss Grant taught science to both homerooms; the other teacher taught social studies to both homerooms. The three fourth-grade teachers grouped students by achievement for mathematics across their three homerooms. The result was a complex schedule that left Miss Grant with little scheduling flexibility.

Mrs. Parker, one of three sixth-grade homeroom teachers, was a middle-aged European American woman with a family of her own. Her family was very important to her; she had changed from full-time teaching to substitute teaching for several years when her children were young so she could be with them. She and the other two sixth-grade homeroom teachers had developed a complex schedule that involved each of them teaching students from all three homerooms. Mrs. Parker taught three social studies classes, which encompassed all the sixth graders. Like Miss Grant, she had little flexibility in scheduling her classes.

At the time of my study the school district was becoming increasingly interested in cooperative learning. During the summers of 1988 and 1989, new teachers in the school district received a full day of training in cooperative learning as part of their orientation. Soon after the focus year, a task force recommended that ability tracking be replaced in the middle grades by cooperative learning. A staff development specialist in the school district reported that in 1990 some form of cooperative learning was being used in all of the district's schools.

The atmosphere at the school was generally supportive of cooperative learning, although, as discussed in chapter 4, the math lab director discouraged Miss Grant from using cooperative learning in the spring. Prior to this study the principal and several teachers had participated in cooperative learning workshops, and the principal had given a workshop at the school on the Jigsaw method of cooperative learning. Before this study began, three teachers in the school, including one of the teachers in the focus classrooms, were using cooperative learning on a regular basis.

At the beginning of the focus year, Mr. Harris announced that he had included cooperative learning in the official school objectives for the year. Cooperative learning was part of two in-service sessions at the beginning of the fall semester. The first workshop presented a broad framework based on the Learning Together method (D. W. Johnson, R. T. Johnson, & Holubec, 1986) and demonstrated various techniques that teachers could use for ice breakers, group formation, and instruction. The principal's introduction to the workshop listed what he saw as the most important benefits of cooperative learning: it builds self-esteem, citizenship skills and caring for other people. He added that it also helps achievement, critical thinking, attitudes toward school and subject matter, and liking for classmates. The second workshop consisted of the *Circles of Learning* video (D. W. Johnson & R. T. Johnson, 1983), which presented the Learning Together method.

However, Mr. Harris did not push for a major schoolwide implementation of cooperative learning in one year. He planned to implement cooperative learning over several years, with teachers participating voluntarily, at their own speed. Thus, teachers had considerable latitude in deciding how and when to use cooperative learning, and students had varied experiences of working in cooperative learning groups.

Four

Teams-Games-Tournaments
in Fourth Grade Mathematics

Miss Grant, the teacher in the fourth grade mathematics class, played a significant role in creating the context for her students' learning of mathematics through cooperative learning. She selected the Teams-Games-Tournaments (TGT) method of cooperative learning, used it according to her pedagogical goals and values, and adapted it in response to various contextual features. It is therefore useful to begin this case study with a discussion of Miss Grant's experience with cooperative learning.

Miss Grant and Her Context

To highlight Miss Grant's learning process and contextual influences on it, I first present a chronology, or natural history (Erickson, 1982), of her learning, focusing on what Miss Grant did and said. I then discuss contextual influences on her learning to use TGT in her mathematics class.

Natural History of Miss Grant's Learning

Miss Grant was a relatively new teacher. She began teaching full-time in fall 1985. After teaching a special education class at another school, Miss Grant came to Maplewood Elementary School. The focus year of this study was her fourth year of teaching. During an interview in the spring prior to the focus year, Miss Grant said that she saw herself as a learner—growing as a teacher and improving each year.

After agreeing to participate in this study, Miss Grant attended a three-hour workshop on cooperative learning in April prior to the focus year. She also initiated discussions with me about cooperative learning from time to time during that spring.

Miss Grant began using cooperative learning soon after the April workshop. Initially, she used the Learning Together (LT) method, which three other teachers in the school had been using, with her homeroom students in science class. Miss Grant's initial goals for using LT were academic. She thought cooperative learning would help her students learn science, and she wanted students to explain things to one another.

Miss Grant soon developed reservations about using LT. Asking students to cooperate appeared to be contrary to school norms focusing on individual effort. Miss Grant was concerned that the school was giving the students contradictory messages about working alone and working together: "We teachers contribute to it. We tell them not to cheat, then to turn around and tell them to share is contradictory."

Miss Grant also wondered aloud if she would continue using LT in science. She felt pressure to teach her students the vocabulary they needed for a science field trip that was imminent and believed that LT would not work fast enough. However, when the field trip was postponed until June, she that "it took the pressure off" and she continued to use LT in science.

In response to her students' behavior, Miss Grant experimented with different combinations of group size and number of worksheets. In the first class I observed, students worked in groups of four, with each student having his or her own worksheet packet. Because students did not work well together in this arrangement, Miss Grant tried having students share one paper per group, but she said that arrangement did not work because the students with the papers did not share with other group members. She then had students work in groups of three, each with his or her own worksheet.

Miss Grant tried several other things to improve students' behavior within their cooperative groups. She reminded the class to work together, admonished her students not just to give one another the answers and conducted some team-building activities. Miss Grant also began awarding points for appropriate cooperative behavior (e.g., helping one another by reading or explaining)—following the practice of several other teachers in the school. Mrs. David, the school's cooperative learning expert, gave Miss Grant copies of charts that identified appropriate behavior and provided examples of award certificates that Mrs. David used to reward the desired behavior. Following Mrs. David's model, Miss Grant had each cooperative learning group select a name and an emblem to put on their group folder. She hung the folders above each group's cluster of desks ("pod") and recorded the group's points in that folder. She gave a reward each week to the individual and the group that got the highest number of points.

Near the end of the school year, Miss Grant reported feeling positive about cooperative learning, and broadened her goals for cooperative learning to include social skills. Miss Grant commented that "if they get one thing from this year, besides the academic, which I want, it's social skills, how to get along."

In the summer Miss Grant took an intensive, three-day workshop on Student Team Learning (STL) offered by its developers. Like other teachers at Maplewood Elementary School, Miss Grant also participated in the two cooperative learning workshops offered at the school.

Prior to the beginning of the focus year, Miss Grant and her principal, Mr. Harris, agreed that cooperative learning would be her professional objective for the year. Mr. Harris also provided money for her to purchase STL materials for fourth grade mathematics and language arts. Miss Grant told me that she had decided to use cooperative learning in mathematics (with the STL materials) and that she might use it in science and language arts.

Continuing her efforts from the previous year, Miss Grant's first use of cooperative learning during the focus year was using LT in science. She started the year with students' desks arranged in groups of five, but said that if five did not work, she would change them. In a class that I observed early in the school year Miss Grant began with a team-building exercise. Then, after whole class instruction, she had teams work together to answer several questions (with one student in each group serving as recorder to write down the group's answer) and to draw a periscope.

Drawing on the models of Mrs. David and Mrs. Parker, Miss Grant developed and displayed in the classroom several charts related to cooperative learning. One chart summarized individual and team responsibilities. Based on the points received for appropriate behavior during cooperative learning, another chart honored teams and individuals who received the highest weekly total, improved the most, or had the highest cumulative total of points. A third chart provided a list of activities from which winning teams might choose their reward: extra computer time, extra library time, free time for reading, planning an art lesson, choosing a class game, or having lunch in the homeroom with Miss Grant.

In Miss Grant's view, cooperative learning was unsuccessful in her science class that fall. In mid-September, Miss Grant told me that she would not be doing cooperative learning in science because the students did not listen and wandered around. Miss Grant also said that she did not have the time for the planning required to use cooperative learning successfully in her science class. Commenting later about the science classes in which she had used cooperative learning, Miss Grant said that the discipline was "awful," that some students were distractions to others, and that cooperative learning had "bombed."

Although Miss Grant did not use cooperative learning again in science that year, she did not give up on cooperative learning. She shifted her attention to using TGT, a form of STL, in her mathematics class.

Learning to Use Teams-Games-Tournaments in Mathematics

At the beginning of the focus year Miss Grant's mathematics class comprised 24 students: 13 European Americans (5 girls and 8 boys), 5 African Americans (4 girls and 1 boy), 5 Asian Americans (3 girls and 2 boys), and 1 Hispanic American girl. Six of these students (Julita, Kyon, Larry, Philip, Rosanna, and Veata) were second language learners. Only Philip was in an English as a Second Language (ESL) class during the focus year; he was considered an advanced ESL student.

As previously reported, Miss Grant's "high math" class comprised fourth grade students with the highest prior mathematics performance. This class met five days a week in the morning, immediately before lunch, for 50 minutes. On Thursdays the students went to the "math lab" for assessments.

In late September 1988, Miss Grant said that she hoped to begin using cooperative learning in mathematics by October, but that it took time to learn about the individuals in the class for group placement. Miss Grant also commented that she was feeling time pressure because a university course she was taking required a lot of work.[1] She told me that TGT appealed to her because she had obtained a set of materials developed for use with TGT and other STL methods, which meant that she would not have to develop materials on her own.

Despite her concerns, Miss Grant began to use TGT with her mathematics class at the beginning of October. She presented new material early in the week. The students generally had one team study session (called "practice" by Miss Grant) mid-week and a tournament session on Friday. Miss Grant said she would have liked to have two days a week for team practice in her mathematics class, but did not because her students went to the math lab for assessments one day a week.

Miss Grant selected curriculum materials for TGT from the materials provided by the developers. These materials comprised question and answer sheets for the practice and tournament sessions. Miss Grant based her selection on the topics she was currently teaching or on previously-taught topics that she believed the students needed to review.

During the first practice sessions students sat facing one another in teams of four students. The teams selected team names. Miss Grant changed the teams several times during the year. Almost all teams had at least one second language learner.

In an early practice session Miss Grant explained to the class that in practice sessions they were not competing against one another: "If . . . someone doesn't understand, it's your responsibility to make sure they learn." She explained that they would compete later in the week in tournaments to bring points to their team. She also summarized their individual and group responsibilities, reading from the chart on the wall. Individuals were responsible for trying, asking their team members for help, and being courteous.[2] Teams were responsible for solving their own problems, asking her a question only when no one on the team could answer it, helping teammates, consulting with other teams, using a voice only heard by teammates, and becoming quiet when she used the quiet signal. When Miss Grant started using TGT, she combined it with awarding points for appropriate behavior, a feature she had used with LT in her science class. (The charts that Miss Grant had put up for LT in science, which were related to assigning points for appropriate cooperative behavior, were still up on the walls.)

Miss Grant soon found that four-member teams students easily got distracted during practice sessions. To deal with this she allowed team members to challenge one another during practice sessions, so they all would be working on the problems at the same time. When this did not solve the problem of student distraction, Miss Grant soon had the teams work in pairs as a way to keep all students involved.

Students participated in tournaments on Fridays. In the tournaments, members of different teams competed against students with similar mathematics performance. Although the first tournament groups contained four students, Miss Grant switched almost immediately to groups of three, which she found worked better.

For the students' first tournament session Miss Grant explained that students should keep the cards for questions that they answered correctly. The student who did not have the answer sheet could challenge the student answering the question, and challengers would gain or lose a card depending on whether a challenge was successful. Miss Grant recorded the number of cards each student won. She assigned points to individual students according to their relative ranking in their tournament group (the highest scorer received 60 points, the middle scorer received 40, and the lowest received 20). Each week she added together the points earned by members of each team, and she designated teams as Super, Great, or Good, depending upon their relative ranking, with the top team (or two top teams if they were close) being designated the Super Team. Super, Great, and Good teams got certificates for their ranking. The Super Team got an additional reward (for example, extra computer time or extra library time).

In mid-October, shortly after Miss Grant had begun using TGT, she mentioned to me informally that she thought TGT was working well, and that the students enjoyed it, seeing it as fun. She was concerned, however, about the competition in the tournament part of TGT because she thought students already had enough competition in school.

Miss Grant's initial uses of TGT were designed to address her pedagogical goals. During an interview in late October, Miss Grant talked extensively about her experiences and views related to cooperative learning. She said that she had several goals for using cooperative learning in her mathematics class. She saw it as a good way to get drill done. She added that the students looked at TGT as fun, and that she would like the students to enjoy mathematics. Miss Grant said that she wanted all the students to learn the material, and she saw the peer incentives in TGT as helpful motivation for some students. She also wanted the students to pass their weekly assessments in the math lab.

Miss Grant identified several problems, or "pressures" in her words, that she experienced with TGT in her mathematics class. After using TGT several times in her mathematics class, Miss Grant said she was concerned that the STL materials did not fit exactly with the school district's mathematics curriculum, and she needed to make sure that the students were on track with regard to the mathematics program. During our interview in October, Miss Grant was concerned about whether the work students did in cooperative learning would carry over into their mathematics assessments. In this regard, Miss Grant commented that the director of the math lab was "on her back" because she was supposed to "cover" the fifth grade mathematics curriculum. The math lab director was concerned that TGT was slowing the class down.

Miss Grant identified lack of time as another problem with TGT. She felt that she had to devote too much time to preparation, even though she was using materials from the TGT developers. "Getting it on a roll" also took time.

In spite of these problems with TGT, Miss Grant decided to extend her use of it to her language arts class in December. She thought TGT would improve the students' social skills and help those students who had difficulty with language arts.

In December, Miss Grant made several changes in how she used TGT in her mathematics class. Lack of time was a major factor contributing to these decisions. She stopped giving rewards other than certificates to the weekly Super Team(s). Miss Grant explained: "When you give students time out to use the library or time to use the computer, then you've got to make up whatever you teach to the rest of the class." She also discontinued giving points for good behavior, and during Christmas break, she took down the cooperative learning charts that were related to assigning and rewarding behavior points. Miss Grant found keeping the necessary records and making additional certificates too time-consuming. "The record keeping . . . requires a lot of time. Just to get the rewards filled out [takes time], and then, they should be colored. Students don't want a blank piece of ditto paper. They want something attractive." After making these modifications, Miss Grant continued using TGT in her mathematics class for the rest of the year in essentially the same way, which she felt "worked" for her.

During the second half of the focus year, Miss Grant typically would begin a TGT class with direct instruction. Next, she would explain the worksheets that the students would use during their practice session. Finally, during the practice session, which comprised the last half of the class, students worked in their teams to solve problems on the worksheets.

In practice sessions the four-member teams divided into two pairs. Students took turns working practice problems, selecting a card from a pile to determine which problem to solve. The partner with the answer sheet would tell the problem solver whether an answer was correct or incorrect. In addition, the partner with the answer sheet would sometimes help the problem solver arrive at an answer. These interactions between the practice partners will be discussed more fully below in the section of this chapter regarding the students' experience of TGT.

Tournaments were held among three-member groups. As Miss Grant had done in the first half of the year, she selected the competitors by ability so that each student would have an equal chance of earning points for his or her team. Team scoring remained as it was at the beginning of the year. She did not use the "bumping" system suggested by Slavin (1986).

During our interview in late April, I asked Miss Grant what she had learned over the past year about using cooperative learning in her classrooms. She said that she learned a lot about individual students by being able to watch them work in groups. She also learned that her mathematics students liked being part of a team and had a sense of identity with their teams; however, her language arts students did not identify with their teams to the same extent. When cooperative learning works well, she said, students can carry the ability to work together into other areas of the classroom.

She also learned that there are some "snags" in cooperative learning. She said some students and teams got upset because of the competitive aspects of TGT.

> As soon as it's competitive, which TGT is, [some students] . . .
> are upset and frustrated by it. When they don't get a card,
> [or] point, that's when the discipline problems start, because
> they're upset. . . . [Getting recognized as a] Good Team is like
> losing to the students. . . . I never see a lot of great smiles
> when they get that Good Team.

She also said that one student can disrupt the whole group: "If one [student] wants to be silly and doesn't want to do [the work and] the others are followers, then that person basically can get the whole team not to do the work."

Contextual Influences

Contextual features influenced Miss Grant's decision to use TGT in her mathematics class, how she learned to use it, and how frequently she used it—all of which affected students' learning.

Miss Grant's decision to use TGT in her mathematics class was influenced by her professional objective for the year, time constraints, her perception that there was a good fit between the developers' materials and the district's curriculum, and her beliefs about students' motivations.

Miss Grant needed to use cooperative learning because, in collaboration with her principal, she had identified it as her professional objective for the year. When cooperative learning "bombed" in her science class, she moved on to her mathematics class.

As previously reported, Miss Grant thought drill and practice were necessary for her students to master the mathematics curriculum. She believed that TGT would help motivate her students to do the necessary drill and practice.

Time also influenced Miss Grant's selection of TGT for her mathematics class. Because teachers had limited planning time under their contract, Miss Grant could not engage in extensive planning unless she contributed her personal time to the process. Because she was taking graduate courses and was planning to get married after the school year ended, Miss Grant had little personal time to devote to planning or preparation of class materials. The TGT method appealed to her because it offered previously-developed curriculum materials that seemed to address the topics the school district required her to teach.

A wide array of contextual features also influenced how Miss Grant used TGT in her mathematics class. These features influenced the tasks she assigned, how she structured the practice sessions and tournaments, and how she approached students' social skills.

The school district's curriculum and instructional management system and the TGT materials influenced the tasks Miss Grant presented to the students in the practice sessions. The district's approach stressed that students should learn specific mathematics objectives in sequence. An objective could be a skill such as "identifies common factors of two numbers." Following the district's instructional management system, teachers taught material related to objectives, administered tests regularly to see if students met the objectives, and retaught the material if necessary. The TGT materials available to Miss Grant were compatible with the district's focus because the materials presented discrete problems that focused on specific mathematical procedures and included many mathematical topics that the school district required Miss Grant to teach.[3]

Many contextual features influenced how Miss Grant conducted the team study and tournament sessions in TGT. Miss

Grant's definition of her students' activities during TGT team study sessions as "practice" was influenced by the school district's approach to mathematics, which Miss Grant saw as involving her teaching an objective, students' practicing it, students being assessed on it, and her reteaching the objective if necessary. As discussed above, TGT was consistent with this approach.

Miss Grant's use of TGT in her fourth grade mathematics class was also influenced by the way other teachers at Maplewood School had used cooperative learning and by her own prior experiences with cooperative learning. For example, drawing on Mrs. David's model and her prior use of behavior points with LT, Miss Grant initially incorporated giving points for appropriate behavior into her use of TGT.

Miss Grant's pedagogical values influenced how she used TGT in her mathematics class. Because many students were upset and sometimes became behavior problems when they perceived that they or their team had "lost" in TGT, Miss Grant tried to temper the competitive aspect of TGT by announcing team awards the week following the Friday tournament sessions rather than at the end of the Friday class. Because she did not believe in giving food "treats" as rewards, Miss Grant initially used rewards such as computer time or library time as additional rewards for teams achieving Super Team status.

Lack of time was again an important contextual feature. Miss Grant discontinued awarding points for behavior because of the time involved in keeping the necessary records and making attractive award certificates. She did not use the bumping system and stopped giving extra rewards to Super Teams because of time constraints. The bumping system involved more recordkeeping and depleted instructional time because students would have to form different tournament groups each week. Miss Grant stopped providing rewards beyond certificates because the other rewards took students away from regular instruction.

Students' behavior also influenced how Miss Grant structured the practice sessions, moving from groups of four, to groups of three with challenging, to pairs. Challenging was part of the TGT tournaments, and Miss Grant used it briefly in practice sessions as a way to keep all students in the practice sessions more focused on the task.

Miss Grant's approach to developing students' social skills was also influenced by contextual features. At the beginning of the focus year she drew from Mrs. David's model, posting charts that listed individual and group responsibilities and assigning behavior points and giving rewards to top teams. However, Miss Grant stopped doing that within three months because of the time involved in keeping the records and giving related rewards.

Miss Grant conducted no explicit social skills training the way Johnson and Johnson (D. W. Johnson, R. T. Johnson, & Holubec, 1986) recommend for their Learning Together method of cooperative learning. This is not surprising. No other teacher at Maplewood School conducted explicit social skills training. Moreover, social skills training is not part of the TGT model, and Miss Grant could have expected negative responses from the math lab director and principal if she took time away from mathematics to teach social skills.

Contextual features contributed to the "pressures" Miss Grant experienced and influenced how frequently she used TGT. Miss Grant's use of TGT practice sessions once a week was influenced by the school schedule. Because the fourth grade teachers had decided to group their students by past performance for mathematics, all three teachers had to coordinate the schedule for their classes, leaving little room for modification. On Thursdays, Miss Grant's students went to the math lab during that period. She said that she would have liked to have practice sessions twice a week but had insufficient time for it. Frequent modifications in the school schedule interfered with Miss Grant's use of cooperative learning. Events such as swimming lessons and performances—events designed for "enrichment"—made it difficult to plan or to carry out plans.

Mathematics had a special role in Maplewood Elementary School. In districtwide standardized tests of students' mathematics performance, Maplewood's students had a pattern of performing well. The principal was proud of the students' performance and wanted to maintain the school's good record. Because students' mathematics performance was important to the principal and the school district, Miss Grant had very little leeway regarding the topics addressed or the approach used in her fourth grade mathematics class. Moreover, the pressure to have her students perform well in the math lab assessments was even stronger because she had the "high" mathematics class, with a charge to complete the *fifth* grade curriculum with these students.

One day a week, students went to the school's math lab where the director assessed students' knowledge of key objectives, based on their answers to test questions. The director of the math lab sent each mathematics teacher and the principal periodic reports on each student's achievement on key objectives and the cumulative achievement for the mathematics class.

Miss Grant commented informally several times in February that she felt pressure from the math lab director and the principal to have the students perform well on the mathematics assessments. In fact, the math lab director wanted Miss Grant to stop using TGT in mathematics and spend the time on teaching, reteaching, and testing. On at least two occasions in the spring Miss Grant decided not to do cooperative learning in order to review material with students before mathematics assessments. In March she said that, because the TGT materials did not cover all the areas she'd be teaching in the near future, she'd probably use cooperative learning every other week.[4]

In sum, many contextual features influenced Miss Grant's learning to use TGT in her mathematics class. Because contextual features changed over time and interacted with her use of TGT, Miss Grant's learning process was ongoing. Even after Miss Grant had developed a relatively stable pattern of practice with TGT in her mathematics class, she needed to continue to negotiate contextual features as she sought to identify what "worked" in her classroom.

Students and their Context

Contextual features influenced learning opportunities and students' interactions in Miss Grant's mathematics class. In the first section that follows, I examine the students' learning processes in terms of their tasks and interpersonal interactions. In the second section, I explore other contextual features that influenced their interactions and learning.

Learning Mathematics

TGT in Miss Grant's mathematics class emphasized procedural mathematics. Students practiced tasks that involved comprehension questions and convergent thinking,[5] with the "correct" answers presented on answer sheets. Students were not expected to explain the processes by which they arrived at their answers.

Students frequently answered their questions correctly without any assistance, and the interactions around a particular question could be very brief.

Excerpt 4.1

(Kyon and Kanika exchange question and answer sheets.)

. . . .

(Kyon picks a card from the pile.)

Kyon: Seven [saying the question number]. [The question is "A person with a fever might have a temperature of: A. 38°C, B. 76°C, C. 100°C."]

(Kyon looks at question sheet and then at chart on blackboard [which has a large thermometer with both Celsius and Fahrenheit marked on opposite sides of it].)

Kyon: The first one [her answer].

Kanika: Yes. Seven (showing Kyon the answer sheet).

Kyon: Alright, uh ah, uh ah!

When the "reader" gave a correct answer, the other student generally gave some confirmation that the answer was correct. These episodes were similar to the I-R-E (initiation-reply-evaluation) sequence Mehan (1979) identified as a prominent feature of much teacher-student interaction. In these episodes the reader read a printed question (initiation) and offered an answer (reply); the other student then said whether the answer was correct or not (evaluation).

When the reader gave an incorrect answer, the student with the answer sheet informed the reader that the answer was wrong. This provided an opportunity for the student with the answer sheet to explain why the answer was wrong. Students could also help one another prior to an answer being given, for example, after the reader displayed difficulty or explicitly asked for help. The nature and occurrence of such help was a focus of my analysis of the students' interactions during TGT practice sessions.

The TGT practice sessions present a mixed picture of students' helping interactions. Students did help each other learn mathematics. I observed student pairs complete 262 practice questions. Of those practice questions where I could tell whether their answers were correct ($N = 257$), readers gave the correct answer without any help 62% of the time. Of the remaining 98 questions, readers got 56 questions correct after receiving some form of help—either from their partner, the teacher, or through self-help. In 50 of these 56 instances, the help was provided by peers. Thus, TGT practice sessions provided students with the opportunity to arrive at a correct answer, even when students could not answer questions on their own.

The percentage of beneficial help increased over time. In the first 4 practice sessions (out of 11), students got help that resulted in their giving correct answers for 44% of the questions they did not answer correctly on their own. In the last 4 practice sessions, students got such help for 71% of the questions that they did not answer correctly on their own.

In a review of research on helping participant structures in small groups in mathematics classrooms, Webb (1991) suggested that help can be viewed as a continuum, from elaborated explanations to telling the answer, with other kinds of help fitting between the two extremes. As discussed in chapter 2, she found that giving explanations correlated positively with academic achievement, and that receiving answers or a lower level of help than requested is negatively correlated with achievement. Webb found no clear patterns for receiving explanations or for intermediate kinds of help.

Across the 50 instances of successful peer help in Miss Grant's mathematics class, 50% involved some kind of explanation, while 8% involved only giving the answer. Giving background information accounted for 13%. Feedback, hints, and guesses accounted for 28%. Over the course of the school year, students seemed to learn to give explanations rather than just the answers. Explanations accounted for 30% of the successful help in the first half of the practice sessions and 67% in the second half. Giving answers accounted for 19% in the first half, and 0% in the second half.

The following examples illustrate the extreme ends of the help continuum. In Excerpt 4.2, Kyon explained to Rosanna how to solve a problem after Rosanna said that she did not know how to do it. (Note that Kyon's procedural explanation to Rosanna in Excerpt 4.2 and Kim's procedural explanation to Nancy in Excerpt 4.4 are consistent with the overall procedural approach to mathematics embodied in the class.)

Excerpt 4.2

(Kyon and Rosanna exchange the question and answer sheets, and Rosanna picks a card.)

Rosanna: Twenty-three [card number]. [The question is "Compare the fractions 3/12 and 6/24. Write $<$, $>$, or $=$."]

Kyon: All the same [she is not providing the answer, but seems to be commenting on the similarity of many of the problems].

Rosanna: Cause you don't get them.

Rosanna: (( )) [at this point Rosanna is making funny faces and seems to be talking in nonsense words].

(Rosanna and Kyon laugh.)

Rosanna: Look at your face!

Kyon: Look, do you know how to do it?

Rosanna: Yes, no, I don't know.

Kyon: Okay, Okay. Numerator, Okay? Three times 2 is 6.

Rosanna: Right.

Kyon: And then if 12 times 2 is 24, it both works out. So what's the answer?

Rosanna: Both works out?

Kyon: Yeah. So what's the answer?

Rosanna: Equal.

Kyon: Right.

(Rosanna laughs.)

In contrast, Excerpt 4.3 illustrates students giving and receiving an answer.

Excerpt 4.3

(Kim and Nancy exchange question and answer sheets.)

. . . .

(Kim draws a card.)

Kim: Twelve [number on her card]. [The question is "The temperature on a warm summer day may be: A. 98°C, B. 2°C, C. 30°C."]

Nancy: Ah (using a funny voice)!

(Pause)

(Kim looks at the blackboard where a large thermometer with both Celsius and Fahrenheit degrees is displayed.)

Kim: (laughs) Whoa! No way! (pause) I'm not sure if, whether it's "B" or "C".

Nancy: Pick one. Very close. (pause) The last one you said.

(Kim looks at large thermometer again.)

Nancy: Kim, the last one you said.

Kim: Huh? C.

(Nancy nods "yes.")

Kim: That's the one I thought it was but I wasn't sure.

Nancy: Well, you got it.

Frequently, students received more than one kind of help as they tried to answer a question. In Excerpt 4.4, Kim provided Nancy with background information, allowed Nancy to guess, and then explained how to arrive at the answer to the problem.

Excerpt 4.4

(Kim and Nancy exchange question and answer sheets.)

(Kim gives Nancy a card from the pile.)

Nancy: Five [question number].

Kim: I know the answer (patting the desk).

Nancy: (reads) "If the temperature reaches 35 degrees Celsius (pause) tomorrow, will it be, will it be cold, warm, or hot?" (pause) 35 degrees ((Look at this.)) (Looks at large thermometer on the blackboard that has both Celsius and Fahrenheit marked on it.)

(Pause)

Nancy: Cold gets nearer to zero, right?

Kim: Yes (nodding). (Leans over Nancy's paper and points.)

Nancy: Warm?

Kim: No.

Nancy: Hot?

Kim: Right.

Kim: Okay. I'll give it to you [meaning she would count it as correct]. See look. I'll explain it. Okay. Normal warm temperature is 35 degrees Celsius. You look over there, over there, and look at the thirty and you see where it would be over on the Fahrenheit. (pause) Okay?

Kim: I'll give it to you.

Nancy: Okay, thanks.

Kim: You gave me one. (laughs)

Even giving and receiving answers was not always a simple process. Students sometimes gave their peers answers *after* providing some other kind of help, as in Excerpt 4.5, where Joshua used Socratic-type questions before giving Blanca the answer.

Excerpt 4.5

(Blanca and Joshua exchange question and answer sheets.)

(Blanca draws a card. [The question is "Write the word or symbol for the unit of metric measure that best fits each example. The width of a bug: Word _____ Symbol _____. "])

. . . .

Blanca: "The width of the bug" [reading the question]. Centimeter is the, uh, width. (pause)

Blanca: Mrs. Walker! [mistakingly calling her homeroom teacher instead of Miss Grant]

Philip: Miss Walker? (giggles)

Joshua: Miss Grant.

Blanca: Miss Grant?

Philip: You call [her] Miss Walker every time.

(Blanca waves her hand, trying to get Miss Grant's attention. When she does not come over to their table, Blanca puts her hand down.)

Joshua: You have a bug, any bug. What would you use? Any kind of bug.

Blanca: Centimeters.

Joshua: Hmm. (pause) Pick an ant. What would you use to measure an ant?

Blanca: Centimeters.

Joshua: Well, what do you choose? CM, KM, MM, or M?

Blanca: (( ))

Joshua: MM?

(Blanca nods.)

Joshua: (Makes sound like a bell.) Right!

The complexity of the social processes involved in Excerpts 4.3, 4.4, and 4.5 suggest that the students were doing more than just providing help to one another. As I discuss later in this chapter, students' interactions during practice sessions were influenced by their definitions of these sessions as "games." Webb's (1991) categories, which identify kinds of help related to learning, do not account for all aspects of the students' interactions.

Students also engaged in "self-help," talking aloud to themselves as they worked through a difficult problem. While students can silently "talk" to themselves in individual work, the cooperative learning context allowed students to talk to themselves out loud, which seemed to be helpful to the students, as Excerpt 4.6 illustrates.

Excerpt 4.6

(Charlie and Larry switch question and answer sheets.)

(Charlie draws a card from the pile and begins to figure answer to his question. [The question is "What is 2 2/3 as an improper fraction?"])

Charlie: Seven, 7/3 [his answer].

Larry: What number?

Charlie: Wait. Twelve. No. Eleven [his question number]. (pause) Wait. Whoa, whoa, whoa, whoa. I did, 2 times 3, 6 (pause) 7, 8 [talking to himself]. Eight thirds [his answer].

(Larry nods "yes.")

In addition to help with specific questions, students also helped one another by clarifying the immediate task or another assignment. While not directly related to learning, such help could keep the student from going down a fruitless path or losing time trying to determine what they needed to do in an assignment.

However, task-related peer help was not always forthcoming when needed. Of the questions for which I could determine the accuracy of students' answers, in 42 episodes the readers never answered the questions correctly. In 36 of these episodes readers did not receive any help in understanding the problem from their peers. I consider these to be "missed opportunities" because by answering the question incorrectly, the students clearly demonstrated a need for help. Such missed opportunities (N=36) occurred frequently in comparison to beneficial peer help (N= 50). In Excerpt 4.7, Philip did not help Larry understand why his answer was wrong.

Excerpt 4.7

(Philip and Larry switch question and answer sheets.)

(Larry selects a card and begins to work on his question. [The question is "What is the length, in centimeters, of the pencil shown below?"])

(Larry measures the pencil and Philip leans over and watches him.)

Larry: Sixty-nine [his answer] (pause) sixty-nine centimeters.

Philip: Wrong, wrong, 12 centimeters, only 12. [laughs] What you talking about?

Larry: Dag, man, I dunno.

Philip clearly missed an opportunity to help Larry understand why his answer was wrong.

Contextual Influences

As indicated in the previous section, the students' tasks and interpersonal interactions (particularly their helping behaviors) influenced the students' learning. Other contextual features also were important influences on their learning and interactions. These features included the curriculum and materials, the participant structures established by Miss Grant, Miss Grant's definition of the practice sessions, the students' own definition of the practice sessions, and the students' social skills (or lack of social skills).

Although the students helped each other to a degree, two contextual features in particular seemed to inhibit the cooperative learning process. The emphasis on getting the correct answers provided little encouragement for giving explanations. In addition, the idea of games seemed to take over the practice sessions, prompting the students to compete for points, or to be the first to complete the practice session, rather than encouraging students to assure that all team members understood the mathematics questions and could answer them correctly.

Materials and Curriculum

The questions presented to the students in TGT practice sessions consisted primarily of simple numerical problems and multiple choice questions with a few word problems. Most of the questions involved computations or multiple choice answers. Examples included: "Which metric unit would you use to measure the length of a pencil: a. millimeters, b. meters, c. centimeters;" "What is the least common multiple of 4 and 6? Do not include 0;" and "13/15 − 5/15 = _____." Some worksheets had "problem solving" questions at the end. An example: "There were 373 hamburgers for 45 hungry children. How many hamburgers did each one get? How many hamburgers were left over?" The "correct" answer for each question was presented on an answer sheet. Answering the questions involved convergent thinking and comprehension, and embodied a procedural approach to mathematics.

These kinds of mathematics questions were consistent with the school district's curriculum, which emphasized a procedural approach to mathematics and measured students' progress through their answers to similar kinds of questions. The questions also worked well as preparation for the TGT tournament sessions, which involved identifying which students answered the most questions correctly in a competitive context.

Participant Structure Established by Miss Grant

After some initial trials, Miss Grant arrived at a consistent structure for TGT practice sessions. Pairs of students worked together. One student had the question sheet and the other the answer sheet; between them was a pile of cards face down with the question numbers on the cards. When it was a student's turn, the student would pick the top card from the pile, read the number on it, and then answer the corresponding question on the problem sheet. The other student had the answer sheet and would tell the student who worked the problem whether his or her answer was correct or not. This can be considered a "helping" participant structure, as opposed to a collaborative participant structure. Students were not working together to solve a problem, rather one student had a problem to solve and the other student, who had the answer sheet, could provide help.

Miss Grant's Definition of the Team Study Sessions

Miss Grant characterized the TGT team study sessions as practice, consistently referring to them as "practice," "team practice" or "practice sessions" when she spoke to the students. By defining the team study sessions as practice, Miss Grant focused on these sessions as preparation for the TGT tournament sessions and for the assessments in the math lab, both of which rewarded students for answering the maximum number of questions correctly. As discussed earlier, Miss Grant told the students when they began using TGT in their mathematics class that when their partners answered a question in a practice session incorrectly, the student with the answer sheet should explain to the partner how to solve the problem correctly.

Students' Definition of Team Study Sessions

A central issue in understanding the behavior of any group of students is the students' own definition of the situation, their "motive" in activity theory terms (Leont'ev, 1978, 1981). This helps us to understand the kinds of helping behaviors the students gave, the missed opportunities for help, and why a partner rarely gave help after a reader answered a question incorrectly.

Although Miss Grant defined the team study sessions as practice, her students defined the practice sessions of TGT as competitive games. In one "game" resembling the tournaments, the students competed with each other to get the most "points" (indicated by the number of cards they kept because they gave correct answers). In all but one practice session students counted and compared the number of cards each student had, discussed how many cards each had, or commented about wanting to "beat" someone by having more cards.[6]

For example, in the first practice session Nancy and Kyon, members at the same team but in different pairs, compared the number of cards they had after Nancy's partner left to examine a chart on the wall:

Excerpt 4.8

Nancy: How many cards do you have, Kyon?

Kyon: Is that all your cards?

Nancy: (counting her cards aloud) Two, three, four, five, six.

Nancy: How many?

Kyon: Huh?

Nancy: How many?

Kyon: First, how many? [wants Nancy to tell first]

Nancy: Six.

Kyon: Seven.

At the end of the same practice session, Kim, Nancy's partner, said, "OK, we're done. You beat me" (meaning that Nancy accumulated more cards for correct answers than she did). After Nancy left the table to turn in her cards, Kim counted her cards aloud.

In another example, the competitive spirit was illustrated when Frank commented to his partner Philip in the first episode of their practice session: "You gonna lose. . . . You gonna lose." Throughout the session Frank and Philip continued referring to the number of cards each had obtained. After Miss Grant announced that practice was over, Frank said to Philip: "Let's count," and they each counted their cards. Each had eight cards. Frank then said into the microphone on their desk, talking as if he were a sports announcer: "Everybody, it's a tie! Eight to eight, and the champions are Frank and Philip. Here! Yay! (claps) Yay! Everybody, that was a close game. There was no tie breakers [sic]. And the winners are Philip and Frank! Everybody, that was a close game. Anybody coulda won. Till next time, this is Frank Clark, your speaker" (laughs).

Frank's competitive spirit was not limited to his own partner. He also checked several times with Charlie, a member of the other pair in his team, about how many cards Charlie had, and he also asked a pair of girls at another table how many each had.

Another indication of the importance of "points" was that students negotiated what "counted" as a point. In one episode Philip wanted to redo a problem after he answered it incorrectly. His partner (Jack) would not agree until Philip said, "It doesn't count [as a point for me] if I get it right again."

In a few episodes a spirit of reciprocity developed around "giving points," i.e., counting an answer as correct when it was incorrect and allowing the erring partner to keep the card. In one episode,

Kim's question required her to read the temperature from a picture of a thermometer. Her first answer was "seven"; the correct answer was thirty-seven. The thermometer on the question sheet had 35 as the first number on the thermometer; at subsequent marks just the unit digits were printed (6, 7, 8, etc.). Nancy told Kim that her answer was wrong and gave her a hint for the correct answer. Kim then saw her error:

Excerpt 4.9

Kim: Oh, see. It says thirty-five. I didn't see the thirty-five there. Thirty-six, thirty-seven.

Nancy: (to Kim) Okay. I'll give it to you.

Kim: Oh, good.

Nancy: 'Cause you didn't see it.

A few minutes later Kim reciprocated by not "counting" Nancy's first answer (which was incorrect) and allowing her second answer (which was correct) to "count," thus giving Nancy the point (see Excerpt 4.4 above).

The importance of "getting points" seemed to mean that once a student gave an answer (and either did or did not get a point), he or she was unlikely to receive help from another student. As mentioned above, the students gave 42 incorrect answers in the practice sessions. In only 6 of these episodes did students provide help to their partner after the partner gave an incorrect answer, with only 3 of these episodes involving explanations. If learning or winning the tournament were the students' goal, incorrect answers would have motivated students to help their partners understand how to answer the questions. These students did not seem to interpret incorrect answers that way. Once an answer was given, it was time to begin the next round of the game.

The students' competitive spirit and interest in getting "points" at times seemed to inhibit their willingness to encourage one another and to behave honestly. An episode involving Frank and Philip shows how their competition affected their peer support. About eight minutes into the practice session, Frank seemed accidentally to walk away with Philip's card. Philip responded, "Gimme my card. That's my card." Frank tossed it to him and then drew a card from the pile. Philip then said to him, "I wish you got it wrong." An exchange later in the same episode strengthens this point. Frank had been working on his problem silently, and then tried to peek at the answer sheet while Philip was not looking.

Excerpt 4.10

Frank: (laughing) Oh, I'm in trouble, 'cause when I check it, I get, I get one, not a four.

Philip: Just say it.

Frank: I don't wanna get it wrong.

Philip: What's the answer?

Frank: See, if I, I keep on checking it, I always get a one.

Philip: (giggles) Get a one? Just say it!

Frank: I'm gonna get it wrong.

Philip: Huh?

Frank: I'm gonna get it wrong.

Philip: So what?

Frank: I don't wanna be a loser.

(Frank raises his hand.)

Philip: I don't want you to ask Miss Grant. You ask Miss Grant, you gonna get it right. Then Miss Grant gonna tell you the answer.

Miss Grant came to their table and helped Frank rework the problem and see his error, with the result that the answer he gave Philip was correct. After Miss Grant left, Philip and Frank continued to talk:

Excerpt 4.11

Philip: I hate you.

(Frank giggles.)

Philip: From now on, nobody can ask Miss Grant.

Frank: Okay.

Philip: But that doesn't count. Put it [card] back.

Frank: No.

Philip: That isn't fair. You had Miss Grant do it for you!

Frank: Okay. I do it over? I do another one?

Frank then proceeded to work another problem, this time without help from Miss Grant.

Frank's attempt to cheat by peeking at the answer sheet was not an isolated incident. In three practice sessions students cheated or tried to cheat, and in a fourth, one student asked the other if he wanted to cheat but the student declined. As Frank's comments indicate, this behavior seemed to be related to the students' desire to get more cards.

In a different kind of "game," pairs of students strove to finish their pile of cards before the other pairs, i.e., to "be first." The "finish first game" was visible in students' efforts to get their partners to work faster. In over half of the practice sessions students made references to getting done fast or to the amount of time left. In four practice sessions students explicitly compared their speed (measured in number of cards finished) to another pair. For example, in one practice session Kyon said to Rosanna, "Hurry up! They're done." In another instance, Veata said to Matthew, "Hurry up, 'cause, look, they're beating us." At the beginning of another class Barika said to Melinda, "Come on, Melinda. (pause) Let's try to speed up and work. We wanna be the first ones to finish at least."

The students' "finish first game" also seemed to influence their learning. The desire to finish first may have contributed to the pattern that giving help usually occurred *before* a student gave an answer. Giving help before a student offered an answer would have speeded up the pair overall and thus may have helped them win the "finish first game." Providing help after a reader had answered incorrectly would have slowed down the pair and reduced their chance of winning the "finish first game."

The "points game" and the "finish first game" seemed to eclipse team spirit as a motivating factor in the students' behavior during practice sessions. When a student gave an incorrect answer or had difficulty with a question, neither the student trying to answer a question nor his or her partner ever referred to the importance of learning how to answer the problem correctly for the sake of their team.[7] Team spirit, which the developers of TGT present as a primary motivational device in TGT (Slavin, 1986), was not a significant motivator in Miss Grant's mathematics class.

Competition in TGT, the School, and the Larger Community

We can understand students' definition of the practice sessions as competitive games by examining contextual features of these sessions. The tournament component of TGT seemed to provide the model that the students extended to the practice sessions. In the tournament sessions students represented their teams in competitions against members of other teams, earning points based on the number of cards (questions answered correctly) that they won.[8]

The way in which Miss Grant rewarded the winning teams may have deemphasized the team. At the end of each Friday's tournament session she recorded how many questions (represented by the number of cards) each student had answered correctly. Miss Grant did not immediately tally team scores or announce team awards, opting to share that information the following week.[9] This delay, and Miss Grant's removal of external rewards for the Super Team, may have contributed to the students' diminished focus on team spirit.

Maplewood School's use of the school district's system for mathematics instruction may have contributed to the development of the "points game" during the practice sessions. The creation and use of the math lab, which assessed students' knowledge of mathematics objectives once a week, and the weekly reports of each students' scores, which Miss Grant sometimes shared with the students, created a context which emphasized passing (or "accumulating") as many objectives as possible.

That the students chose to extend the competitive approach from the tournament sessions to the practice sessions was not surprising given the individualism and competition that pervades our schools and society (Goldman & McDermott, 1987; Tobin, Wu & Davidson, 1989). That broad societal context presented a situation in which it was easy for the students to define the practice sessions as competitive games.[10]

Students' Social Skills

Cooperative learning groups, even those as highly structured as the TGT practice sessions and tournaments, are social situations as well as learning situations (see Erickson & Shultz, 1992). As discussed above, students' social relationships influenced students' learning by contributing to students reciprocating in "giving points" (Excerpts 4.9 and 4.4) and to students being less than supportive (Excerpts 4.10 and 4.11).

The students themselves saw social skills as important to their cooperative learning groups. When I asked students what they would tell a new student about how to be a good group member, almost all the students mentioned social skills. They said that good group members should be respectful, not talk too much, not yell, not laugh when others get an answer wrong, and not fight. They also mentioned that students should study hard, listen to the teacher, do their homework, pay attention, try their best, and help one another.

Lack of social skills contributed to bad feelings within cooperative learning groups. When I asked the students what others do in their groups that makes them feel mad or angry, more than half of the students mentioned behaviors related to social skills. They said that they got mad when students called them names, made fun of them when they got an answer wrong, distracted them by humming or kicking them, bragged about the points they had, or told them that their answer was wrong when it really was right.

When I asked what they did when other students did these behaviors, the most frequent answer involved responding verbally in some way. Students said they would say "that's not really very nice" or "how would you like it if someone did that to you," or they would "tell him to stop it" or "tell 'em they shouldn't do it." A few students said to ignore it and keep working or "stay calm."

As discussed earlier, Miss Grant reviewed with the students at the beginning of the year appropriate behavior for their groups, and she awarded points for appropriate behavior early in the school year. However, she did not explicitly teach social skills related to working in the TGT groups. Students' behavior and their responses in the interviews indicated several areas where explicit instruction might have aided students' working relationships and learning.

Using the six categories outlined in chapter 1, the final section of this chapter will summarize the contextual influences on cooperative learning in the fourth grade mathematics class. However, before proceeding to that discussion, the effects of cooperative learning are examined.

Outcomes of Cooperative Learning

The discussion so far has focused on processes, primarily around TGT in Miss Grant's mathematics class. As discussed in chapter 1, I also examined outcomes. However, for several reasons (see chapter 1 and the Appendix), the quantitative comparative data are "messy" and not based on comparable classes; therefore, the results should be interpreted with caution.

Mathematics

In an interview in late April Miss Grant said that overall she would give cooperative learning an 8 on a scale of 1 to 10. Miss Grant thought cooperative learning was effective in eliminating the monotony that often attends individual drill and practice. She also found that cooperative learning helped her to know how individual students were doing with the problems.

The students interviewed saw two major benefits to the practice sessions. Some students said that the practice sessions and tournaments helped them learn math. Rosanna said that with groups "it's easier to learn, than to be alone and not to know what to do." Jack said, "You learn a lot together. . . . and you learn more faster if you work together." Kanika said that in the practice sessions, "someone can help us if we don't really understand it." Students also said that the practice sessions helped them prepare for tournaments or tests. Kanika said of the practice sessions, "It's like a challenge for you to get ready for the tournament." And Julita said that she thought Miss Grant had them do practice sessions and tournaments "so we could do our best in our tests in the math lab." (Although the students said during interviews that they thought the practice sessions helped them to learn mathematics and to prepare for tournaments or tests, these benefits did not seem to be the primary motivators of their speech and behavior during the practice sessions.)

Miss Grant's students continued to work "above grade level," according to the school district's standards. The school district's expected on-grade-level range for the second quarter of the fourth grade was between 72 and 105 objectives completed; Miss Grant's class had completed an average of 112 objectives.

I compared Miss Grant's mathematics class to the other two fourth grade mathematics classes on the number of mathematics objectives completed. However, because the fourth grade mathematics classes were "tracked" by students' mathematics performance, the classes are not comparable. Raw score comparisons are the most difficult to interpret, but gain scores do provide a measure of how much each class changed, independent of their starting points. Miss Grant's mathematics class ($M = 12.6$, $SD = 2.7$) completed more mathematics objectives within the first two quarters of the year than the other two mathematics classes ($M = 10.3$, $SD = 4.2$; and

$M = 8.9, SD = 3.4), F(2, 56) = 5.89, p < .01$. However, this is not surprising given Miss Grant's class was the "high" mathematics class.

Broader Comparisons

Previous research indicates that cooperative learning often influences positively students' self-esteem and attitudes toward school (Slavin, 1990). Because fourth grade students at Maplewood School experienced several methods of cooperative learning in various classes (see chapter 3 and the Appendix), this exposure to cooperative learning outside their mathematics classes could have influenced their self-esteem and attitudes toward school. In an effort to detect this kind of influence, I compared students with the most and least experience with cooperative learning in terms of self-esteem and attitudes toward school as well as students in the three mathematics classes (see the Appendix for details).

Analyses of the quantitative data indicate that measures of self-esteem and attitudes toward school showed no differences between the three fourth-grade mathematics classes, either in raw scores or in gain scores, that could be clearly attributed to TGT. Moreover, there were no differences between students who received the most and the least cooperative learning overall.

Students' views of the place of TGT in their experience of Miss Grant's mathematics class is useful in understanding TGT's apparent lack of effect on their self-esteem and attitudes. I asked students in interviews what they would tell a new girl or boy who asked them, "Tell me about your math class. What do you do? How does Miss Grant teach it?" Students most frequently mentioned the math lab or math assessments, followed by discussions of recent class content, and then comments about aspects of cooperative learning, primarily referring to it in terms of tournaments or games. Cooperative learning was not *the* defining feature of students' experiences in their mathematics class. These perceptions, the patterns of peer interactions in the TGT practice sessions, and the fact that the TGT practice and tournament sessions accounted for no more than two of the students' five weekly mathematics classes, help us understand why TGT had no measurable effect on students' self-esteem or attitudes toward school.

I expect that similar contextual features contributed to the results of the most to least comparison. Based on my general observations in the school and interviews with teachers, cooperative learning was not the defining feature of any fourth grade class.

Discussion

TGT in Miss Grant's mathematics class presents a mixed picture. Students had opportunities to learn procedural mathematics. They enjoyed TGT practice sessions and, through their interactions in the practice sessions, students aided one another in getting the correct answers. The frequency of their help increased over time. However, less then half of the peer help given involved explanations, and students frequently missed opportunities to provide their peers help when they needed it.

Miss Grant said she would give TGT an 8 on a scale of 1 to 10. The class seemed to meet the school district's criterion for number of objectives passed, although the director of the math lab and the principal were not happy with the students' progress. TGT and cooperative learning more broadly did not appear to influence students' self-esteem or attitudes toward school.

Contextual features help us understand these patterns. The six categories of contextual influences, introduced in chapter 1, provide a useful way to understand contextual influences on Miss Grant's learning and on her students' interactions and learning. (I discuss contextual influences within these categories further in chapter 7, where contextual influences on the two focus classes are compared.)

All six categories of context were important influences on Miss Grant's learning processes. Her task, learning to use TGT in her mathematics class, presented numerous challenges that were not addressed when she was taught about cooperative learning.

Miss Grant was influenced by various psychological and technical tools. The tools, which provided "scripts" or models from which she drew, included: TGT as an existing cooperative learning structure, books about TGT and cooperative learning, her training and experience with cooperative learning, her prior experience using cooperative learning, and published curriculum materials.

Miss Grant's interpersonal context did not involve an extensive or active local "community of practice" regarding cooperative learning. She did not engage in ongoing interactions with adult "experts" or "peers" to learn how to use TGT in her mathematics class. The closest parallel to expert assistance for Miss Grant was informal consultations she had with Mrs. David and what she heard from other teachers about how they or others had used cooperative learning previously in Maplewood School. As discussed above, students' behavioral and verbal responses to using TGT were important influences on her learning to use TGT, contributing to her modifying aspects of TGT in mathematics and extending her use of TGT to her language arts class.

Individual and social meanings were also central to Miss Grant's learning. For example, her goal of using TGT to help motivate students to practice mathematics influenced how she learned to use TGT and what students learned in the practice sessions. Her agreement with Mr. Harris that using cooperative learning would be her professional goal for the year increased her personal stake in learning to use cooperative learning successfully.

Local cultures and institutions also influenced Miss Grant's learning. Maplewood School provided a generally supportive climate for teachers' use of cooperative learning. The high stakes meaning of mathematics, especially in the school but also in the larger community, created pressures for Miss Grant. The lack of planning time, the schedule of classes, pullouts, modifications in the school schedule, and problems with integration between existing materials and the required curriculum constrained her use of cooperative learning in her classes.

The influence of larger cultures and institutions can be seen in the school district's procedural approach to mathematics and in the pervasiveness of competition in the school and larger educational community. Aware of these larger cultural patterns, Miss Grant expressed some ambivalence regarding competition in her classes. She expressed concerns about asking students to cooperate in the context of school norms that supported competition, but was disturbed enough by the competitive aspects of TGT that she modified the scoring system to make TGT less competitive.

Miss Grant seemed to have a view that was compatible with the contextual analyses performed here. In our interview in April, Miss Grant said of her use of cooperative learning: "I've adapted to my own way of doing things." Later in the interview, when I asked about her overall evaluation of cooperative learning, Miss Grant said, "it's not going to work with everything; the teacher and the class will make it. . . . It depends on the situation."

The six categories of contextual influences also are useful in discussing how context influenced students' learning within TGT practice sessions. The explicit focus of the students' learning was procedural mathematics. The mathematics tasks Miss Grant assigned during practice sessions involved convergent questions, usually with numerical (nontextual) problems, with the "correct" answer provided on an answer sheet. These tasks did not require students to perform complex mathematics or to explain the processes by which they arrived at their answers.

The "scripts" offered by TGT for practice sessions (team study) and tournaments, and the "tools" provided by TGT question sheets and answer sheets structured the students' learning of mathematics. The tournament component of TGT seemed to influence students' definition of the practice sessions as competitive games. Although not directly related to their learning of mathematics, the question cards were indirectly related to their learning after the students began using them to count "points" during practice sessions.

Students' peer interactions and relationships were central influences on students' learning. Miss Grant set up the TGT practice sessions as helping participant structures, with one student in a pair checking the answer sheet while the other student tried to answer a question. In approximately half of all episodes, students answered their questions correctly without any help. In the remaining episodes, students provided help about half the time, and in about half of these instances students provided explanations in response to a peer's problems. However, much of the peer help was less than optimal; in addition, "missed opportunities" occurred frequently.

Students saw social skills as important to their experiences of TGT. To help foster students' social skills, Miss Grant discussed a list of acceptable behaviors for cooperative learning sessions, but this did not seem to provide sufficient support for students to develop optimal social skills.

Miss Grant's and the students' meanings are both relevant in understanding the students' learning. Although Miss Grant explicitly told her students to explain how to solve a problem correctly if their partner gave an incorrect answer, her definition of team study as practice sessions seemed to emphasize students' answering the maximum number of questions correctly. Students' definition of the practice sessions as competitive games was a contextual feature that was a central influence on their peer interactions and learning. The "points game" and the "finish first game" contributed to the frequent missed opportunities, students' rarely giving help after their partners gave an answer, students' lack of encouragement to one another, and students' cheating.

The weekly assessments in the math lab in Maplewood School and the related weekly reports probably contributed to students' emphasis on individually accumulating "points" during the practice sessions. There is a striking similarity between the math lab's emphasis on individual students passing as many objectives as possible and the students' goal of accumulating the most "points" during practice sessions.

The high value placed on competition in the broader society (and in the school) made it easy for the students to define the practice sessions as competitive games. The school district's curriculum and system for teaching mathematics emphasized procedural mathematics, which definitely influenced how Miss Grant defined the tasks her students needed to learn.

Although variations among students based on ethnicity, race, or gender were not a focus of the analysis here, patterns in Asian American students' interactions illustrate the kinds of influence possible from ethnic or gender cultures. Asian American students stood out in their interest in explaining and understanding the mathematics problems (albeit in a procedural manner). Although they accounted for 25% of the students in the videotaped observations, Asian American students produced 55% (17 instances) of explanations given by peers to one another. (See Kyon in Excerpt 4.2 for an example.)

Despite the importance of contextual features, they were by no means unilinear "causes" of how Miss Grant learned to use cooperative learning or how her students learned in the mathematics class. As I discuss further in chapter 7, contextual features were interwoven and not "separate" influences. For example, features of TGT, Miss Grant's use of TGT, students' definition of the practice sessions as games, and the widespread norm of competition in the school and society all influenced students' interactions during practice sessions.

Miss Grant characterized some of the aspects of context as "pressures" on her, suggesting that they exerted an influence, but that she also had choices. In fact, Miss Grant did not always change her behavior in response to pressures she felt. Although the mathematics coordinator wanted her to stop using TGT in mathematics altogether, Miss Grant only reduced its frequency. Although Mr. Harris wanted the fourth grade mathematics classes to be mixed ability classes, Miss Grant and the other fourth grade teacher persuaded him to approve classes based on past mathematics achievement.[11] Miss Grant clearly exercised agency. Students' agency is most clearly seen in the centrality of their definition of the practice sessions as games.

The contextual analyses presented here may appear to stand in contrast to the fidelity approach, which seeks to identify whether a teacher implemented an innovation according to preset criteria. As discussed further in chapter 8, I do not view a teacher's adaptations of an innovation as inherently good or bad. The issue is whether particular changes contribute to or detract from the desired processes and outcomes.

However, I think a contextual perspective can aid those approaching an innovation from the fidelity perspective because context helps in understanding how a teacher learned to use an innovation in a particular way, and how and what the teacher's students' learned. As shown below, contextual features may also help explain the influences of particular fidelity criteria.

Miss Grant met the TGT fidelity criterion of individual accountability through the tournaments, individual quizzes administered in class, and weekly individual assessments in the math lab. This criterion fit very well with the individualized system for mathematics the school system was using at the time.

Miss Grant addressed the criterion of team recognition or rewards by giving teams rewards based on teams' relative tournament rankings. However, the impact of team rewards as a motivator may have been diminished by Miss Grant's decision to delay giving team awards until the week after tournament sessions and by her decision in December to eliminate rewards beyond certificates. These decisions were influenced by time constraints and by her goal to reduce the competitive aspect of TGT because some students were very distressed when their team "lost." Students' definition of the practice sessions as competitive games also seemed to diminish the impact of team rewards.

Miss Grant's use of TGT had a mixed record on "equal opportunities for all," which the TGT manuals (Slavin, 1986, 1994) presented as a fidelity criterion. High and low achievers within the class could contribute equally to their team score because they competed with students performing at about the same level, although Miss Grant did not use the bumping system suggested for TGT. Lack of time—both time she would need to determine which students needed to move to which tournament tables and time for students to form new tournament tables each week—contributed to this decision. By assigning scores to teams based on their relative rankings rather than on their attainment of specific criterion scores, Miss Grant departed from the recommended procedures. Her decision was influenced, as discussed above, by her wish to create a positive experience for her students. If Miss Grant had used the suggested criterion scores to assign Super Team, Great Team, and Good Team ratings, very few teams would have earned recognition, especially early in her use of TGT. For example, if Miss Grant had applied the TGT manual's (Slavin, 1986) criterion to the first tournament in October, two teams would have achieved Super Team, but none of the other four teams would have received any reward. In the second tournament, two teams would have earned Great Team, and two Good Team.

A contextual feature that may partially account for Miss Grant's lack of complete fulfillment of the TGT fidelity criteria is the limited amount of training she received in cooperative learning and in the TGT method. Although Miss Grant had participated in a three-day workshop offered by the developers of TGT, she had no onsite support as she learned to use TGT in her mathematics classroom. However, I would venture to say that most teachers using TGT and other STL cooperative learning methods in everyday classrooms probably have had less training about these methods than Miss Grant and that few teachers receive the benefit of onsite support as they learn on-the-job to use these methods in their classrooms.

Although fidelity criteria are important, this chapter indicates that a fidelity perspective by itself would overlook many significant influences that contribute to cooperative learning's success or failure in everyday classrooms. This case study has provided many examples of how goals, values, meanings, constraints, and competing pressures can influence how teachers use cooperative learning and how students learn within it. Perhaps the most compelling example was the students' definition of practice sessions as competitive games—an understanding that was inconsistent with Miss Grant's instructions to the students and that worked at odds with TGT's assumption that team spirit would motivate the students to teach each other. Viewing practice sessions as games, the students became more interested in winning points or finishing first in the practice sessions than helping their teammates learn the mathematics needed to succeed in the tournaments.

The examples of contextual influences discussed in this chapter suggest that in the challenging world of everyday classrooms, teacher training that does not help teachers address contextual influences may not play a controlling role in a teacher's use of an innovation, and how a teacher uses an innovation will not necessarily determine its effects on students. (See chapter 8 for further discussion of training issues.) Many other aspects of context, including the meanings and values of the students, will influence the effectiveness of an innovation in everyday classrooms.

Five

Learning Together in Sixth Grade Social Studies

Mrs. Parker used the Learning Together (LT) method of cooperative learning (D. W. Johnson, R. T. Johnson, & Holubec, 1986) in her social studies class. In contrast to Teams-Games-Tournaments (TGT), which is highly structured, Learning Together is based on general principles. (See chapter 2 for a fuller discussion of the two approaches.)

Mrs. Parker and Her Context

Natural History of Mrs. Parker's Learning

Mrs. Parker was an experienced, highly regarded teacher, who had well-established routines of practice before she introduced cooperative learning into her classes. The focus year was her eighth year of full-time teaching and her seventh at Maplewood Elementary School.

Mrs. Parker had been introduced to Learning Together a year before this study during a summer course on special education. The course included a short section and film on the LT method of cooperative learning. Mrs. Parker pursued LT further on her own, with informal consultation from Mrs. David, the special education teacher in the next room, who was already using cooperative learning.

Mrs. Parker initially used one aspect of LT early in the school year prior to this study. Her purpose was to address the pedagogical need that her students were not completing their homework. Mrs. Parker hoped that group rewards in LT would motivate students to help one another get organized and complete their homework on

65

time. She assigned students in her homeroom to groups, and each morning she awarded the groups a point for each group member who completed his or her homework assignments. Mrs. Parker periodically tallied the points and provided a reward to the group with the highest number.

Mrs. Parker soon expanded her use of cooperative learning to provide group rewards for completing "bellwork" (assignments given for the time after students arrived and before the bell rang) and for other desired school behavior. She later extended the use of points and group rewards to content area instruction. In spelling, Mrs. Parker awarded points to groups based on how group members performed on spelling tests. However, she soon stopped this when students cheated in order to get higher grades and more points.

After having success with using group rewards for behavior management, Mrs. Parker incorporated another feature of LT—students' face-to-face interaction—into her use of cooperative learning. In her reading class Mrs. Parker had students read to one another, without using group rewards in any way. In a social studies class comprising her homeroom students, Mrs. Parker had students work together in groups on academic tasks, assigned different roles to members of each group, and provided group rewards for appropriate behavior. As a result of her continuing discussions with Mrs. David about cooperative learning, Mrs. Parker based her system for awarding and recording group points on Mrs. David's model.

At the end of the academic year before the focus year of this study, Mrs. Parker explained her ideas about cooperative learning in social studies:

> I try to stress to them [the students] that. . . . they should help each student in the group locate clues that will lead to the answer, to listen to each other's ideas, and together come up with a group product. . . . I think that if you teach someone something, you retain that information longer. That's why cooperative learning is good—each student can benefit from the group working together. . . . Maybe that's a better way of learning than just memorizing things, doing it by rote, and not having any real meaning with it.

Like other teachers at Maplewood Elementary School, Mrs. Parker participated in two inservice cooperative learning workshops the week before classes started in the focus year. The first workshop presented a broad framework for cooperative learning based on the

LT method, demonstrating various techniques that teachers could use for ice breakers, for group formation, and for instruction. The second workshop consisted of the *Circles of Learning* video about the LT method.

At the beginning of the focus year, Mrs. Parker used cooperative learning according to the pattern she had established at the end of the previous year. She assigned students in her homeroom to four member groups. Each group had their desks pushed together into a "pod," with two desks side by side and each pair facing the other pair.

Mrs. Parker gave groups points for bellwork and homework that was finished on time. She also awarded points to groups when they were well behaved, did classwork on time, completed long-range assignments on time, got quiet at the right times, or walked in the halls quietly. She used the group reward system for spelling to encourage students to help one another study for quizzes, with groups earning points based on group members' scores on the spelling tests. At the end of each two-week period Mrs. Parker totaled the points for each group, and then rank ordered them. She then posted group names on the cooperative learning chart as Super Team (highest), Great Team, Average Team, Most Improved Team, or Could Do Better Team (lowest). The super team could select from a list of rewards.

In language arts and reading, where the abilities of Mrs. Parker's students were considered average or above, she sometimes had students work in pairs or groups, with one student reading aloud for the other(s). Mrs. Parker sometimes told students they could help one another answer questions at the end of a chapter. Her most extensive use of cooperative learning was in the social studies class.

Learning to Use Learning Together in Social Studies

Mrs. Parker taught all three sixth grade social studies classes. Unlike the fourth grade mathematics classes, the sixth grade social studies classes were heterogenous in terms of students' past performance. The focus social studies class comprised Mrs. Parker's homeroom students.

At the beginning of the school year the focus social studies class included 23 students: 8 European Americans (6 girls and 2 boys), 7 Asian Americans (3 girls and 4 boys), 5 African Americans (all girls), and 3 Hispanic Americans (1 girl and 2 boys). Eight of these students (Carmela, Daniel, Hak Soo, Jane, Manuel, Peggy, Sung Min, and Woody) were second language learners. All but one of the second language learners had "graduated" from ESL classes.

The focus social studies class met once a week on Tuesdays, for a double period about ninety minutes long. This class was the first class after lunch and recess, and it was the last before school was dismissed for the day. During the first half of the class, Mrs. Parker usually taught or reviewed course material. During the second half, students usually worked in their cooperative learning groups.

Students sat facing one another in heterogeneous groups of four. Mrs. Parker changed the groups several times during the year. Almost all groups included one or two second language learners.

Near the beginning of the focus year Mrs. Parker said that her goal for using LT in her social studies class was "having the students work together to learn and to become successful." She thought that learning to work well with other people would be important for students' future success in their adult occupations.

> I think our young people don't have the same values, they don't have the same structure, as I did, or, I mean, [as] some generations. I think if maybe I can give them a little taste of helping each other, and not thinking only of "me," but thinking of other people too [that would help them]. And if I can do that in a roundabout way—I mean, you can talk to them about it, but actually making them do it I think would give more of an impact. . . . I think it's important that they learn to work together. Not all people are compatible, but you have to learn to tolerate. And you have to learn to help, and give and take. And, I think they have to start young. I think they have to learn that because, I don't know, I think something's missing from our children these days.

At the beginning of the school year Mrs. Parker established the rules to be followed in the cooperative learning groups. She passed out copies of a list of class rules from Kagan (1985), discussing each item with the class. Individuals had responsibility for trying, for asking for help from their group, for helping others in the group, for courteous behavior (for example, no put downs), and for fulfilling a specific role in the group (recorder, checker, materials gatherer, or reader). Groups had responsibility for asking "group" questions (i.e., those which no one in the group could answer), for helping one another, and for using soft voices. Aside from reminding students of the expected behaviors (usually after a group had violated the expectations) and implementing one team building activity in December,

Mrs. Parker did not instruct the students in small group skills nor did she have the groups process their group functioning. However, Mrs. Parker did establish a reward system for group behavior at the beginning of the year. She explicitly monitored group behavior, and publicly assigned points to groups according to how well the members of a group worked together. The group with the highest number of points could select from the list of possible team rewards, which included eating lunch with the teacher in the classroom, a "free" homework assignment in spelling or English, 30 minutes on the computer, an extra 20 minutes of library time, being teacher's assistant for one day, staying in for recess and playing a board game, or receiving a free milk at lunch.

At the beginning of each cooperative learning lesson Mrs. Parker outlined the tasks that were to be accomplished and if student roles were important she explained who was to do what to accomplish the task.

While working in cooperative learning groups, students usually completed individual worksheets, which involved reading text on the worksheet and answering convergent, comprehension questions based on the text they had read.[1] A typical example focused on "The African Experience." A worksheet presented information about Africa. Questions, whose answers were to be found from reading that worksheet, included: "Where was the evidence of earliest man found? When did the Ishongo people live? What significant contribution did the Ishongo people make to learning?"[2]

Students also performed assignments designed to improve their map skills. One example focused on longitude. The beginning of the worksheet reviewed information about longitude, parallels, and meridians. Students were expected to answer questions like the following: "Locating a place on a map can be easier when you know its longitude. This is especially true when the place is on or near a printed longitude line. Circle the following cities on the map and name them below: a. City in Morocco at 10° W, b. City in Nigeria at 10° E, c. City in Kenya near 40° E."[3]

When students completed a worksheet, Mrs. Parker expected them to place the worksheet in their individual social studies notebooks in the prescribed order. Mrs. Parker collected the students' notebooks at the end of each grading period. She saw this activity as helping the students to learn to be organized—a view she expressed directly to the students in April, as she reviewed what they had done so far in the class:

Some of you worked hard on your notebooks and some of you
didn't wait 'til the last minute to get your notebook together.
This is the type of thing you'll be doing next year, maybe not
in all your classes but certainly more than just one. You will
have to keep notebooks for more than one class. I hope you
will have learned this year how to organize yourself and how
to get your papers together. Some of you have progressed a
great deal from the beginning of the year. You have really
come a long way, you've organized yourself and you know
what's expected. . . . So hopefully you will be prepared, not to
go in and be shocked and surprised when a teacher requires
you to hold onto papers from the beginning of the year. Now
in lower grades the teacher hands back a paper, and you look
at it. Usually it goes in the trash right away, and you don't
think anything more about it. You will need to keep papers
because you may have tests that cover a lot of information. So
I think you will do a good job. Most of you are well organized.

Although one of Mrs. Parker's goals for using LT was to help students learn, her instructions to the class emphasized the tasks to be
completed during the class rather than what was to be learned. For
example, in a class early in the fall she told the students:

We're going to see a filmstrip on population and then you
will have time to work on this worksheet. . . . First I would
like you to work on this map and worksheet, then go back
and do anything that you have not done. This is the last
thing that will go in your notebook [for this grading pe-
riod]. . . . Then in your groups have the reader read; [and
then] answer the questions. You will have to answer these
questions on the back.

In April as the class began a new unit on Greece, Mrs. Parker told
the class about their assignment for the cooperative learning groups:

Now, what we're going to do, is back on pages 98 and 99, is
what we talked about Western Civilization. . . . I want you
(and this will be the first thing that will go in your notebook
for Greece) to write a definition for what is meant by Western Civilization. . . . Include some things that it says in the
book, but *don't copy* from the book. Put it in your own words.

Throughout the year, students took quizzes and tests individually. There were no group rewards for group scores on tests or quizzes.

Mrs. Parker soon began to introduce changes into the routine in her social studies class that used LT. By November Mrs. Parker had decreased her use of points for good group behavior, commenting to me that she made this decision because the students no longer needed points to work well together. However, Mrs. Parker continued informally to monitor the groups by circulating around the room during cooperative learning and to make suggestions to groups that were having problems about how they could work together more successfully.

In December Mrs. Parker had her students do a team building activity, Survival in the Desert (see Kagan, 1985). She hoped it would help them see the benefits of working together rather than alone. In this exercise students were asked to imagine that they were the survivors of a plane crash in the desert. Students were given a list of items salvaged from a plane wreck, and were asked to rank the items in order of their importance to their survival. The students first performed the exercise individually, then as a group, and later compared these rankings to a survival expert's ranking. The exercise assumed that the group's rankings would be a closer match to the expert's than any individual student's rankings, thus indicating to the students the benefits of cooperation.

Mrs. Parker usually had students complete worksheets that she had used in previous years. Thus, the content and nature of the cooperative learning tasks differed little from the work that her students the previous year had done individually. The worksheets that Mrs. Parker used in the fall required her students to answer convergent comprehension questions, with a presumed single "correct" answer.

However, in March Mrs. Parker developed a new task, which involved students interviewing each other about the projects they had just completed about Egypt. Students were to ask one another in their groups what they did, where they got their information, who helped them, and what important facts they had learned. Then each interviewer shared with their group what he or she learned about another student's project. Finally all the members of a group contributed from what they had learned to a "web" about Egypt. This assignment had more than one "correct" answer, i.e., it involved divergent questions.

Mrs. Parker was so pleased with how the new task worked, that she told Mrs. David about it. She then modified other tasks to make them more divergent and cooperative, with many of the new tasks requiring analysis or synthesis. For example, Mrs. Parker had each group develop a definition for city state. Then, using pictures of Athens and Sparta, each group predicted what they thought life had been like in the two city states. The groups then put these predictions on large paper charts, which were posted on the wall and discussed by the whole class.

Mrs. Parker's experience of using activities with more divergent questions in LT seemed to influence how she thought about the goals for using cooperative learning. In response to my question in May about how cooperative learning was meeting her goals, Mrs. Parker responded that one of her goals was for her class to be able to work together in a setting where they felt comfortable and where they could gather information together (rather than her giving the information to the class):

> I think it's important for the students to develop the skills of research, working together and looking for a common answer or a common goal. I think for the most part they have done that. . . . I like it. I think it works. It's good for the students and it's a good way of teaching them responsibility and working together.

Throughout the focus year Mrs. Parker set up three different participant structures for assignments that used LT. One was the "group reading" participant structure, in which she told students to read the text of a worksheet together. The other two participant structures involved students answering content-related questions. One was a "helping" participant structure, in which she told students to help one another, without any requirement to arrive at a joint answer.[4] The other was a "cooperative" participant structure, in which students jointly created their answers.

Contextual Influences

As with Miss Grant, contextual features influenced Mrs. Parker's decision to use LT in her social studies class, how she learned to use it, and how frequently she used it—all of which influenced her students' learning.

Mrs. Parker was already using LT in her social studies class when the principal and I agreed that I would conduct this study at Maplewood Elementary School. Mrs. Parker's training in cooperative learning, her prior use of it, the school's history of using cooperative learning, and feedback from her own use of LT all influenced her decision to use LT in her social studies class during the focus year.

If Mrs. Parker was to use any method of cooperative learning, the choice of LT was not surprising. Mrs. Parker's prior training in cooperative learning had focused almost totally on the LT method. Mrs. David, the school's cooperative learning expert, knew about LT, used aspects of LT, and drew upon LT when she advised Mrs. Parker and other teachers regarding cooperative learning.

A number of contextual features influenced how Mrs. Parker used LT. These features influenced the tasks she used, her goals for the LT classes, how she structured LT, and her approach to students' social skills.

For most of the focus year, students' tasks in LT consisted of completing worksheets that Mrs. Parker had used in previous years. These commercially-produced worksheets fit with the curriculum requirements of the school district. According to the developers of the LT method, one of its benefits is that it can be used with existing curriculum materials (D. W. Johnson, R. T. Johnson, & Holubec, 1986).

Lack of time was a factor in Mrs. Parker's choice of the existing materials. The amount of time involved in planning and using cooperative learning was a concern for Mrs. Parker. She commented in October of the focus year that she did not use cooperative learning in her other social studies classes because of the time and paperwork involved. When I asked Mrs. Parker in May what she would tell another teacher about cooperative learning, she said that it was a lot of work, implying that it required a considerable investment of time.

Mrs. Parker's goals for her students provided a context for her use of LT in social studies. At the beginning of the focus year, she told me that one of her primary goals in using cooperative learning in social studies was for her students to learn to work together and to expand their focus beyond themselves to their fellow students. Mrs. Parker also said that from her prior use of LT in social studies, she saw LT as beneficial because students helped one another organize their assignments, homework, and notebooks. In November, in response to my question about how she would explain cooperative learning to another teacher, Mrs. Parker identified cognitive benefits of cooperative learning, stating that cooperative learning gave "the groups a bit more freedom in discovering things or learning things." However, these cognitive benefits of cooperative learning did not seem to be a major goal of her use of LT at the beginning of the focus year.[5]

Mrs. Parker was concerned that her students learn the social studies content of their LT sessions, and she said that was a goal for her use of LT. (The content was included in individual quizzes and tests.) However, in her instructions at the beginning of LT sessions, Mrs. Parker stressed to the students that they were to finish their assignments and to have complete, well ordered notebooks. These goals were influenced by several contextual features, one of which was the meaning of social studies in the broader context of the school and school district. Because students' social studies achievement was not the focus of districtwide standardized testing (indicating its relatively low importance), there was no external measurement of what students learned in social studies. Consequently, other goals could compete with students' learning of social studies content.

One of Mrs. Parker's goals arose out of her expectation that the following year, when her students would be in middle school, teachers there would require the students to keep their completed work in a notebook for the duration of a grading period and to turn in the notebook to teachers in an organized manner at the end of the grading period. To help them develop the organizational skills they would need, Mrs. Parker required her students to maintain individual social studies notebooks.

The school district had a social studies curriculum that teachers were expected to follow. For the sixth grade the curriculum included Africa, ancient Egypt and Greece, and map skills. Teachers were expected to "cover" this material. This requirement, together with lack of flexibility in scheduling, contributed to Mrs. Parker's emphasis on finishing the assignments.

Mrs. Parker's emphasis on finishing assignments, in contrast to understanding the content, is not unusual. After reviewing studies on the nature of academic tasks, Doyle and Carter (1984) concluded that "teachers' and students' attention in classrooms is often dominated by concerns for maintaining order and finishing assignments" (p. 129). Given the ubiquitous emphasis on "covering" material from central district offices, the emphasis on finishing is not surprising.

As Mrs. Parker used LT in her social studies class, her goals for LT changed. As mentioned above, she focused initially on helping her students work together. Later, after she had assigned tasks that required students to generate knowledge, her goals expanded to include the cognitive benefits of LT. A feedback loop developed between Mrs. Parker's goals for LT and her use of LT. She tried a component of LT. If she found the component helpful, she included it in her goals for LT, and then used the component in other areas. A dramatic example in her social studies class was her addition of divergent tasks after a semester of using convergent tasks.

Several contextual features also influenced how Mrs. Parker structured her use of LT in her social studies class. Mrs. Parker's training influenced her to assign students to specific roles in LT. Use of student roles is presented by the developers of LT as a way to achieve positive interdependence among group members (D. W. Johnson, R. T. Johnson, & Holubec, 1986).

As discussed earlier, Mrs. Parker used two different participant structures (helping and cooperative) for assignments that required students to answer questions. Several contextual features seemed to contribute to her decisions about when to use these participant structures.

Student "pullouts" contributed to her use of the helping participant structure. During the LT sessions Mrs. Parker made frequent reference to modifications in the school schedule that interrupted cooperative learning activities, requiring her to recompose groups. Students regularly left her social studies class to participate in enrichment experiences or meetings for school projects. These "pullouts" also resulted in students being at different places in completing a task. In such situations, Mrs. Parker used helping rather than cooperative participant structures. As will be seen later in the chapter, these interruptions also had a direct impact on students' behavior in cooperative learning.

The nature of the task also influenced the participant structure that Mrs. Parker established. Some tasks were cooperative in their very design (for example, the interview task described earlier), so Mrs. Parker used a cooperative participant structure for these.

Student behavioral responses were a recurring contextual influence in Mrs. Parker's decisions about how to use cooperative learning. As discussed above, she curtailed giving students points for good group behavior in December because students were working well together without them.[6]

Students' verbal comments about cooperative learning also seemed to play a role in Mrs. Parker's continued use and expansion of cooperative learning. For example, Mrs. Parker said in April of the focus year that students liked cooperative learning, implying that the students' enjoyment of LT was a reason that she continued to use it. Mrs. Parker made a similar comment in November, indicating that part of the reason she continued to give points for students' spelling test grades was that they liked receiving them.

Contextual influences were also important in how Mrs. Parker approached students' social skills. Mrs. Parker addressed students' social skills in three ways: by monitoring their group interactions, by giving points for good group behavior, and by leading the students through a team building exercise early in the school year. Contextual features influenced her selection of these approaches and how she did them.

Mrs. Parker's use of points for good group behavior was an extension of her earlier uses of behavior points. Her interpretation of cooperative learning as involving behavior points seems to be clearly related to her initial exposure to cooperative learning in a special education class. Given the behavioristic emphasis within special education at the time, it is not surprising the Mrs. Parker's initial uses of cooperative learning was as a behavior management tool.

The local use of cooperative learning, particularly Mrs. David's, also influenced how Mrs. Parker used LT. For example, Mrs. David provided wall charts and ideas for a system of recording behavior points.

As discussed in chapter 2, social skills training and group processing of group functioning are a hallmark of the LT method (D. W. Johnson, R. T. Johnson, & Holubec, 1986, 1993a). Although Mrs. Parker gave behavior points and conducted one team building exercise, she did not provide ongoing training in social skills nor did she require groups to process their interactions.

Lack of time influenced this decision. As mentioned above, Mrs. Parker commented several times about the amount of time involved in preparing for LT. Social skills training would have required Mrs. Parker to devote more time to planning, especially since none of her training in cooperative learning addressed this component of LT, and might have prevented Mrs. Parker from "covering" all of the required social studies curriculum. Mrs. Parker was concerned also that all three of her social studies classes get the same exposure to the material before quizzes and tests. If she provided social skills training for her homeroom students (the only social studies class in which Mrs. Parker used LT), then her homeroom class would have devoted less time than her other social studies classes to the subject matter.

Contextual features also influenced how frequently Mrs. Parker used LT in social studies. Mrs. Parker thought that successful use of LT depended on having her whole class together. Frequent student pullouts for resource help and other reasons limited the number of times each week that Mrs. Parker thought she could use LT.

As happened with Miss Grant, Mrs. Parker's learning process continued throughout the school year. Contextual features continued to influence how she learned to use LT and to interact with her use of it.

Students and their Context

Mrs. Parker's use of LT provided her students with opportunities to learn social studies. In this section I examine how her students enacted cooperative learning in their social studies class and how contextual features influenced them.

Learning Social Studies

Most LT sessions in Mrs. Parker's social studies class required students to read worksheets or texts and then to answer questions derived from that reading. As discussed earlier, Mrs. Parker set up three different participant structures in LT in her social studies class: reading, helping, and cooperative.

In the reading participant structure one member of the group read aloud from a worksheet while the others followed along silently. Typically, group members took turns reading sections of the worksheet.

Most (72%) of the students' nonreading tasks involved convergent questions at the comprehension level (e.g., matching or fill in the blank), based on information from the preceding text. About 22% of the nonreading tasks involved divergent comprehension questions (e.g., generating ideas from pictures about a cultural group they were studying). In the spring some episodes involved divergent questions that required analysis or synthesis (4% and 2% of the total nonreading tasks, respectively).

The helping participant structure in the sixth grade social studies class was much less structured than the helping participant structure in the fourth grade math class. In the sixth grade, students did not alternate answering questions aloud, nor was an answer sheet available to them. Students worked on their own and could help one another as needed or requested.

The following excerpt occurred in a helping participant structure. Students had been working on different questions. Doria asked for help with the second part of the following question: "A. What metal is thought to have advanced the culture of Western Africa? B. In what area was it first used?"

Excerpt 5.1

Doria: (to Hak Soo) And what's this one? (pause) What's this one (showing her worksheet to Hak Soo)?

Hak Soo: (reads) "In what area was it first used?"

Kathleen: (to Hak Soo) Is the same thing?

Hak Soo: Yeah, the same thing, right here, "found in Begin, Nigeria."

The cooperative participant structures involved students working together to produce a common answer or complete a task. In the following excerpt, Mrs. Parker had set up a cooperative participant structure, and the group was trying to answer the question, "What significant contribution did the Ishongo people make to learning?"

Excerpt 5.2

Tonya: (to her group) Number three. "What significant con- tribu- contri-"

Sung Min: I already got that one.

Tonya: (to Sung Min) Hold it. (then reads aloud to herself) "What significant contribution did the Ishongo people make to learning?" Uh—

Tonya: (to her group) Where is the Ishongo thing? Okay. La-la-la-la-la. "Archaeologists found—" (reading from text).

Daniel: (to group) "What significant—"

Sandra: Three.

Tonya: "What signi-"

Daniel: "What significant contribution did the Ishongo—"

Tonya: They made and used a simple abacus counting frame.

Sandra: (to Tonya) Where, where?

Daniel: (to Sandra) On number three.

Tonya: (to group) A simple abacus counting frame.

Sung Min: (to Tonya) I know.

Daniel: (to group) A simple abacus counting frame. I put that for number two.

Tonya: (to Daniel) Huh?

(All write.)

Daniel: (to himself, while writing) Used, a simple, abacus, count-

Sung Min: (to Tonya) What did you—what did you put for three?

Tonya: (to Sung Min) The Ishongo people used a simple abacus counting frame.

Daniel: (to group) Frame.

Daniel: (to Sung Min) It's on your sheet, uh, right here, counting frame, right here (points to it).

Sung Min: (to group) So what should I put?

Daniel: (to Sung Min) Used a simple abacus counting frame.

Sung Min: (to Tonya) They—What did you put—?

. . . . [Students begin to discuss the answer to another question, and this discussion is interspersed with discussions about the focus question here.]

Sung Min: They used—

Tonya: (to Sung Min) The Ishongo people used abacus, a counting frame.

. . . .

Sung Min: Used a simple abacus counting frame.

. . . .

Tonya: (to Sung Min) You don't have to put "simple" in there.

Daniel: (to Tonya) Well, I just put it.

Tonya: (to Daniel) No, you didn't.

Daniel: (to Tonya) Oh yeah. Oh yeah.

Sung Min: (to Tonya) So what should I put, "Ishongo people—"?

Tonya: (to Sung Min) (reading her answer) "Used, used abacus, a counting frame." That's all I said.

Sung Min: (to Tonya) Abacus counting frame?

Tonya: (to Sung Min) Abacus, a counting frame.

In this excerpt, the group worked cooperatively, with multiple students talking about the answer, although there was little real discussion of the content of the answer.

Because helping and cooperative participant structures led to different kinds of student interactions, I examine the two participant structures separately.

In almost all of the nonreading episodes (73 out of 74) that Mrs. Parker set up with a helping participant structure, the students worked in a parallel manner, providing help to each other only if requested.[7] In one episode they worked in an associative manner, meaning that students talked aloud and shared ideas as they worked on the same question. Thus, when the sixth grade social studies students were told to help one another they almost always enacted this structure in the least cooperative way.

One measure of the success of a helping participant structure is the degree to which the students actually help each other. By this measure, the helping participant structures were less than completely successful. In 34 episodes (46% of the total), a student provided some kind of help to another student; in 40 episodes (54% of the total) the students provided no help to each other. In four instances a student asked for help in answering a question but did not receive it.[8]

Fifty-three percent of the instances of helping behavior involved providing answers to the workbook questions. Other kinds of help included giving hints (22%), giving background information (17%), and providing explanations (8%). As discussed in chapter 4, these categories are based on Webb's (1991) research.

Excerpt 5.3 shows a student giving the answer to another student. It was part of an assignment in which Mrs. Parker wanted the students to label their individual maps with the places she had listed on the overhead projector. She told students to help one another by checking to see that everyone in the group had all the places marked. Students in the focus group were working in a parallel manner, and Mrs. Parker came to their table and urged them to work together. One member of the group, Adam, was further along than the others in his group. When he finished his map, soon after Mrs. Parker visited the table, he helped Woody, as shown in the following excerpt.

Excerpt 5.3

Adam: (to Woody) Tunisia, you don't have. Woody, Woody, Woody! Tunisia? It's right here (pointing to it on the map).

Woody: (to Adam) This is Tunisia?

Adam: (to Woody) T, U, N, I, S, I, A [spelling "Tunisia" as Woody writes it on his map].

The following excerpt is from earlier in the same class. Peggy helped Adam by providing a hint to him.

Excerpt 5.4

Adam: (to group) Where is Sardinia? That's that other island.

Peggy: (mumbles to Adam) It's on the Mediterranean.

In the next excerpt Carmela provided background information Ronald needed to answer the following question: "Use the line scale to measure the distances between the following places. Give the distance in either kilometers (km) or miles (mi.). . . . From Tangier, Morocco, to Constantine, Algeria (north coast) _____."

Excerpt 5.5

Ronald: (to group) Morocco, where is Morocco?

(Carmela points on his map.)

Ronald: (to Carmela) Oh, thanks.

Ronald: (to himself) Tangiers, Morocco to—Algeria.

In the following excerpt, from the same episode as the previous excerpt, Ronald explained to Tonya how to answer the following question: "In the drawing, the equator and two other parallels cross over Africa. What are the latitudes of the two other parallels? _____ _____ "

Excerpt 5.6

Tonya: Hold up, look. This says "In the drawing, the equator and two of the—"

. . . .

Tonya: (to Ronald) Hey, isn't this 20 and 4—Hey isn't this 20 ((and—here))? I don't know what that (( )) (showing Richard her worksheet).

Ronald: (to Tonya) On the map, the big map, look and see which ones, which of these two lines down here cross through Africa.

Tonya: (( ))

Unlike the fourth grade mathematics class in which explanations increased over time, all of the explanations in the sixth grade class occurred during one class session in the first half of the year. Providing background information and help other than answers also decreased over time.

One hundred and thirty-eight of the episodes set up by Mrs. Parker had cooperative participant structures. How students cooperated during these episodes is a measure of the success of the cooperative participant structure. In 48% of the episodes Mrs. Parker set up as cooperative participant structures students worked cooperatively during the whole episode, as in Excerpt 5.7 below. In this excerpt the group was generating ideas about characteristics of Egyptian farming families based on a drawing of them. Each group had one paper on which to record their group answers; Kathleen was the recorder in this excerpt. The focus of this episode was the idea that the climate was hot; it overlapped with the end of another episode as Kathleen recorded the group's idea that the houses of the Egyptian farming families were small.

Excerpt 5.7

Tracy: And there ((are)) not very many, very many trees so it's probably very hot.

Kathleen: Very hot. The houses are, very—(writing).

Sung Min: (to Tracy) There are trees, okay (pointing to the picture).

Tracy: (to Sung Min) Alright.

Sung Min: (to Tracy) Why do you say there's not a lot of—I see a lot of trees.

Tracy: (to Sung Min) There are *not* very many.

Sung Min: (to Tracy) ((Uh huh. I think so.))

(Sung Min shakes his head in disgust.)

Tracy: It's probably hot.

Kathleen: It looks hot. Look what they're wearing.

Sung Min: I know. It's very hot. You can show that it's very hot 'cause it just wears a little skirt. (giggles)

Kathleen: The houses are very small [repeating the earlier idea]. And the, climate—

Sung Min: Is very hot.

. . . . [Mrs. Parker gives instructions to the whole class.]

(Pause)

Manuel: I think I'll go to the bathroom.

(Manuel leaves the group.)

Kathleen: 'Cause they're wearing—

Sung Min: Just write the facts first. That's what they said.

Kathleen: Okay. Hold on.

Sung Min: I don't want (( ))

(Sung Min throws a wad of paper at Kathleen in frustration. She doesn't react but pushes the wad away. Sung Min picks it up again.)

Sung Min: I feel ((stupid.)) Heh heh heh heh. Hey look. Annoying (mumbles)

(Pause)

Sung Min: Okay. They were very hot, though.

Kathleen: Okay. That's—I wrote that. That's what I wrote.

(Kathleen passes sheet to Sung Min to show him what she wrote.)

This excerpt illustrates how in a cooperative participant structure students worked together to produce a joint answer.

In 52% of the episodes Mrs. Parker set up with cooperative participant structures students worked associatively or in parallel for at least part of the episode—i.e., the cooperative participant structure "deteriorated." Prior to the following excerpt, Mrs. Parker had told the students to arrive at their answers together. Students in the group were working on different questions (i.e., not working cooperatively) when Tracy began to focus on question 5, "Why do you think large parts of North Africa are unpopulated?"

Excerpt 5.8

Tracy: Yep. Now what? You're already on number 5.

. . . .

Allison: No, I'm not! I'm just getting number 4.

Tracy: Oh.

. . . .

Allison: "Why do you think large parts of North Africa are unpopulated?"

Tracy: Number 4. I'm on number 4. "What are some factors that contribute to a dense population in Africa." I have no idea. Number 5, "Why do you think largest, large parts of North Africa are unpopulated?"

. . . . [c. one minute]

James: What's number 5?

Nakisha: I haven't the slightest idea.

Tracy: Oh, it's, it's your choice, I mean number 5, "Why do *you* think large parts of North Africa are unpopulated?"

. . . . [The assistant principal, who recently arrived at the class to substitute while Mrs. Parker attended a meeting, comes over to the group and engages them in a conversation about the deserts in Africa.]

Allison: I skipped number 5 and number 6 too [in response to Nakisha's question about whether she skipped number 4].

. . . .

Nakisha: Populations. What do you think—Number 5.

. . . . [c. two minutes]

Tracy: Five [question number].

Woody: Five is in your own words. Read, Allison, "Why do you think large parts of North Africa are unpopulated?" Look on the ((north parts)).

. . . .

Allison: Because (pause) because it's in the middle of Africa. I don't know.

In this example, students never focused on the content of question five. The many discontinuities in the transcript (indicated by ". . . .") and the relatively long periods of time between segments related to the question are typical of episodes when students worked in a parallel or associative manner.

Given the potential benefits of cooperative participant structures to the quality of students' discussions, it is significant that cooperative participant structures appeared to be somewhat "fragile" in this classroom. In about half the episodes in which Mrs. Parker set up a cooperative structure, the students either did not work together cooperatively or stopped working cooperatively.

In both helping and cooperative participant structures students engaged in self-help and gave each other procedural help. Self-help involved students "thinking aloud" as they engaged with the substance of their social studies assignment. Procedural help involved conveying information needed to complete a task. For example, in one episode that involved labelling a map, Carmela asked Ronald if they had to label the Red Sea. Ronald answered, "No, you don't have to label that, you just leave it blank."

Throughout the year, students also received help during LT from Mrs. Parker. In these interactions her focus was on helping the students understand the material, not on finishing the task. She explained concepts that students did not understand and engaged groups in Socratic-type dialogues to help them arrive at an answer. The following excerpt is an example of the latter kind of help. The group had been working together to answer the following question: "Find the word 'density' in your dictionary. In your own words, explain what is meant by a 'low population density.'" They had found a definition of density but had been unable to apply it to the concept of low population density. Mrs. Parker engaged them in a conversation to help them make that application.

Excerpt 5.9

Mrs. Parker:. . . . What does dense mean?

Woody: Thick.

Tracy: Nuh uh, Density means, I don't know, I just now looked it up but I don't remember, dense means, dense means, density means—

James: "The quality of state of being dense" (reading from dictionary).

Tracy: *Or* state of being dense.

Mrs. Parker: Okay. Can—now do you know what dense means?

(Tracy shakes her head, indicating no).

Mrs. Parker: No, sometimes definitions in dictionaries—

Tracy: Tell you to look up the other word.

Mrs. Parker: Okay, they will tell that it's, is but if you don't know what the base word means then, you're no better off.

Tracy: I looked it up that one too, but I forgot what it was.

Mrs. Parker: Okay, what does the base word dense mean? You got it there?

Allison: Yeah, It says thick or stupid, that's what mine said.

(Tracy is standing to look at dictionary on Nakisha's desk.)

Nakisha: It's right here.

Mrs. Parker: Okay, read it.

//Nakisha: "Marked by comp- compact or crowding together of parts."

//Woody: Thick head, dense.

Mrs. Parker: Okay, crowding together of parts, so what do you think dense population is going to be?

//Tracy: A lot of people

//Woody: Low dens- Yeah.

Mrs. Parker: Okay. What do you think a low population density would mean?

Woody: That no people—

Tracy: Not that many people, not that many people—So just put "not that many people—"

Mrs. Parker: Okay, live in an area. Answer in a complete sentence. . . .

(Mrs. Parker leaves the group.)

In this instance and many others students working together and aloud made their problems more visible to the teacher, allowing her to intervene and help as needed.

Contextual Influences

The previous discussion shows how tasks and interpersonal interactions influenced students' learning of social studies. Other contextual features that influenced the students' interactions and learning included: the participant structures set up by Mrs. Parker, students' definition of LT, the predominant competitive ethos, the materials provided, the kinds of questions posed on the materials, and interruptions to their group activities.

Participant Structures

As the preceding section shows, the three participant structures Mrs. Parker set up (reading, helping, and cooperative) involved very different kinds of student-student interactions and thus presented students with different opportunities for learning social studies. In the reading participant structures, students usually took turns reading aloud the assigned material.

In the helping participant structures, students almost always worked parallely. The most common form of help was to provide the answer.

In cooperative participant structures, students worked cooperatively during the whole episode about half the time. In the other episodes they worked parallely or associatively, converting cooperative participant structures to helping participant structures.

Students' Definition of Learning Together

Students' "meanings," particularly their definition of the task at hand, are central to understanding how the sixth grade students enacted the three participant structures comprising LT in Mrs. Parker's social studies class.

The students' active role in shaping their own learning environments through the meanings they negotiated can be seen clearly in the reading participant structure. Mrs. Parker had assigned roles (materials gatherer, reader, writer, and checker) to individual students in each group. However, during the reading participant structures students negotiated how the reader role was enacted, usually deciding to share the task. The following instance illustrates this kind of negotiation.

At the beginning of the reading segment Jane began to count the number of paragraphs, so they could be divided among group members. Then Sandra pointed out that they had two worksheets to read, not just the one Jane had counted. Jane began to recount the paragraphs. Sandra asked "Who's the reader?" Jane answered, "Me," and Daniel echoed, "Jane is." The group members then counted the number of paragraphs in both sheets combined. Jane counted 12 and Sandra said, "There's 17. So you get to read four paragraphs (pause) each." Then Sandra announced that she was going to start reading. Before she did, however, Jane explained that the last reader needed to read the instructions that follow the reading. Daniel responded, "I'll read, I'll read last. I'll read this page" (pointing to the last page). Sandra disagreed with him, "Nun-um." Jane then got them moving: "Just go. Who's gonna start?" Sandra began, and the group members took turns reading the three pages of text.

In the helping and cooperative participant structures, students' spontaneous comments indicate that the students' main focus wason completing the assigned tasks within the class period rather than on learning or understanding the material.[9] This was manifested in statements about wanting to finish the task, in skipping difficult questions, in copying answers rather than discussing them, and in apparent lack of concern about answering the questions correctly.

Excerpts 5.10 and 5.11, which are from the same class, illustrate students' interest in finishing their assignments. Prior to these excerpts, the group had been struggling with the task of explaining in their own words "low population density." Mrs. Parker had come over to their table and helped them with that task (see Excerpt 5.9 above). After Mrs. Parker had left the group, they had trouble with question four ("What are some factors that contribute to dense populations in Africa?") and considered skipping it:

Excerpt 5.10

Woody: Skip number 4.

Allison: No.

Woody: No?

Nakisha: It's not good to skip it. You have to come back to it anyway.

Although the group eventually decided to address question four, their discussion emphasized the need to finish the question rather than understand it. Five minutes later, after a side discussion with the assistant principal, the issue was revisited:

Excerpt 5.11

Nakisha: Who knows the answer to number 4?

Woody: Nobody.

Tracy: I don't. I skipped it.

Nakisha to Tracy: You've got to come back to it, so what's the sense in skipping it?

In the following excerpt, the group has been waiting for Doria to finish writing answers to questions on a worksheet so they could proceed to read a worksheet together. The students' lack of interest in understanding is reflected in multiple comments.

Excerpt 5.12

Doria: I'm done. Let me see if my answers are correct.

(Doria starts comparing her answers to Allison's.)

Allison: I might be wrong.

Nakisha: We don't care as long as it's completed.

Allison: Good, she's not complaining, 'cause I don't know if I'm right or not.

Doria then continued to compare her answers with Allison's, changing some of her answers to match Allison's, without discussion of the content when they differed.

Students frequently "celebrated" being finished. For example, when one group had finished a worksheet task involving circling specific areas on their maps, Tracy exclaimed: "We're finished, we're finished. I already found everything!"

Students' focus on completing tasks can be understood in the larger context of the assignments. Many of the activities done in the cooperative learning groups involved students filling in worksheets, of which each student had a copy, and which were to be added to their social studies notebooks. As discussed above, Mrs. Parker emphasized the importance of completing assignments, and she collected the notebooks at the end of each grading period. When Mrs. Parker graded the notebooks she rewarded completeness and organization, but gave no credit for whether the worksheets were completed correctly. Answering the worksheets correctly was rewarded to the extent that it enabled students to learn information on which they were tested.

Competition in the School and Community

As discussed above, students usually enacted nonreading helping participant structures in either a parallel or associative manner, minimizing their cooperation. This is not surprising given the competitive and individualistic ethos that predominates schools and society in the United States (see Goldman & McDermott, 1987; Tobin, Wu, & Davidson, 1989). Because cooperative learning was a new experience for these students, it is not surprising that they reverted to the least cooperative forms of interaction in the helping participant structures.

Cooperative participant structures also seemed "fragile." Several contextual features seemed to contribute to break downs in cooperative participant structures.

Separate Answer Sheets

Using separate answer sheets meant that students could easily "drift" into answering questions on their own. Most of Mrs. Parker's worksheet exercises involved separate answer sheets, one reason for this being Mrs. Parker's goal that students learn to keep notebooks. Although the separate answer sheets may have advanced this goal, they seemed to have had the unintended consequence of reducing cooperation.

Kinds of Questions

Another contextual feature that seemed to influence the breakdown of cooperative structures was the difficulty of the question. There seemed to be a bell curve relationship between difficulty of the task and the level of students' cooperation. If the tasks were too easy or too difficult, cooperation "broke down," and students worked on their own. The optimal task seemed one that challenged the students, but not excessively.

Convergent comprehension questions (for example, Excerpt 5.2) were often "too easy" to require cooperation and generated little constructive conversation.

The following excerpt illustrates a cooperative participant structure breaking down when the students encountered a task they found too difficult. For the students' first assignment in a unit on ancient Greece, Mrs. Parker asked the students to work in their groups to write a definition of Western Civilization. In her instructions to the class Mrs. Parker reminded the students that two pages of their textbook had discussed Western Civilization and that in the previous unit on ancient Egypt they had written a definition of civilization. In the excerpt below, Sandra's comment focused the group on the task at hand. After generating one idea for their definition, the group stopped working together. Jane's comment about the paucity of information in the text is an indicator of the difficulty they encountered.

Excerpt 5.13

Sandra: (to group) Are we gonna work together or what?

Jane: (to Sandra) Yeah.

(Jane finishes writing, and then reads silently from the textbook.)

Jane: Okay, um, Western Civilization is a combination of, uh, like lots of, um, civ-, lots of—

Daniel: Combination of many civilizations.

Jane: (whispers) Yeah.

(All are writing.)

Sandra: Is what?

Daniel: Combination of many civilizations.

Sandra: (to Carmela) You writing it down?.

(Carmela writes.)

Jane: Combination, of— (writing)

Daniel: Combination of *many* civilizations.

(All are writing.)

Jane: They sure don't give you enough to write on. Mm, mm!

Daniel: ((Can—tee))

Jane: (to group) Let's work separately?

Sandra: Hmm?

Jane: (to group) Let's work separately.

Sandra: I don't care.

(Students work independently and quietly.)

On another occasion the transition from working together to working separately took longer. The group had successfully answered several questions from the worksheet (some with help from Mrs. Parker). Then they began to work on the question: "What are some factors that contribute to dense populations in Africa?" The students found this question difficult, they either suggested skipping it or actually skipped it (see Excerpts 5.10 and 5.11), with the result that the students no longer worked cooperatively.

Within the same kind of participant structure, divergent tasks (i.e., tasks that had more than one answer or the possibility of more than one answer) generated more complex discussions than tasks that involved identifying the one "correct" answer. In the following excerpt the group worked on a divergent comprehension task. Drawing on what they had just seen in a filmstrip and the information represented in a drawing of an "ancient Egyptian farming family," the group was supposed to work together to generate a list of "facts" about the farming family. The drawing showed two men plowing and two men planting in a field; houses and palm trees were in the background. The group had one copy of the drawing, and there was one recorder for this episode. The focus of the episode was the group's discussion about the nature of the work portrayed in the drawing.

Excerpt 5.14

Sung Min: (to Tracy) Alright. The farming family has to work very hard [trying to focus the group by generating the first idea].

. . . . [Group discusses what they are supposed to do.]

Kathleen: What does the picture look like it's doing?

Tracy: Uh, they're working very hard.

Kathleen: Yeah. They're working to plow the soil. See they're, they're plowing the soil. So they're, they're plowing the soil.

. . . . [Manuel introduces a new idea about their houses.]

Kathleen: And, and then while they're plowing, some workers are planting the seeds.

. . . . [Manuel returns to his idea about their houses and the group discusses the requirements of the assignment.]

Tracy: They're working for a living? Working for a living.

Kathleen: Oh, wait. You want me to write it? [i.e., act as the recorder]

Tracy: Yes. (Tracy hands Kathleen the paper.)

Kathleen: Oh, what's the title? Farming fam—(reading paper to find her place) Um um um um. (writes) Um.

Tracy: The picture shows, that they're working for, a living.

Kathleen: Wait, what shall we write? The picture shows that they're *plowing* the soil—

Sung Min: They're working very hard.

Manuel: Yeah.

Tracy: They're plowing the soil for their garden so they can work so they can eat, so they can sell, so they can live.

((Sung Min)): Oh, sure. (small laugh)

(Sung Min shakes his head.)

Tracy: Well, I'm serious. It does say that here.

(Pause while Kathleen writes.)

Sung Min: (( ))

Kathleen: Hmm. The soil, right? Plowing the soil (writing) (pause) With—

Sung Min: The kids, the kids put the seeds in.

Kathleen: While, um, while, while the, servants, right?

Tracy: No. No. They're, they're kids.

Sung Min: (to Kathleen) Kids, or children.

Sung Min: The kids are putting the seeds in.

Tracy: I don't think, I don't think, um. The farm- ers, the farm people have, servants.

Sung Min: No, that's right.

Tracy: I don't think they do. They may.

(Mrs. Parker observes the group.)

Tracy: I'm not sure. Alright. Hey, and also the—

Kathleen: Um. The picture shows that they are working hard on farms while the children are planting the seeds.

Tracy: Right. Yeah.

Kathleen: Is that what they're doing?

Tracy: Yeah. And working with the ((legumes)) so they can live, so they can eat, so they can sell their food, so they can—

Mrs. Parker then intervened in the group, asking for another idea.

Discussions concerning the answers to divergent questions contrast with discussions about answers to convergent questions. The divergent questions, as illustrated in Excerpt 5.14, contributed to extensive discussion about the content of the answers. The convergent questions, as illustrated in Excerpt 5.2 above, led to extensive talk, but little discussion of the content of the answers.

Students' Social Skills

In helping participant structures and in cooperative participant structures, the students were not as cooperative as they might have been. As discussed in chapter 2, the developers of LT (see D. W. Johnson, R. T. Johnson, & Holubec, 1986, 1993a) stress that, for LT to succeed, students need to learn the social skills to work in small groups.

Mrs. Parker's students agreed that social skills are important in LT. When I asked students what they would tell a new student about how to be a good group member, almost all the students mentioned social skills. They said students should be nice and listen to others; students should not be bossy or stuck up; and they shouldn't get mad at things other students say to them. Just as frequently, the students mentioned the need to help and cooperate with one another. They said students should help others, ask for help when they need it, stay together and not get ahead of others, cooperate, and take turns reading. Most students also mentioned that it was important to stay on task, do their work, and behave.

Lack of social and cooperative skills led to negative feelings within the LT groups. When I asked students what others did in their groups that made them feel mad or angry, most students mentioned behaviors that involved other students failing to use appropriate social or cooperative skills. Students said they got angry or mad when others talked too much or at the wrong times, fought or argued, or yelled at or teased the student answering. They also got mad or angry when other students did not do their work and asked for answers, did not bring in their homework (which meant that a group did not get points), rushed them, did not cooperate, or did not help them.

When these kinds of behaviors occurred, students seemed to have a limited range of responses. When I asked what they would do when other students made them mad or angry, most students said that they would relax or ignore them, or that they would tell them (verbally or nonverbally) to do the opposite of what they were doing.[10] For example, students would tell others to finish their homework (if they had not completed it) or to be quiet (if they were talking too much). Kanika's discussion of how different teams responded to someone who did not bring in their homework illustrates how students frequently responded to one another:

> At my old table, we used to, if you didn't bring in your homework, we'll [sic] give you the silent treatment for five minutes and we don't talk to you 'til five minutes is over. . . . But not at my table now. They don't want to do that. They don't think it's funny, or fair. So at that table we just yell at them. We say, 'You dummy! Why didn't you do your homework?'

As I discussed above, Mrs. Parker had explained to students the kind of social behavior she expected of them in the groups. To reinforce these standards she awarded points for appropriate group behavior during the first half of the school year. After she discontinued awarding points, Mrs. Parker still monitored the groups and intervened when she thought it necessary. However, she did not explicitly teach social skills in her social studies class.

Interruptions in Class

For the cooperative participant structures in Mrs. Parker's class to be effective, students needed to be working on the same question or task. Various contextual features increased the likelihood that cooperative participant structures would break down by causing disruptions in individual students' work. Students were "pulled out" of social studies class for enrichment or other school-related activities. The "pullouts" not only presented a problem for Mrs. Parker in terms of group size and composition, but also disrupted students' efforts to work together cooperatively.

School rules designed to maintain order in the halls provided another source of disruption. To minimize the number of students in the hall, the rules prohibited more than one student at a time from leaving the classroom to get a drink of water or go to the bathroom. It was difficult for a cooperative participant structure to continue when group members departed one-by-one during an LT session.

Students created some disruptions themselves. As discussed above, students negotiated in their groups how they would read text on the worksheets. Usually their decisions led to sharing the oral reading task. However, at times the students decided to read individually and in silence, usually because of some problem with a student's reading. When the students read separately, they usually began answering the questions at different times, thereby inhibiting cooperation. For example, in one case Tonya took the first turn at reading. Sandra and then Sung Min soon complained that Tonya was reading too fast. Daniel offered to read first but Tonya initially refused to yield her position. When she said, "Go! Who's reading?" Sandra responded, "Nobody, we're reading to ourselves." Sung Min concurred, and the group members then read individually. As students finished reading they began to work individually on the questions, even though Mrs. Parker had told the class to work together in their groups. When Mrs. Parker saw what had happened she told the group to reread the passage together and work on the questions together.

The last section of this chapter will summarize and classify the various contextual features that influenced cooperative learning in the sixth grade social studies class. However, before proceeding to that discussion, I examine the results of cooperative learning.

Outcomes of Cooperative Learning

Although my focus was on processes and contextual influences on them, I also examined outcomes of cooperative learning in Mrs. Parker's social studies class and in the sixth grade classes generally. (See chapter 1 and the Appendix for methodological discussions.)

Social Studies

In an interview in May of the focus year, Mrs. Parker said that she basically was happy with how cooperative learning had worked in her social studies class. "For the most part I think it's worked very well," although she added that there were instances where groups wouldn't work together in spite of everything she tried. Mrs. Parker said she thought that the cooperative learning class had done better academically than her two other classes. However, she added that the Monday class, which did not use cooperative learning, had met fewer times than the other classes because school had been closed on many Mondays that year due to snow or holidays. She also thought that most of the students had learned to work well together. "My goal is for them to work together to accomplish the material. And I think for the most part that we've done that. . . . .I feel good about how the students work together and how they feel about each other." She also was pleased with the particular units where students gathered information on their own because she wanted them to develop research skills.

When I asked whether cooperative learning had helped her students with motivation, she gave a qualified response:

> In some ways it has. . . . I think it's helped the lower students, the students who have more difficulty, because they know that they're not by themselves, that they have a way of getting help and it's right there. . . . And I think that for some of the higher students, it's fun to teach others.

Students enjoyed cooperative learning in Mrs. Parker's class. When I asked why they liked it, most said that they liked getting help with the course content. Tonya, for example, said "Your group helps you do things. If you don't understand, the people in your group will help you." Sung Min said "If somebody doesn't know how to do it, we can just tell him and work in groups, and we can tell how we do them." Several students mentioned procedural help and social issues as reasons for liking cooperative learning. Thep stated, "If you forget to write down your homework you can always ask somebody that's in your group. . . . If you've been in the bathroom or something, and then you come back, and you don't understand what's happening, you can always ask them." Manuel stressed the social aspect: "It's fun working in groups because you get to talk a lot."

I compared the grades that Mrs. Parker awarded to students in her LT social studies class with the grades she awarded to students in her other two social studies classes. On the test students took at the end of the first quarter, Mrs. Parker's LT class ($M = 78.0$, $SD = 21.0$) did not perform differently than the other two social studies classes ($M = 76.5$, $SD = 20.3$; and $M = 77.1$, $SD = 24.4$), F $(2,56) = .02$, $p = .98$. On the second quarter test the LT students ($M = 79.6$, $SD = 24.9$) performed better than the other two classes ($M = 67.4$, $SD = 19.3$; and $M = 64.8$, $SD = 20.7$), F $(2,52) = 2.41$, $p = .10$. On the third quarter test the LT students ($M = 78.5$, $SD = 11.2$) and students in the second class ($M = 78.8$, $SD = 9.1$) performed better than the third class ($M = 67.9$, $SD = 15.6$), F $(2,56) = 5.13$, $p = .01$. This pattern of results suggests that the effects of LT on students' learning of social studies were positive during the second quarter. However, as discussed above, Mrs. Parker thought that one of the non-LT social studies classes had less time for social studies than the other two classes, which may have contributed to the class's weaker performance.

Broader Comparisons

As discussed in chapter 4, previous research indicates that cooperative learning often has a positive influence on students' self-esteem and attitudes toward school. Because sixth grade students at Maplewood Elementary School experienced several methods of cooperative learning in various classes (see chapter 3 and the Appendix), their experiences with cooperative learning in other classes could have influenced their self-esteem and attitudes toward school. Consequently, for these broader measures, I compared not only the three social studies classes but also students with the most and least overall experience with cooperative learning during the focus year.

On measures of self-esteem and attitudes toward school, the raw score and gain score data indicate that there were no differences between the LT social studies class and the other social studies classes that showed benefits of LT. Similarly, there were no differences between students with the most and least experience with cooperative learning that indicated benefits from cooperative learning.

Students' views of the role of LT in their social studies class shed some light on the overall pattern of "no significance" across outcome measures. I asked Mrs. Parker's students what they would tell a new student about their social studies class and how Mrs. Parker teaches it. Most students responded by recounting specific activities done in social studies class: reading a book, filling in the map, drawing, taking notes, putting their papers in a notebook, and watching videotapes. Students also mentioned frequently the content of their lessons: Egypt, civilization, and Africa. Some students added their emotional response to the class, stating whether they liked it or not, or whether they thought it was fun. Only three students spontaneously mentioned anything about LT or their groups. In response to my followup question asking if there was anything else she would tell a new girl, Nakisha said, "We work in groups." Carmela, also responding to a followup question, said, "She'd [Mrs. Parker] probably give us a sheet of paper, we could do on, Africa. Then we could do it together in our tables or, we could, do it separately." Mrs. Parker's students did not view LT as the major defining feature of their social studies class.

Moreover, students had LT in social studies for the equivalent of one class period a week. Consequently, it is not surprising that it seemed to have little impact on their self-esteem or attitudes toward school.

I expect that similar contextual features contributed to the lack of effects in the most to least comparisons. My general observations in Maplewood School and interviews with teachers indicate that cooperative learning was not a defining feature of any sixth grade class.

Discussion

The LT approach to cooperative learning, as used by Mrs. Parker and enacted by her students in the sixth grade social studies class, presented opportunities for students to work together in three different participant structures. It also afforded Mrs. Parker opportunities to observe students' work and to help them as needed. In the helping participant structures students usually answered their worksheets in a parallel fashion, minimizing their task-related interactions. When students helped each other, they usually gave answers, rarely explanations. In approximately half of the episodes with a cooperative participant structure, the students worked cooperatively throughout the entire episode. In the other half they worked parallelly or associatively for part or all of the episode. Thus, the students' enactment of the LT method was not maximally productive.

Mrs. Parker was generally pleased with the outcomes of LT in her social studies class. She thought that the LT had helped her students learn social studies and that most of the students had learned to work well together. Outcome measures indicated that the students who experienced LT did better on social studies tests in the middle of the school year than those students who did not experience LT, although Mrs. Parker said that one non-LT class had met less often than the LT class. Other outcome measures indicated that LT and cooperative learning more broadly did not appear to influence sixth graders' self-esteem or attitudes to school.

All six categories of contextual features are helpful in understanding how Mrs. Parker learned to use LT in her social studies class. As occurred with Miss Grant, Mrs. Parker's task of learning to use LT in her social studies class presented challenges beyond what she had been taught about cooperative learning.

Several "tools" influenced Mrs. Parker's decision to use LT and how she learned to use it in her social studies class. The LT method itself and books about it and other forms of cooperative learning offered her "scripts" and influenced her use of roles in the LT groups at the beginning of the year. Her prior training about cooperative learning and her prior use of cooperative learning influenced her use of points for good group behavior. The availability of commercially-produced worksheets (coupled with a lack of planning time) influenced Mrs. Parker's decision to use these materials with LT.

Like Miss Grant, Mrs. Parker had a limited "community of practice" as she learned to use LT in her social studies class. Although Mrs. Parker obtained ideas from Mrs. David (for example, using points to reward good behavior), students' responses were a major influence on Mrs. Parker's learning to use LT in her social studies class. For example, she stopped giving points for good behavior in social studies after students seemed to work well together without it, and she implied that she continued to use LT because students enjoyed it.

Individual and social meanings also were important influences. Mrs. Parker's goals for her social studies class (that they learn the required social studies content and organizational skills, and to work well together) influenced her emphasis on students finishing assignments, her use of points for group behavior, and her requirement that each student maintain a social studies notebook.

Mrs. Parker was influenced by several aspects of the local school culture. The general meaning of cooperative learning within the school created a positive environment for her use of LT. Because social studies was not a "high stakes" subject, Mrs. Parker had more latitude in her use of LT than Miss Grant had in her use of TGT. She could pursue other goals for her students beyond learning social studies, leading to unintended consequences. For example, students' use of individual answer sheets for their notebooks, which resulted from Mrs. Parker's goal that her students develop organizational skills, seemed to reduce their cooperation during LT.

As mentioned above, the lack of planning time was another feature of the local culture that contributed to Mrs. Parker's use of existing worksheets and her minimal emphasis on social skills training for her students. The many interruptions in the schedule and the pattern of frequent pullouts influenced how frequently Mrs. Parker used LT and contributed to the frequency with which she used the helping participant structure.

Many features of the local school culture were also a reflection of larger cultural patterns in the district and national educational communities. For example, social studies is generally not a "high stakes" subject, and teachers routinely indicate lack of time is a constraint in using educational innovations. Mrs. Parker's perceptions of middle school norms (and thus the need to prepare her students with particular kinds of organizational skills) were at least related to regional patterns in the school system. The school district's emphasis on completing the required curriculum influenced her emphasis on "covering" the required material.

Mrs. Parker herself saw context as relevant to how she used cooperative learning. In our interview in May, when Mrs. Parker knew she would be teaching in a new school during the coming year, I asked how she would use cooperative learning there. Her response shows the contextual features she saw as important:

> I haven't really thought it completely through. I'll probably do cooperative learning in social studies. I don't know. It depends on the groups of students, the situation at the new school, and how things develop. I might do something different, or branch out. I think I would keep it in social studies and I might include it in other subject areas, like math or reading. I don't know. I'll have to see how the groups are set up and how the year is going to be, or (laughs) how I think it's going to be.

The six categories of contextual features also are central to understanding students' learning and interactions during LT. Within her focus on social studies during LT, Mrs. Parker presented her students primarily with comprehension questions to answer on worksheets; later, in the spring semester, she presented some more complex tasks. Other features of the students' learning tasks (e.g., degree of difficulty and convergent vs. divergent questions) influenced the likelihood that students would cooperate successfully on a task. Divergent questions led to more complex discussions than convergent questions.

The "scripts" offered by LT and the commercially-produced worksheets available to Mrs. Parker were important "tools" as the students learned social studies in her class. The individual notebooks students maintained in Mrs. Parker's class and related individual worksheets seemed to diminish students' helping and cooperation.

The three different participant structures used by Mrs. Parker contributed to different patterns of student interaction and related learning. However, the students did not always enact the participant structures as Mrs. Parker set them up. Although LT afforded the students opportunities to help one another, the way the students enacted nonreading helping participant structures minimized the amount of helping among them and often involved students giving answers rather than explanations. Cooperation among students broke down in approximately half of the episodes with a cooperative participant structure. Students' lack of well-developed social skills seemed to have contributed to some negative feelings and difficulties in students' interactions in LT.

The meanings that Mrs. Parker and her students attributed to assignments influenced how students interacted and learned, and what they learned. Mrs. Parker announced to her students that their goal was to complete the assigned tasks, and her students generally accepted this definition, with the result that during LT completing the assignments seemed to take priority for the students over learning the subject matter. Mrs. Parker's requirement that students keep individual notebooks and her grading of them also contributed to students' emphasis on completing assignments rather than learning social studies content. Students' active role in defining tasks was evident in the reading participant structures, where students negotiated how they would carry out that assignment.

The meaning of social studies as a "low stakes" subject in the school (and larger community) allowed for competing goals, and thus influenced what students learned. The frequent interruptions and pullouts during social studies class disrupted students' cooperation.

The competitive ethos in the school and larger society was a likely influence on students' pattern of minimal helping during nonreading participant structures and the fragility of cooperative participant structures. The culture of the middle school influenced Mrs. Parker's decision to include organizational skills as a goal for her students, which led to individual worksheets for the notebooks and seemed to inadvertently diminish students' helping and cooperation. Finally, the school district's emphasis on "covering" the required curriculum influenced Mrs. Parker's emphasis on students' completing their assignments, which seemed to diminish an emphasis on learning social studies.

Contextual features were interwoven in Mrs. Parker's use and students' enactment of LT. In almost all cases more than one contextual feature was useful for understanding a particular pattern related to students' learning. A good example is the influence of competing goals in Mrs. Parker's social studies class. Mrs. Parker wanted students to learn to develop organizational skills and to work together because she saw these as important for their future. She also wanted them to learn social studies, but what she emphasized to the students was that they should finish the assigned tasks. This message was influenced by the district's emphasis on covering the assigned curriculum and by Mrs. Parker's requirement that each student maintain a notebook, which in turn was influenced by her perception of the culture of middle school. These various goals could influence and compete with one another because social studies was a "low stakes" subject in the school and larger educational community.

Contextual analyses are useful in examining how LT in Mrs. Parker's social studies class met the fidelity criteria advocated by the developers of LT. As discussed in chapter 2, the developers of LT (D. W. Johnson, R. T. Johnson, & Holubec, 1986, 1993a) provide five fidelity criteria for LT: positive interdependence, face-to-face interaction, individual accountability, small group social skills, and group processing. Analysis of Mrs. Parker's social studies class from the fidelity perspective is complex because there was considerable variability in how she used LT over the focus school year.

To achieve positive interdependence Mrs. Parker assigned group members different roles (materials gatherer, reader, recorder, and checker). However, students did not always enact these roles as Mrs. Parker intended. For many tasks Mrs. Parker told the students to arrive at their answers together, presumably intending to create a common goal. However, because students often used separate answer sheets (in order to be able to put them in their individual notebooks), students could (and often did) complete their sheets without arriving at a common answer. For most of the fall and a few times in the spring, Mrs. Parker created group rewards by assigning groups points for using good group processes, but she stopped doing this on a regular basis when she thought the students no longer needed the rewards to work well together. (There were no group rewards for group scores on tests or quizzes.) Mrs. Parker occasionally used other ways of creating positive interdependence. Two tasks in the fall involved sharing a globe or atlas; the web task in the spring required students to obtain and present information about each other's projects; and several other tasks in the spring required the members of a group to prepare a common answer sheet.

At first glance, LT in Mrs. Parker's class would appear to meet the positive interdependence requirement presented in the *Circles of Learning* book she used. However, analyses presented in this chapter indicate that what Mrs. Parker set up did not always have its intended effect because of contextual influences.

Using the Johnsons' current approach to positive interdependence (which requires goal interdependence, and finds goal interdependence with reward interdependence to be preferred), an observer would probably conclude that goal interdependence did not occur frequently. Mrs. Parker's admonition to her students to work together may not have communicated effectively to the students that they would "sink or swim together." Although Mrs. Parker rewarded students for working well together at the beginning of the school year, she did not provide reward interdependence for learning the subject together.

Although the participant structures that Mrs. Parker set up were intended to elicit helping or cooperative peer interactions, the students' actual processes of peer interaction were influenced by many other contextual features that often reduced the helping and cooperation that occurred. Tasks that were too easy or too difficult for the students appeared to inhibit cooperation. The press to "cover" the curriculum and the emphasis on finishing the assigned tasks seemed also to emphasize individual effort rather than helping or cooperation. Mrs. Parker's view of the organizational skills that her students would need for middle school led her to emphasize the importance of completing and organizing individual notebooks, which had the unintended consequence of interfering with students' cooperation in learning the course material. Pullouts, classroom interruptions, and school rules for leaving the classroom contributed to "breakdowns" in cooperative participant structures. Achieving the kind of "promotive interaction" the Johnsons (D. W. Johnson, R. T. Johnson, & Holubec, 1993a) now advocate was not an easy task in Mrs. Parker's social studies classroom.

Mrs. Parker held the students individually accountable for learning by administering individual quizzes and tests that included material covered in the cooperative learning groups. She also held students accountable individually for completing their worksheets and including the worksheets in their notebooks. However, Mrs. Parker did not hold students accountable for answering worksheet questions correctly. Rather than collecting and grading worksheets as students completed them, she decided to have students compile their worksheets in individual notebooks across each grading period. The time required to grade the worksheets may have contributed to her decision.

The Johnsons' two final fidelity criteria hold that students need to be taught small group skills and given time for the groups to process their functioning. Although Mrs. Parker did neither of these, she made a number of efforts in the area of students' skills for group work. At the beginning of the school year Mrs. Parker established the rules to be followed in the cooperative learning groups in her social studies class. She monitored groups during cooperative learning and reminded them about her expectations when they strayed from her intent. In the first half of the year, she regularly gave groups feedback at the end of the class on how well they had worked together. She assigned points, which were accrued toward a group reward, to those groups that had worked well together. She continued to monitor groups' work together and give them verbal feedback even though she eliminated giving points for good behavior mid-year.

Mrs. Parker's training about LT did not show her how to teach her students small group skills; nor did she have local models for explicitly teaching small group skills. Mrs. Parker did follow Mrs. David's model of monitoring small groups and awarding points for good group behavior, until she thought that her students no longer needed the points as motivation to work well together.

In summary, what Mrs. Parker did partially met the Johnsons' criteria as presented in the 1986 edition of *Circles of Learning*. She would have fared less well against the Johnsons' current criteria, which are both more extensive and more specific about what is required.

Although fidelity criteria may be important, they are not enough to understand what happened in Mrs. Parker's classroom. First, what the fidelity criteria are and how to determine whether they have been met is not always clear. Developers have changed fidelity criteria over time, and multiple observers could make different judgments about whether the criteria have been met. Second, fidelity criteria tend to focus on what the teacher does. Contextual analyses indicate that class structures and activities that outwardly appear to satisfy fidelity criteria may not actually succeed in doing so. Third, fidelity criteria are not the only relevant features. Contextual features other than those suggested by fidelity criteria influenced what Mrs. Parker and her students did. The contextual analyses presented in this chapter indicate that fidelity criteria can usefully be viewed as contextual features among many others that contribute to what happens when LT is used in everyday classrooms.

Six

Acquiring English in Content Classes

Approximately 25% of the students in Miss Grant's mathematics class and 35% of the students in Mrs. Parker's social studies class were second language learners. A few of the students were taking a class in English as a Second Language (ESL); most had "graduated" or transitioned from ESL classes. These second language learners were still acquiring both the conversational and academic English needed in order to fully participate in their content classes (see Collier, 1987, 1989, 1995; Cummins, 1981).

Student-student interactions in cooperative learning can present students with a range of opportunities for acquiring English. Second language acquisition theorists see cooperative learning as beneficial to second language learners because it may provide opportunities for second language learners to participate in conversations they can understand, hear language that is modified to meet their needs, and produce language understandable to others.[1] Most studies examining cooperative learning and second language acquisition (e.g., Bejarano, 1987; Long, Adams, McLean, & Castanos, 1976; Doughty & Pica, 1984, as cited by Long & Porter, 1985; Pica & Doughty, 1985; Sharan, Bejarano, Kussell & Peleg, 1984), have been field experiments, which generally have supported the proposition that cooperative learning facilitates second language acquisition.

As with studies of cooperative learning in general, few studies examine what happens in everyday classrooms when second language learners participate in cooperative learning groups.[2] This chapter focuses on second language learners' opportunities for acquiring English during cooperative learning in the two focus classrooms. I paid particular attention in the naturalistic data to second language learners' explicit opportunities for acquiring academic

107

English, language that would not typically be heard outside the classroom, including lexical items and specialized grammatical structures more commonly found in academic prose. I examined instances when students exhibited problems with academic English or made links between academic and nonacademic knowledge. (See the Appendix for an elaboration of the methods used.)

Acquiring English in Fourth Grade Mathematics

Miss Grant knew that second language learners were a focus of this study. Although she saw cooperative learning as potentially beneficial to her second language learners, aiding their second language acquisition was not a goal for her use of cooperative learning. However, Miss Grant said that she thought cooperative learning would be good for ESL students: it would help them learn new vocabulary, and it would give them experiences of success by helping them finish the tasks. She said that ESL students were often behind in science because they were pulled out of science for ESL class.

Six of the students (Julita, Kyon, Larry, Philip, Rosanna, and Veata) in Miss Grant's mathematics class were second language learners. Only Philip was in an ESL class during the focus year; he was considered an advanced ESL student. In the cooperative learning groups these students exhibited few grammatical problems with basic English, except Philip. The observational data were consistent with the students' scores on formal language proficiency tests as the beginning of the school year. On the Idea Oral Language Proficiency Test (IPT I), four scored as fluent English speakers, one as a limited English speaker, and one (Philip) as a non-English speaker.[3] On the reading component of the Language Assessment Scales Reading and Writing test (LAS R/W), five scored as competent and one (Jonathan) as limited. On the writing component of the LAS R/W, two scored as competent, three as limited, and one (Philip) as nonliterate.[4]

Second language learners had few positive opportunities (N=31) supporting their acquisition of academic English in TGT practice sessions in Miss Grant's mathematics class (see Table 6.1). The most frequently occurring category (N = 22) was "self help," which involved students reading a question aloud before or during working a problem. Such reading aloud might have helped the second language learners process the text. In one example, Kyon read her question aloud ("There are 60 minutes in an hour. What part of an hour is 20 minutes?") after picking a card.

Table 6.1
Frequency of Positive Opportunities for the Acquisition of Academic Language

Kind of Opportunity	Fourth Grade Math	Sixth Grade Social Studies
Academic Terms	–	38
Lexical and Conceptual Explorations	2	10
Homonyms	–	8
Para-academic Knowledge	2	4
Self-help	22	4
Conventions of Written English	2	3
Being Invited To Do More	1	2
Difficult Academic Concepts	2	2

Second language learners had a few other opportunities in their peer interactions to produce language that would help them acquire academic English. Rosanna explained the concept of multiples, a difficult academic concept; Larry explained how to interpret the answer sheet (para-academic knowledge) and some of the conventions of written English; Philip "played" with English by linking the number 16 to Joe Montana, a football player whose jersey number was 16; and Larry gave a "complete" answer to a word problem after being prompted to do so by a peer.

Second language learners had some positive opportunities through help they received from their peers. Philip was the recipient of Larry's explanations of how to interpret an answer sheet and the conventions of written English; Larry was part of a conversation in which Philip linked references to the number 16.

There were three instances when second language learners asked for help with academic language issues and did not get the assistance they requested. In Excerpt 6.1 Philip did not seem to be able to help Larry understand the instructions.

Excerpt 6.1

(Philip takes the answer key.)

Larry: I've got twenty-four [his card number].

(Larry takes worksheets and starts to read problem.) [The question says "the length of your math book" followed by two blank spaces with "word" and "symbol" over the columns. The general instructions for this section are on the previous page: "For items 22–25, write the word and the symbol for the unit of metric measure that best fits each example." Larry had not read the previous page.]

Larry: What? [re. problem] I don't get this. (pause) What are you supposed to do?

(Both Larry and Philip look at the question sheet.) [They both seem confused.]

. . . .

(Larry looks toward the blackboard, where Miss Grant is standing.)

(Larry works on problem, measuring his math book. Philip holds answer sheet.)

Larry: Oh my God. Twenty-five? [his answer]

Philip: (( )) I don't get it.

Larry: It said "Measure your math book." (( ))

(Larry leaves table and goes to Miss Grant for help. Philip remains at his desk looking at the question sheet. After 30 seconds, Larry returns.)

Larry: Now, I know. Now I know how to do it.

In Miss Grant's mathematics class there were no instances of second language learners receiving negative messages from peers about their language abilities during the practice sessions.

Contextual Influences

That Miss Grant's goals did not include second language acquisition was an important contextual feature for second language learners' opportunities to acquire academic English in the TGT practice sessions. Miss Grant did not consciously structure the tasks with second language acquisition in mind, nor did she provide any guidance to the students about how they might help one another acquire English.

As discussed in chapter 4, the school district defined mathematics in a procedural manner, and Miss Grant defined the team study sessions as "practice." Students' defined the practice sessions as competitive games. These various definitions of the situation suggest that students would see little need to explain or elaborate the processes they used to arrive at their answers. Thus, little oral academic language was required unless students tried to help their peers understand a problem. As discussed earlier, such help did not occur as often as it might have.

The nature of the tasks provided also was important. As discussed in chapter 4, many of the tasks were numerical problems, with little text-based literacy involved. (For example: $1/10 + 4/10 = $ _____.) Some were multiple choice problems. (For example: The temperature on a cold winter day may be: (a) 25°C, (b) 1°C, (c) 40°C.) A few tasks were word problems, called "problem solving" by the students. (For example: Bob has 16 pencils. 1/4 of them are red. How many red pencils does Bob have?)

Research indicates that an important aspect of context for learning a second language is students' identification with the group associated with the new language (Gardner & Lambert, 1972). Students are much more motivated to learn a second language when they identify with the native speakers of the language.

Information from the interviews gives some insight into the second language learners' identifications, which seemed to support their acquisition of English. When I asked them who their best friends were, none of the second language learners identified only students of their own ethnic group. All of the six second language learners I interviewed included at least one native English speaker among their best friends. The second language learners seemed well integrated in multi-ethnic friendship groups, of which native English speakers were a significant part. The second language learners did not exhibit strong bonds of primary affiliation to their own ethnic group in their friendship patterns in school.

I also asked the second language learners where they would like to live when they grow up. Five of the six said they would like to live in the United States. When I asked why, they said that they like it here or that their friends are here. Philip, recently arrived from Taiwan, said that he did not want to return to Taiwan because "if you don't do your homework, they will hit you. . . . the United States is more clean. . . . the house is bigger. . . . [and] everyone has his own car." The one student (Julita) who did not answer the United States said she would like to live in the Philippines because she missed it, but she added that if she went back there, then she would miss her friends here. She seemed torn between the two places.

The demographic context of the community and school seemed to contribute to the pattern of cross-ethnic friendships. Because the community was so diverse, with minimal ethnic enclaves, there was pressure for students to form cross-ethnic friendships because there were no or few members of their own group in their class, grade, or community.

Outcomes of Cooperative Learning

The comparative component of the study broadened the focus of investigation in several ways. The quantitative measures I used examined both conversational and academic English. Because fourth grade students at Maplewood School experienced several methods of cooperative learning in various classes (see chapter 3 and the Appendix), these experiences outside of their mathematics classes could have influenced their acquisition of English as a second language. Consequently, I compared students with the most and least experience with cooperative learning in addition to comparing the three mathematics classes (see the Appendix for details).

I compared Miss Grant's mathematics class to the two other mathematics classes on quantitative measures of English oral proficiency, reading, and writing. In comparing raw scores and gain scores, there were no differences that indicated a positive benefit of TGT on these measures. Similarly, comparing students with the most and least cooperative learning did not result in any substantive differences between those receiving differing amounts of cooperative learning.

As discussed above, Miss Grant's students did not see TGT as a defining feature of their mathematics class. Moreover, second language learners were friends with native speakers of English and identified with the United States. Given these patterns, perhaps it is not surprising that cooperative learning had no measurable impact on the second language learners' English skills.

Acquiring English in Social Studies

Like Miss Grant, Mrs. Parker knew that second language learners were a focus of this study. In an early interview Mrs. Parker indicated that she saw LT as potentially helpful to second language learners, offering them opportunities to develop vocabulary, improve comprehension, and reduce their anxiety about reading aloud. However, Mrs. Parker did not have second language acquisition as a goal for using cooperative learning in her social studies class, and did not encourage students to use LT to help second language learners acquire academic English.

Eight of Mrs. Parker's students (Carmela, Daniel, Hak Soo, Jane, Manuel, Peggy, Sung Min, and Woody) were second language learners. All but one had been mainstreamed from ESL classes. (The student in ESL had been placed there when he transferred to the school in the middle of the focus year.) Based on the students' performance on the Idea Oral Language Proficiency Test (IPT I) at the beginning of the focus year, four of the second language learners were fluent English speakers, two were limited English speakers, and one student was a non-English speaker. On the Language Assessment Scales Reading and Writing (LAS R/W) six second language learners scored as competent and one scored as limited. In the cooperative learning groups, the students exhibited few problems with their word usage or grammar in basic English.

Across all three participant structures set up by Mrs. Parker, the LT method provided a wide range of positive opportunities for second language learners to acquire English.[5] Students received and gave help with academic terms, difficult academic concepts, and para-academic knowledge. They heard and produced lexical and conceptual explorations, and homonyms. They received help with the conventions of written English. They also spoke aloud for self-help and were invited to produce more language. See Table 6.1 for a summary of the frequency with which each occurred. Examples of the most frequent categories follow.

Help with academic terms was by far the most frequently occurring category. These instances occurred as one student read aloud and others followed along during group reading of a worksheet. The words that proved problematic included general polysyllabic words (e.g., development, efficient), specific content words found primarily in academic contexts (e.g., matrilineal, monarchies), and special proper nouns generally found only in a social studies context (e.g., Athens, Ishongo, Agora). Assistance included initial decoding of words, explanation of word meaning, or clarification of pronunciation.

In one example, native speaker Doria received help with decoding and the meaning of a word from second language learner Hak Soo:

Excerpt 6.2

Doria: Hak Soo, what's this word?

Hak Soo: Religious.

Doria: Religious?

Hak Soo: Religious beliefs.

Doria: What?

Hak Soo: Religious!

Doria: Briefs. Isn't that briefs?

Hak Soo: Belief!

Doria: Beliefs?

Hak Soo: When you believe in something.

Doria: Beliefs?

Hak Soo: Yeah!

Doria: Oh.

Hak Soo: Beliefs, what that is, things you believe in.

Doria: Oh, okay. "Many Africans believe." Oh, it says, "What were some of the beliefs of Africans?" "Many Africans believed in a supreme God." It gave you my answer right there. I popped it up.

Help with para-academic knowledge involved help with issues that were not a direct part of the academic content but that helped students understand task instructions or sociolinguistic norms. In the following excerpt, second language learner Jane received help from second language learner Daniel.

Excerpt 6.3

Sandra: (rapidly reads task instructions) It says, "Each sentence below has one word or term that makes the thought incorrect. Underline the incorrect word, and write the correct term for this statement in the blank. See the example."

Jane: I don't understand it.

Daniel: Oh! I get it! See? ' Cause this (pointing to example) is an incorrect word. That's not supposed to be the teacher. You underline it, that's incorrect, and you write what it's supposed to be, soldier. "In Sparta, to be a soldier was the highest honor."

Jane: Oh!

If Jane had been asked to do this exercise on her own, it is likely that she would have encountered difficulty and fallen behind the other students. However, with help from Daniel, Jane quickly understood what the assignment required.

Second language learners also received help with the conventions of written English, which included receiving help to produce a timeline and to spell words correctly. In the following example a second language learner received help with spelling:

Excerpt 6.4

Hak Soo: Is "a lot" a separate word?

Jessica: It's a separate word. Two separate words.

This example is interesting because not only did native speaker Jessica supply the requested information, but she also corrected Hak Soo's inaccurate phrasing of his question. Hak Soo referred to something he believed might be two words as one word ("a separate word"), while Jessica replied using the correct form ("two separate words").

Second language learners' exposure to and use of lexical explorations, conceptual explorations, and homonyms offered opportunities for acquisition of creative language. Lexical and conceptual explorations refer to those instances when students linked familiar words to unfamiliar academic words or concepts to help clarify their meaning. In one example, a group was studying the differences between drawings of poor ancient Egyptian farming families and wealthy ancient Egyptian families. They noticed that the poor farming families ate basic foods such as barley, bread, and fish, while the wealthy families not only used gold and silver dishes but also ate more unusual foods such as duck, antelope, fruits, and honey. In an effort to characterize the food of the wealthy families, second language learner Sung Min suggested several alternatives to Kathleen (who was writing down the group's answers) before settling on "gourmet foods:"

Excerpt 6.5

Sung Min: They ate great foods.

Kathleen: I know.

Sung Min: The foods they ate were better.

Kathleen: I know.

Sung Min: They ate gourmet foods. (pause) They ate mostly gourmet foods.

Sung Min seemed to be extrapolating from what he knew was an appropriate contemporary term for expensive food and applying it to the ancient Egyptian context.[6]

Homonymic references extended the meaning of on-task activities by providing another way for students to make connections between an on-task activity and something academically 'unrelated' but phonologically and culturally connected. Frequently, these analogies interjected a pun into the learning experience. One example occurred when a second language learner interjected a homonymic reference into the group's efforts to identify the lake region in Africa. A native English speaker listed several lakes: "Lake Chad, Lake Rudolph, Lake Tangaka [Tanganyika]." Second language learner Woody immediately began singing the song "Rudolph the Red-Nosed Reindeer." Nakisha, a native English speaker, said: "I knew somebody was gonna sing that," and laughed.

Cooperative learning groups allowed students to talk aloud to themselves—i.e., produce "private speech"—as a way of helping them solve problems. An example occurred in April when second language learner Hak Soo sounded out "Med-i-terr-a-ne-an" as he wrote the word as part of an answer. Later in the same class, Hak Soo thought aloud about ancient Egyptian clothing: "Very simple. Very exotic. Exotic. Exotic." He seemed to be absorbing and rehearsing the word "exotic," adding it to his linguistic repertoire as the rest of the group worked.

Another way that second language learners were helped in their language output occurred when peers asked the second language learners to produce more language, to think more. In the following excerpt, Carmela (who was so quiet that her name only appears in some transcripts of her group one or two times) was asked to contribute more language to the group's efforts during a challenging exercise. The group was making a list of predictions about life in Athens by looking at a picture. They seemed to run out of ideas and they realized that Carmela had not yet contributed. Jane then invited Carmela to contribute:

Excerpt 6.6

Daniel: Number 4. (sigh) Let's see.

Jane: It's your turn.

Carmela: There weren't a lot of women?

Jane: What?

Carmela: There weren't a lot of women there.

Jane: Okay.

Although Carmela first stated her answer in a questioning tone, she became more confident after she was asked to restate her response. Jane, one of the informal leaders of the group, then acknowledged the acceptability of the answer for the group to write down.

Although the positive opportunities for second language acquisition that cooperative learning afforded were undoubtedly helpful to the second language learners, only 71 positive opportunities occurred during a total of 8 3/4 hours of interaction in cooperative learning groups. While this may be more opportunities than would have occurred during a teacher-led class, it does not seem that this was as "rich" an environment for second language learners as it might have been. Over half (53%) of the positive occurrences involved second language learners either receiving or giving help with academic terms (see Table 6.1). While help with academic terms is clearly important, it does not involve *complex* academic language.

Students missed opportunities to help one another. These occurred when second language learners unsuccessfully asked their peers for language-related help. For example, after being asked to identify the factors that contribute to the formation of densely populated areas in Africa, second language learner Woody sought help:

Excerpt 6.7

Woody: Factors? What are factors? I know what they are in math.

Nakisha: What are what?

Woody: Factors.

Tracy: (to James) James.

James: What?

Tracy: Have you ever lived in Johnsonburg? [mispronouncing Johannesburg]

James: No.

Woody's request for help was never answered. Instead, the group responded to Tracy's question and discussed Johannesburg. It is possible the students did not know the meaning of factors, they did not know how to explain it, or they simply chose to ignore the question.

In some instances, second language learners received negative input from their peers about their linguistic capabilities or academic needs. In the example below Sung Min sought clarification of his earlier query about the group's next task. Native speaker Sandra contradicted Sung Min in a loud voice and, when he complained, responded with a derogatory comment about his language ability.

Excerpt 6.8

Tonya: It said you answer the questions in the bottom.

Sung Min: *This,* right? (gestures towards paper)

Sandra: No, you have to answer *these* first.

Sung Min: Okay, Sandra, you don't have to yell at me. You don't have to yell at me.

Sandra: He can't understand anybody. (laughs)

Such instances occurred infrequently. Missed opportunities occurred 5 times and negative input occurred 3 times. However, their presence suggests that cooperative learning did not reach its full potential for supporting second language learners' acquisition of academic language.

These findings present a mixed picture. While cooperative learning offered positive opportunities that supported the acquisition of academic language, positive opportunities for acquiring academic language occurred relatively infrequently, and the opportunities that did occur were skewed toward simpler aspects of academic language. Some opportunities were missed; a few resulted in negative input.

Contextual Influences

Many contextual features influenced second language learners' opportunities to acquire academic English: the embeddedness of academic English, students' and Mrs. Parker's definitions of the task, various features of the task, participant structures set up by Mrs. Parker, and students' enactment of the participant structures.

Because Mrs. Parker's goals for her social studies class did not include second language acquisition, she did not consciously structure her class to help second language learners increase their proficiency in English. As a result, second language learners' opportunities for acquiring academic English were embedded within content-oriented interactions. The contextual features that influenced these interactions are discussed in chapter 5.

The emphasis in Mrs. Parker's class on finishing the tasks assigned probably influenced the overall frequency of opportunities to acquire academic English. The focus on finishing probably inclined students to complete the tasks assigned as soon as possible instead of assisting their peers with English, which would have delayed completion of the task.

The reading participant structure was an exception. Because groups often read together, errors or problems could slow everyone down. Consequently, it is not surprising that most opportunities for academic language acquisition occurred during the reading participant structure, in which one student read aloud while the others followed along silently. Almost all of the instances of help with decoding academic terms were provided during the reading participant structure.

The content of the assigned task influenced the kind of opportunity for acquiring academic English that second language learners received. For example, when second language learners received help with the conventions of written English, the focus was on spelling or on the timeline register. Second language learners did not receive help with the more complex aspects of written English. This is not surprising given that most of the writing was not connected text, but involved filling in blanks or making lists. Completing the assigned tasks usually did not require the students to write a sentence or a paragraph, so they did not have to deal with more complex issues of writing.

Lexical and conceptual explorations of academic language occurred during tasks that were divergent. An example already mentioned was the assignment requiring the students to list their inferences from pictures of Egyptian families or Greek city states. The divergent nature of the task seemed to have fostered a more generative and creative mindset in the students that led to more creative uses of language.

The students in Mrs. Parker's social studies class also had an important role in creating second language learners' opportunities for second language acquisition. As reported earlier, the students' definition of their task as completing worksheets seemed to inhibit cooperative behaviors generally. The same task definition appeared to have inhibited the students' verbal elaborations and their responses to requests for help. One example occurred in March when the students were recording their inferences about the lives of wealthy Egyptians based on a picture that represented them. After Sung Min mused aloud about how to characterize their food (see Excerpt 6.5), he said to Kathleen: "Just write down that. Who cares? Let's finish this up." His desire to finish the task seemed to halt Sung Min's lexical exploration.

Students' enactment of cooperative participant structures influenced the occurrence of missed opportunities. Except in one case, all instances of missed opportunities for second language acquisition or of negative input occurred while students were operating in what was supposed to be a cooperative participant structure. The remaining instance (negative input) occurred when students were operating in what was supposed to be a helping participant structure. In each instance, the structure established by Mrs. Parker had broken down, wholly or partly, and the students actually were working separately. For example, in Excerpt 6.8, Sung Min received negative input when he sought clarification of the group's next task. Mrs. Parker had told the teams to read a worksheet and answer its questions together, but the focus team could not agree on who would read and did not read the material aloud.

As previously reported, the breakdown of cooperative participant structures was associated with the students' experiencing a task either as too easy or too difficult. Missed opportunities for second language acquisition occurred during such breakdowns. Excerpt 6.7 illustrates such a missed opportunity. Mrs. Parker had told the class to work together to answer questions on their worksheets. The question in this excerpt (What are some factors that contribute to dense populations in Africa?) was difficult for the team. Working individually, various students read the question aloud, for a total of five times, but no one ventured an answer aloud. One student suggested skipping the question. Another, after reading the question aloud, immediately said, "I have no idea," and proceeded to read the next question. In this setting, second language learner Woody's peers did not answer his question about factors.

Difficult tasks that Mrs. Parker asked the students to carry out in a challenging way, i.e., cooperatively, seemed to provide "high potential/high risk" opportunities. While such tasks and participant structures sometimes led to opportunities to learn challenging academic language and provided settings for true collaboration and growth, they also resulted in missed opportunities. It seems that when cooperative structures broke down partially and students were confronted with tasks they found challenging, they were less willing or able to help each other.

Second language learners' attitudes toward native English speakers and toward the United States seemed to motivate them to learn academic English. As discussed above, second language learners' identification with native speakers can provide important motivation to learn a second language. When I asked second language learners who their best friends were, all named students who were not members of their own ethnic group, and all included native English speakers among their best friends. Second language learners in the focus class were well-integrated into multi-ethnic friendship groups, of which native English speakers were a significant part. As previously discussed for Miss Grant's class, the larger demographic context, comprising a large number of ethnic groups, also fostered the formation of cross-ethnic friendships. For students who were not European American or African American, if a student had limited his or her friends to his or her own ethnic group, the student would have had few (if any) friends.

When I asked second language learners where they would like to live when they grew up, all responded that they would like to live in the United States. Their reasons emphasized opportunities here and the students' lack of knowledge of their native country. Kathleen said that "we moved to America because it's better here. We can get better opportunities and there are chances of getting better jobs. And it's just better here, I think." Woody said, "I feel better in the United States because I've never been to Korea."

Outcomes of Cooperative Learning

I compared second language learners in Mrs. Parker's social studies class that used LT to second language learners in the other two social studies classes on measures of English oral proficiency, reading, and writing. There were no differences that indicated a positive benefit of LT.

Because sixth grade students at Maplewood Elementary School experienced several methods of cooperative learning in various classes (see chapter 3 and the Appendix), their experiences with cooperative learning in other classes could have influenced second language learners' acquisition of English as a second language. Consequently, I also compared students with the most and least overall experience with cooperative learning during the focus year. There were no differences that indicated a benefit of cooperative learning, except for the writing test, which indicated that cooperative learning may have had a positive impact on students' ability to write in English. The comparison of the fall (pretest) writing scores were not statistically significant, although the students with the most cooperative learning ($M = 79.0, SD = 11.1$) scored higher than students with the least cooperative learning ($M = 71.5, SD = 12.8$), $F(1,10) = 1.2, p = .30$. The comparison of the spring (posttest) writing scores were statistically significant, with students with the most cooperative learning ($M = 85.3, SD = 9.7$) scoring higher than the students with the least cooperative learning ($M = 70.8, SD = 5.7$), $F(1,10) = 10.0, p = .01$. The comparison of the writing gain scores was not statistically significant, although the difference between the mean gain scores of those who had the most cooperative learning ($M = 6.3, SD = 6.3$) and those who had the least cooperative learning ($M = -.7, SD = 10.9$) seems to be substantively significant, $F(1,10) = 1.8, p = .20$.

Given that students did not see LT (or cooperative learning more broadly) as central to their classroom experience and that second language learners' identified with native speakers and the United States more generally, the general pattern of cooperative learning having no measurable impact on second language learners' acquisition of English may not be surprising. The naturalistic data do not provide clues about why cooperative learning might have influenced the writing skills of second language learners who worked most frequently in cooperative learning groups, especially given the general pattern of no quantitative impact.

Discussion

TGT in the mathematics class and LT in the social studies class were very different in the kinds and frequency of opportunities for second language acquisition. However, neither class seemed to reach its full potential for offering a rich environment for second language acquisition. The categories of contextual features provide a way to examine the role of context on opportunities for second language acquisition in the two classes.

The nature and difficulty of the mathematics and social studies tasks in the two classes influenced students' opportunities for acquiring academic English. For example, in the mathematics class students were presented with few opportunities to read or write academic English related to mathematics. In the social studies class divergent tasks seemed to encourage second language learners to playfully explore English. Because the writing tasks in social studies primarily involved filling in blanks or making lists, second language learners did not have opportunities for learning more complex written academic English.

Both the participant structures the teacher set up and how students enacted them influenced students' opportunities for acquiring academic English. For example, almost all missed opportunities or negative input in the sixth grade occurred during the cooperative participant structure, particularly when combined with difficult tasks. Almost all instances of sixth grade second language learners receiving help with academic terms occurred during the helping participant structure for reading. When sixth grade students opted to read alone in social studies rather than as a group, they removed opportunities for second language learners to get help with their reading, and they inhibited cooperation in subsequent tasks because they completed their reading at different rates.

Several different kinds of meaning were important. In both classes the teachers did not have second language acquisition as an explicit learning goal for students, although they both thought that cooperative learning would help the second language learners in their classrooms. This meant that opportunities for second language acquisition were "embedded" within opportunities presented for learning content. As such, second language acquisition opportunities were influenced by some of the same contextual features as students' opportunities for learning content.

Miss Grant's definition of the team study sessions as practice and the students' definition of them as competitive games inhibited students' use of elaborated academic language. Similarly, in the sixth grade, Mrs. Parker's and her students' emphasis on finishing the assignments likely diminished second language learners' opportunities for acquiring academic English. In contrast, second language learners' cross-ethnic friendship patterns and identifications with native speakers and the United States seemed to motivate them to acquire English.

This latter pattern was influenced by the demographic context of the community where there were few enclaves of particular ethnic groups, thus encouraging cross-ethnic friendships.

Although cooperative learning did not seem to reach its full potential in these classes, this does not mean that cooperative learning cannot provide a rich environment for second language acquisition. For example, Gutierrez (1992, 1994, 1995) documented that collaborative groups in everyday content classes (language arts classes using a process writing approach) can be productive environments for second language acquisition.[7]

Many educators have suggested ways to address the needs of second language learners in content classes. For example, recent efforts to integrate language and content in content classes (Crandall, 1993; Short, 1994; Spanos, 1989) and to team second language teachers with grade level teachers suggest that supporting second language acquisition in content classes could be a productive instructional goal for teachers with second language learners in content classes.

While these various ideas offer ways for teachers to address the needs of second language learners in content classes, context will influence how these ideas are used in everyday classrooms. Gutierrez' (1992, 1994, 1995) work, discussed above, supports this point. Her study of successful collaborative groups occurred within a larger study of seven primary classrooms that included Latino students who had recently transitioned from Spanish to English. She found that how teachers used the process writing approach in their classrooms influenced the kinds of opportunities Latino students had to learn English literacy. Moreover, Gutierrez (1992) reported that:

> the way in which teachers constructed and implemented writing activities (task) was shaped by the nature of classroom talk (discourse), the social roles teachers and students assumed or were assigned (social arrangement), and the way in which their interaction was organized (physical arrangement). . . . [Moreover,] certain configurations of these sociocontextual features accompanied, or were constitutive of, three distinct types of instructional scripts or methods used to implement instruction: recitation, responsive, and responsive/collaborative. . . . Thus the effective implementation of the intended writing pedagogy was not ensured by the use of writing process materials and activities by experienced teachers. Instead, the nature of writing instruction was determined by the kind of script used to implement the writing process curriculum. (p. 250)

In sum, although theorists have argued and some studies have shown that cooperative learning in content classes can offer rich opportunities for second language acquisition, what actually happens in everyday classrooms is influenced by context. Achieving maximal benefits is not automatic. It requires careful attention, including attention to contextual features.

Seven

Context and Cooperative Learning

This chapter identifies patterns in the case studies using six categories drawn from the cultural-historical tradition. After describing those patterns, I compare my conclusions with the findings of other researchers who have studied cooperative learning. I also present a model of context as a "forest" and suggest possible directions for future studies of contextual influences on cooperative learning and other educational innovations.

Specific Contextual Influences

As reported in chapter 1, cultural-historical theory and research suggest categories of contextual features that influence cognition and learning: task structure and knowledge domain, psychological and technical tools, interpersonal context, individual and social meanings, local cultures and institutions, and larger cultures and institutions (see Jacob, 1997).[1] I use these categories to compare the two case studies, focusing on contextual influences at the school level.

Context and Teachers' Learning

Task Structure and Knowledge Domain

The task Miss Grant and Mrs. Parker faced—learning to use cooperative learning in particular contexts—has a very different knowledge structure than learning *about* cooperative learning, which they had done previously in conventional workshops or university classes. Their learning to use cooperative learning drew on subject matter knowledge, pedagogical knowledge, and curricular knowledge (Shulman, 1986), but went beyond these kinds of knowledge to action in particular contexts. Like other examples of "everyday cognition" in complex work environments, learning to use cooperative learning was a practical activity. "In everyday situations, thought is in the service of action" (Rogoff, 1984, p. 7). To paraphrase Schön (1983), such learning might be considered "learning-in-action."

Psychological and Technical Tools

The Teams-Games-Tournaments (TGT) and Learning Together (LT) methods of cooperative learning constituted "tools" that Miss Grant and Mrs. Parker used in teaching their classes. The teachers learned about these tools through university classes or inservice workshops prior to and during their learning to use cooperative learning in their classrooms. The classes and workshops furnished information *about* one or more methods of cooperative learning (i.e., underlying theory, suggested procedures, guidelines for fidelity) and provided the teachers with firsthand experience as participants in cooperative learning groups.

When the teachers used cooperative learning with their students, each teacher drew on the intellectual tools about cooperative learning provided through her formal training and workshops. For example, Mrs. Parker first learned about the LT method in a special education class. The behavioristic emphasis in special education at that time may have led to an emphasis on the motivational benefits of cooperative learning in contrast to the cognitive benefits, and may have contributed to Mrs. Parker's initial use of cooperative learning— awarding groups points for good behavior to motivate students to complete their homework assignments.

Books about cooperative learning provided additional tools that Miss Grant and Mrs. Parker used in teaching their students. Each teacher possessed a copy of Kagan's (1985) *Cooperative Learning: Resources for Teachers* and copies of materials from their training workshops. Miss Grant owned a copy of Slavin's (1986) *Using Student Team Learning,* and Mrs. Parker had a copy of *Circles of Learning* (D. W. Johnson, R. T. Johnson & Holubec, 1986). The teachers made use of these materials in their classes. For example, Mrs. Parker used the "Survival in the Desert" team-building exercise from Kagan (1985).

The distinction between transmission and acquisition of cultural information (see Eisenhart, 1995) is relevant here. Transmission refers to what is conveyed by "experts;" acquisition refers to what is learned and used. What both teachers acquired through formal workshops or classes was not a verbatim copy of what the experts transmitted; instead, the teachers filtered the information provided by the experts through the lenses of their own pedagogical needs and values.

The teachers' own prior use of cooperative learning also served as an important "tool" for their use of cooperative learning, providing "scripts" for action. Both teachers built their use of cooperative learning during the focus classes on their prior uses, and modified their uses based on their experiences.

Commercially-produced curriculum materials (books, worksheets, etc.) represented important additional "tools" for these teachers. Both teachers used existing materials with cooperative learning. One of Miss Grant's reasons for selecting TGT was that the developers of TGT had prepared materials that she thought would be compatible with the district's curriculum. In the spring, when Miss Grant had difficulty matching the materials with the required curriculum, she stopped using TGT temporarily.

Mrs. Parker made extensive use of worksheets that she had used in previous years. The primary task presented by these worksheets was to require students to answer convergent questions based on factual information presented in the text of the worksheets. If worksheets had been readily available that involved more complex tasks or that were structured for cooperative participant structures, her students might have had a very different experience of cooperative learning.

Interpersonal Context

In the cultural-historical tradition, interpersonal context usually refers to interactions between an expert and a novice, or between a more experienced novice and a less experienced novice, as they jointly perform some activity in which the novice learns. As discussed above, Miss Grant and Mrs. Parker learned about cooperative learning in formal workshops and training sessions. However, they learned to use cooperative learning on the job, where they received little coaching or advice. (As reported earlier, Mrs. Parker, and to a lesser extent Miss Grant, would occasionally consult with Mrs. David, the school's expert in cooperative learning.)[2] Despite Maplewood School's formal commitment to the goal of using cooperative learning, the teachers at the school had a very limited "community of practice" (Lave & Wenger, 1991) supporting the use of this innovation.

Students' responses and behavior contributed significantly to the teachers' learning to use cooperative learning. Miss Grant modified aspects of TGT in response to her students' behavior in the practice teams. Her mathematics students' positive comments about TGT contributed to her seeing it as useful for motivating students to do practice activities and led her to use it with her language arts class. Mrs. Parker started giving behavior points because she wanted to motivate her students to complete their assignments and because she had heard from Mrs. David that giving behavior points would help achieve that goal. Mrs. Parker subsequently stopped giving behavior points in social studies because students' behavior improved and she thought the points were no longer needed. That Mrs. Parker's students liked working in cooperative groups encouraged her to continue using cooperating learning and, eventually, to increase her use of cooperative learning.

Individual and Social Meanings

"Meanings" (e.g., beliefs, goals, values, and understandings) influenced how Miss Grant and Mrs. Parker learned to use cooperative learning in their classrooms. The meaning of using cooperative learning varied for the two teachers. Miss Grant and Mr. Harris agreed that cooperative learning would be her professional goal for the year, which increased her personal stake in learning to use it. Mrs. Parker had no such agreement with the principal.

The teachers' pedagogical goals and values influenced how they learned to use cooperative learning. Miss Grant's main goal for using TGT in her mathematics class was to motivate her students to practice for their mathematics assessments. This led her to the TGT approach, which she thought was consistent with the school district's curriculum and would make practice more appealing to her students.

Clashes among a teacher's goals and values sometimes created conflicts for her and influenced how she learned to use cooperative learning. Miss Grant seemed to be ambivalent about the roles of cooperation and competition in her mathematics classroom. She stated that because competition pervaded students' lives, she was concerned that asking students to cooperate would conflict with social norms; yet, she modified scoring in TGT in order to minimize competition because she thought losing was bad for students' morale.

One of Mrs. Parker's goals was to help her students develop the organizational skills she thought they would need when they went to middle school; consequently, Mrs. Parker required her students to organize their worksheets in notebooks in a precise order. However, her pursuit of this goal seemed to impair the effectiveness of cooperative learning. As reported above, Mrs. Parker's requirement that the students complete separate worksheets, instead of group worksheets, seemed to discourage cooperation among the students, even when the students were supposed to be using a cooperative participant structure.

Local Cultures and Institutions

At the beginning of the focus year of this study, Mr. Harris announced that cooperative learning was a school goal for the academic year and encouraged all teachers at least to try it. This created a general climate that supported teachers' learning to use cooperative learning in their classes. However, because of the principal's stance that teachers should use cooperative learning in their own way and at their own speed, the teachers had no guidance for how or when to use cooperative learning.

The meanings of mathematics and social studies in the school and larger community influenced how Miss Grant and Mrs. Parker learned to use cooperative learning. Mathematics was a "high stakes" subject in the United States, the local school district and the school. Because the principal wanted to maintain the school's record for student performance on standardized mathematics tests, Miss Grant came under pressure to stop using TGT when the math lab director reported that Miss Grant's students were covering fewer objectives than the high math class had covered the previous year.

In contrast to mathematics, social studies was not a high stakes subject. It was not regularly tested by standardized tests, and was considered an "afternoon" (less important) subject. Its status meant that Mrs. Parker had considerable latitude in how she used cooperative learning in those classes.[3]

Miss Grant's experience illustrates how conflicting meanings or goals at the school level can create pressures for teachers. Both the principal and Miss Grant had the goal of Miss Grant using cooperative learning. However, in the middle of the school year that goal seemed to conflict with the principal's and the math lab director's goal of maintaining the school's high performance on standardized mathematics tests. When the math lab director raised concerns about Miss Grant continuing to use cooperative learning, Miss Grant chose to continue using TGT, although somewhat less frequently. Another teacher might have made a different choice.

Lack of planning time contributed to decisions both teachers made. Miss Grant selected TGT partly because materials were available. Without additional planning time, she would have had considerable difficulty using cooperative learning if no materials were available.

The school's schedule, in particular the length of class periods, influenced when teachers did cooperative learning. Interruptions in the school schedule disrupted both teachers' plans. "Pullouts" required restructuring existing groups in both classes and led to breakdowns of cooperative participant structures in Mrs. Parker's class.

Larger Cultures and Institutions

Norms of the larger educational community, in interaction with the teachers' values, influenced both of the teachers. For example, Miss Grant's belief that competition was pervasive in students' school experience and her value judgment that excessive competition was detrimental contributed to her decisions to de-emphasize some of the competitive aspects of TGT. Mrs. Parker's view that her students needed to be able to maintain organized notebooks in order to be successful the following year in middle school contributed to her goal that her students keep social studies notebooks.

School district curriculum requirements influenced both teachers. Following the district's procedural approach to mathematics, Miss Grant's use of TGT emphasized students' arriving at correct answers and did not require students to explain how they arrived at their answers. In Mrs. Parker's social studies class, the district's emphasis on covering the required curriculum influenced her to emphasize completing assignments, which had the unintended consequence of de-emphasizing learning the subject matter.

Context and Students' Learning

The teachers established much of the context in which their students learned. Teacher-influenced aspects of context included the tasks they assigned, the tools they provided, the participant structures they organized, the goals they set, and the social skills training they provided. But other contextual features also came into play. The students themselves were active participants in creating their context and learning opportunities. Their definitions of the situation and how they enacted the participant structures set up by the teacher were important. The local school culture and the larger culture also influenced students' learning.[4]

Task Structure and Knowledge Domains

Miss Grant and Mrs. Parker each defined the explicit focus of her class as academic subject matter—mathematics or social studies. The nature of the tasks the teachers assigned influenced the students' learning opportunities.

The questions posed to students in Miss Grant's mathematics class involved convergent (fill-in-the-blank or multiple choice) questions, with the "correct" answer for each presented on an answer sheet. Students' answers were not very complex, nor were the students asked to explain how they arrived at their answers. Almost all of the questions were numerical problems with little text, although a few simple "word problems" were sometimes included.

In Mrs. Parker's social studies class the primary tasks involved reading and answering convergent questions on worksheets. In the spring semester Mrs. Parker added some tasks involving divergent questions. Tasks that involved divergent questions generated more complex discussions than those with convergent questions.

In Mrs. Parker's class the difficulty of the task influenced students' cooperation and second language learners' opportunities to learn academic English. Tasks that were too easy or too difficult for the students exhibited little cooperation; tasks that were challenging but not too difficult elicited cooperation among the students.

Because many of their students were second language learners, both classes potentially offered the students opportunities to acquire academic English. However, neither teacher made second language acquisition an explicit goal of her class. Opportunities for second language acquisition were embedded in mathematics and social studies tasks, and the nature of the tasks and other contextual features influenced the kinds of opportunities second language learners received for acquiring academic English. The mathematics class offered few opportunities because there was little text presented and students had no need to explain their solution strategies. The social studies class provided more opportunities for acquiring academic English than the mathematics class. However, the opportunities in social studies were not as fruitful as they might have been. For example, because writing tasks in the social studies class primarily involved filling in blanks or making lists, second language learners had fewer opportunities for learning complex written academic English than if the writing tasks had been more complex.

Psychological and Technical Tools

In both classes the instructional materials structured students' tasks. In Miss Grant's mathematics class the question and answer sheets contributed to students' emphasis on providing answers without explanations. The separate worksheets that Mrs. Parker required each student to keep contributed to a similar result in her social studies class.

Other tools also were important. The two different methods of cooperative learning provided different "scripts" for students' learning and peer interactions. In the mathematics class the question cards came to represent "points," which contributed to the students approaching their practice sessions in terms of the "points game." Contrary to what the developers of TGT intended, an incorrect answer in a practice session usually did not motivate the reader to learn from his or her error, nor did it motivate the student with the answer sheet to teach the reader.

As noted above, Mrs. Parker's requirement for individual student notebooks meant that students in her social studies class each used separate answer sheets, which contributed to students' limited cooperation during helping participant structures and to breakdowns in cooperative participant structures.

Interpersonal Context

Cooperative learning researchers have identified certain patterns of student interaction that seem to be productive for learning: giving explanations (Webb, 1989, 1991), constructive controversy (D. W. Johnson, R. T. Johnson, & Smith, 1986), and collaborative guidance and support (Forman & Cazden, 1985). Although the cooperative learning methods that Miss Grant and Mrs. Parker used were designed to elicit peer interactions that supported learning, the students' enactment of the assigned participant structures did not always reach its full potential.

TGT, as used by Miss Grant, provided a helping participant structure for the practice sessions. LT, as used by Mrs. Parker, comprised three different participant structures: a helping structure for reading aloud, a helping structure for answering questions, and a cooperative participant structures for answering questions or doing tasks. These contributed to different patterns of student interactions and different opportunities for learning. For example, almost all instances of students offering second language learners help in the social studies class with academic terms occurred during the helping participant structure for reading. Similarly, missed opportunities and negative input related to second language acquisition occurred during the cooperative participant structure.

Students did not always enact the participant structure set up by the teacher. For example, although Miss Grant wanted students to help one another by providing explanations during practice sessions in the mathematics class, students did not always provide help and when they did, it did not always involve giving explanations.

Moreover, the students in both classes missed many opportunities to provide help to their peers. In the social studies class, students sometimes decided to read alone instead of reading aloud as a group activity. In these instances students completed their tasks at different rates, which inhibited cooperation in performing those tasks. These and other instances when students did not cooperate during cooperative participant structures diminished the benefits of the cooperative participant structure for learning the content of the lessons and contributed to missed opportunities and negative input related to the acquisition of English.

Lack of student social skills may have attenuated the effectiveness of cooperative learning. This is not to say that the teachers made no effort to teach interpersonal skills. Each teacher presented to her students a list of acceptable behaviors in cooperative learning groups. Mrs.Parker expanded her efforts with a team building activity, and began the year by awarding points to groups for good group behavior. However, beyond these activities, neither teacher explicitly taught social skills.

Students in both classes identified social skills as important features of their experience in cooperative learning groups, and their responses in interviews indicated a limited range of possible solutions to interpersonal problems. If students had developed social skills to handle difficulties, such as when questions were too difficult in the social studies class, their interactions might have contributed to more successful learning opportunities.

Individual and Social Meanings

The goals that teachers communicated to the students were important to students' learning. Mrs. Parker's instructions to her class defined the students' goals as the completion of their assigned tasks, and her students accepted this definition.

However, the teacher's definition of the situation was not the end of the story. Miss Grant's mathematics students did not seem to enact her definition of the practice sessions as important preparations for the tournaments and math lab assessments. The mathematics students developed their own definition of the practice sessions as competitive games with the goals of getting the most "points" or finishing first. The students' definition seemed to reduce their motivation to help each other with the subject matter or with academic English.

Other meanings contributed to patterns found in the case studies. Neither Miss Grant nor Mrs. Parker adopted an explicit goal of helping second language learners in their classes acquire English, although they both thought cooperative learning might help these students. Also, in neither class did the students see cooperative learning as a defining feature of their experience in that class.

Local Cultures and Institutions

The school culture also influenced students' learning in the cooperative learning groups. Students' mathematics performance was an important source of school pride; performance in social studies was not. The school's emphasis on performing well on mathematics tests, coupled with the school's use of the math lab, probably influenced students' defining TGT practice sessions as "points games."

Some school norms and patterns—such as school and grade level schedules, interruptions for special activities, pullouts for special student instruction—reduced the effectiveness of cooperative learning, particularly in the social studies class. School norms for "pullouts" and rules designed to preserve order in the halls meant that some students were absent from part or all of their cooperative groups. In the social studies class, the students' absences often resulted in students being at different places in the assignment, which inhibited cooperation within a cooperative participant structure.

Larger Cultures and Institutions

How mathematics was defined (i.e., what mathematics "meant") within the district's mathematics curriculum also influenced what "doing mathematics" involved. During the focus year the mathematics curriculum was somewhat individualized and emphasized students' passing a certain number of objectives each year. In contrast to the current, conceptual approach to mathematics advocated by the National Council of Teachers of Mathematics (1989, 1991), the district's curriculum placed no emphasis on students' solving complex problems as a matter of course or on their learning to explain their solution strategies. The school district's meaning of mathematics was consistent with TGT, which supported drill and practice activities that focused on procedures.[5]

The pervasiveness of competition in American public schools and society (Goldman & McDermott, 1987; Tobin, Wu, & Davidson, 1989) may have influenced students in both classes. In the mathematics class, it probably influenced students' definition of their practice sessions as competitive games, and in the social studies class it may have contributed to the low level of cooperation that occurred during helping participant structures and the fragility of the cooperative participant structures.

The demographic makeup of the community that Maplewood School served seemed to encourage students' cross-ethnic friendship patterns and identification with the United States, perhaps contributing to a positive motivation for second language learners to acquire English.

There was also some evidence that students' ethnic cultures influenced their interactions within the cooperative learning groups. For example, in the fourth grade, Asian American students demonstrated more interest than others in explaining and understanding the mathematics problems.

Moreover, many of the contextual features previously discussed were undoubtedly influenced by features of larger cultures and institutions. For example, the cultures and economics of educational publishing influenced the commercially-produced materials that influenced students' learning. The meanings of mathematics and social studies in the larger educational community and in American society (and the meanings of standardized tests) influenced the meanings of mathematics and social studies in Maplewood School.

As discussed in chapter 1, my data collection and analysis were not focused on the influences of cultures and institutions beyond the school. My analyses here only touch the surface of the possibilities. Future work could explore the influences of district, state and national educational policies; students' gender, ethnic, and peer cultures; and broader societal cultures.

Context in Other Cooperative Learning Research

Few studies have explicitly focused on contextual influences on teachers' and students' uses of cooperative learning. Work by Deering (1992) is the most similar to the present study. His study focused on one teacher's seventh grade mathematics and social studies classes and their contexts across a school year. Deering did not distinguish explicity between contextual influences on the teacher and students, but focused on understanding how cooperative learning classroom culture was constructed and the influences on that culture. The contextual features he found to be most important are similar to the patterns discussed above. Deering's contextual features included: students' conceptions of cooperative learning, students' teammate preferences, teacher's beliefs about schooling and students, teacher's identity, class and group composition, classroom tasks, school policies, stratified assignment of students and teachers to programs, and community values.

Calderón (1994a) reported on interviews with teachers who identified barriers to effective use of cooperative learning: inadequate knowledge to adapt cooperative learning appropriately; pressure to teach to a particular standardized test, to "cover" certain material, to use a particular method of instruction, or to demonstrate dramatic student gains in a short time period; insufficient time for planning; inappropriate curriculum; inflexible school schedules; insufficient time to teach social skills; problem students; grading difficulties; and inadequate or inappropriate supervision or evaluation. These teacher-identified barriers are consistent with patterns identified in this book.

Other studies of the implementation of cooperation learning provide similar evidence of the importance of context. Sharan, Kussell, Sharan, and Bejarano (1984) presented an unusually detailed account of their efforts and "problems" in training teachers to use two methods of cooperative learning (Group Investigation and Student Teams-Achievement Divisions). In rereading this account after conducting the analyses reported in previous chapters, I was struck by the similarity between their "problems" and the contextual influences on teachers that were important in this study. Teachers' difficulties in using cooperative learning were related to their subject matter training and prior teaching experiences, time needed for developing materials and complying with recordkeeping requirements, characteristics of the students, class size, and the length of class periods.

Cohen (1993; Cohen & Lotan 1991) presented similar reports of teachers' efforts to use her Complex Instruction method. Complex Instruction asks teachers to "perceive tasks in terms of multiple abilities and to believe that every student will be good on some of these abilities" (Cohen & Lotan, 1991, p. 11). In a summary article about her overall research program, Cohen (1993) discussed problems she and her team encountered in trying to move Complex Instruction to everyday classrooms: lack of congruence between teachers' and administrators' goals and Complex Instruction's goals; need to demonstrate efficacy of Complex Instruction in terms relevant in the school system (i.e., standardized test scores); need for new curriculum; lack of time by teachers to make needed curriculum changes; need to integrate conventional academic skills into multi-ability curriculum tasks; challenges in integrating other educational goals with goals of Complex Instruction; changes in teachers' role; variability of support by the local principal; and the power of the organizational context of the school in which Complex Instruction took place.

Other work that identifies important characteristics for successful use of cooperative learning can also be read as supporting the importance of context. Hertz-Lazarowitz and Calderón (1994) identified characteristics of the principal, teacher, change agent, school, and central office administrators that they see as critical for cooperative learning's success. Sharan and Shachar (1994) focused on aspects of a school's organization and norms that are important for successful use of cooperative learning, arguing that schools and the classrooms within them must operate using the same organizational model if real change in classroom instruction is to be accomplished. The Johnsons (D. W. Johnson & R. T. Johnson, 1994; D. W. Johnson, R. T. Johnson, & Holubec, 1993a, 1994a), making a similar argument, delineated features of "the cooperative school."

Hertz-Lazarowitz's (1992; Hertz-Lazarowitz & Davidson, 1990) conceptual model, called "Six Mirrors of the Classroom," is also relevant because it draws attention to contextual features *within* classrooms.[6] The model identifies six aspects of the classroom related to the success of cooperative learning: classroom organization, learning task, teacher's instructions, teacher's communication, students' academic behavior and students' social behavior. In this model, the first four aspects are used to understand the last two.

Although this study did not focus on student differences within cooperative learning groups, other research indicates that differences among students can have significant consequences. Research by Kagan, Zahn, Widaman, Schwarzwald, and Tyrrell (1985) and by Slavin and Oickle (1981) pointed to the potential importance of students' ethnic backgrounds on academic achievement in cooperative learning groups. Cohen's (1993, 1994) research indicated that status differences (composed of influences from both inside and outside the classroom) may affect students' expectations of one another in cooperative learning groups, and that these expectations may contribute to unequal opportunities for participation among students in groups.

In sum, although few research studies have focused explicitly on contextual influences on cooperative learning, many reports are consistent with the picture presented here that contextual influences are central to understanding and improving the success of cooperative learning in everyday classrooms.

The Contextual Forest

In addition to providing information about specific contextual features and their influences on the teachers' and students' learning, the two case studies also offer insights into relationships among contextual processes.

The contextual features in the two case studies did not constitute static, unilinear causes of the outcomes observed in the classrooms. Contextual features in these two cases were interwoven.[7] Any particular feature was influenced by other contextual features. For example, to understand the low frequency of student-to-student explanations in each class, we need to understand at least the nature of the task assigned, the participant structure within which the students operated, how the teacher defined the task for the class, and how the students defined what they were doing. To understand these features we need to look at the larger task of which the cooperative learning activity was a part, the approach to cooperative learning used by the teacher, existing printed materials, curriculum guidelines, teachers' time constraints, norms of the larger educational community, and norms of society.

Meanings occurred and recurred among different individuals, classrooms, the school, the school district and the larger society, with varying responses. Participants could accept, modify, challenge, or resist existing meanings; they also could create new meanings. Both teachers accepted the school district's goals for the curriculum in the focus classes. However, Mrs. Parker added the additional goal that her students learn organizational skills, and Miss Grant resisted the math lab director's view of cooperative learning. Students in Mrs. Parker's social studies class accepted her goals that they complete their assignments and maintain individual notebooks. In contrast, students in Miss Grant's mathematics class developed their own definition of the practice sessions as competitive games.

Sometimes meanings conflicted with one another. Miss Grant's definition of the practice sessions and her students' definition conflicted. The meanings related to competition provide another example. The larger society and the school were permeated a competitive ethos; cooperative learning conflicted with this emphasis. Miss Grant seemed to be conflicted about the roles of competition and cooperation, using cooperative learning with some reservations and modifying the scoring component of TGT to reduce the effects of competition among student teams. Students in her room seemed to embrace competition by defining the practice sessions as competitive games, yet they also were upset when their home teams did not receive a "Super Team" award from Miss Grant.

Although the general contextual features relevant to the two teachers' knowledge and use of cooperative learning were similar, their influences on the teachers' learning varied. Mrs. David's practice of awarding points for good group behavior was a contextual feature that seemed to influence both Miss Grant and Mrs. Parker, but the two teachers followed Mrs. David's example in different ways. Miss Grant used group rewards from the outset not only to encourage good group behavior but also to promote academic goals. Mrs. Parker, in contrast, used group rewards initially only to promote her goal of encouraging students to complete their homework. Thus, the two teachers responded to the same contextual feature differently, contributing to different contexts for the students in the two classes.

The saliency of contextual features varied for the two teachers. Miss Grant seemed to feel more "oppressed" by some school-level contextual influences than Mrs. Parker. Miss Grant frequently referred to the pressures she felt: lack of planning time, lack of congruency between TGT materials and the district's curriculum, and pressure to have her students "perform" well on achievement tests. In contrast, Mrs. Parker, a more experienced teacher, never spoke of contextual features as "pressures." Although lack of time was a concern for her, curriculum congruency and students' performance on standardized social studies tests were not concerns for Mrs. Parker.

That external pressures seemed especially salient to Miss Grant, a relatively new teacher, might be understood by examining two different contextual features: the local status of the subject matter and her experience level. While Mrs. Parker used cooperative learning in social studies, Miss Grant used it primarily in mathematics and language arts. Both mathematics and language arts were "high stakes" subjects because students' performance was monitored through standardized tests. Mathematics was especially high stakes because it was viewed as a base for school pride. Social studies, in contrast, was not high stakes.

As a new teacher, Miss Grant may not have developed an extensive experienced-based repertoire of pedagogical tools and knowledge, the ability to evaluate collegial advice, or the status to challenge conflicting directives. Miss Grant's struggle with features of cooperative learning as well as with external contextual pressures is consistent with recent research on student teachers learning to teach conceptual mathematics (Borko, Eisenhart, Brown, Underhill, Jones, & Agard, 1992; Eisenhart, Borko, Underhill, Brown, Jones, & Agard, 1993).

Consistent with what Lave and her colleagues (Lave, Murtaugh, & de la Rocha, 1984) have argued, contextual features in these two classrooms were both stable and created by the participants through their interactions. For example, the curriculum materials could be considered stable contextual features in that they presented certain kinds of text or problems for the students. But the influences of materials also were "created" by the participants. For example, students in Mrs. Parker's social studies class, influenced by her instructions and grading practices, defined their task as completing the worksheets. In another setting the same students might define the task as learning the material presented on the worksheets.

Context and activity mutually influenced one another (see also Lave, 1988; Lave, Murtaugh, & de la Rocha, 1984). TGT and LT were "tools" for Miss Grant and Mrs. Parker. As the teachers learned to use these tools, they changed and expanded their goals for cooperative learning, and their expanded goals helped create new contexts in which the students learned.

Teachers' learning to use cooperative learning and students' learning within cooperative learning were interdependent, each providing a context for the other. The teachers' learning and use of cooperative learning provided part of the initial context for students' learning within cooperative learning. Students' learning and behavior in turn provided a context for teachers' future learning to use cooperative learning. Both teachers said that cooperative learning provided them with opportunities to observe their students doing academic work, which provided valuable information that they used.

Teachers and students thus participated in an interactive "dance," while also being influenced by other contextual features.

Teachers and students were active agents in using cooperative learning. As my discussions above have indicated, both teachers and students constructed meanings and made decisions about how to act, operating within the constraints and pressures of contextual influences.

Discussions of context and cognition often depict context as a series of concentric circles around a "core" activity (cf., Cole, 1996). In one such representation (Cole & Griffin, 1987, p. 7) the core is "Learner, Task and Concept." This core is surrounded by concentric circles that represent "layers" of context. The Teacher/Lesson is the innermost layer, then comes Teacher/Classroom Organization, then Principal/School Organization, and outermost, Parents/School District/Community Organization/Other Sociocultural Institutions. This image implies that the outermost layer influences the next layer, which influences the next layer, and so on.

Because pictorial representations are powerful shapers of thinking (Gould, 1995), such representations should portray features of a phenomenon as closely as possible. While the depiction of context as concentric circles is useful to show the many relevant aspects of context, it suggests that context is separate from the central focus, and it keeps the "layers" separate, implying that more distant layers have an impact on students' learning only indirectly through their impact on intermediate layers. The analyses here indicate that context and learning are interwoven, and what might be considered the central focus in one case (teachers' learning, for example) might become context when viewed from another perspective (e.g., students' learning). Moreover, "distant" contextual features (e.g., societal attitudes regarding competition) can have direct impact on students interactions, not just indirect impact through the intermediate layers. Sometimes the same contextual features can influence *both* teachers' and students' learning in a fairly direct fashion. For example, disruptions in the school schedule made it difficult for the teachers to plan and organize for cooperative learning. The same disruptions also seemed to influence the breakdown of cooperative participant structures in the sixth grade class.

The original meaning of "context" is "to weave together" (Simpson & Weiner, 1989; cf., Cole, 1996). An alternative image to the concentric circles, consistent with the original definition of context, might be a three dimensional ecosystem such as a forest with plants and animals mutually influencing one another. Looking initially just at the plants, each "plant" or group of plants in the forest could be a "center of influence." Some centers of influences are larger than others and "touch" or influence many others, providing context for them—such as shade, shelter, or food; others have smaller spheres of influence. There is no hierarchy of "level of organization;" scope of influence is determined by the extent to which one plant "touches" or otherwise influences others. Influence is three dimensional and multi-directional; it can occur horizontally, diagonally, or vertically. The "spheres of influence" may not be spherical in shape if influence is not the same in all directions. Some influences may be lopsided in one or more directions.

The extent and nature of influence can vary. Some centers of influence may have heavy, dense interconnecting webs radiating from the center. Others' influence may involve only be a few thin, fragile branches.

In addition to interactions between the various plants that influence one another, other, possibly more stable, aspects of the environment also influence the various plants. Thus, local and larger cultures and institutions might be considered similar to physical features such as climate, light, water, and soil. Just as no one set up environmental features is ideal for all plants, so no one context is ideal for learning for all humans.

Bringing animals into the picture adds other dimensions of interrelationships to the already complex system. Like plants, animals are "centers of influence" with varying kinds and ranges of influence. However, animals' mobility and goal-directed behavior produces different kinds of influence.

An obvious and central difference between human and nonhuman components of the system is that humans create meanings (with the result that the same contextual feature can mean different things to different humans) and have agency. Within the ecological analogy this might be considered similar to the way different plants and animals use their environmental resources in different ways.

In contrast to the image of context as concentric circles around a core, there is no visual "center" in the forest image. The observer identifies something as a central focus by choosing to "zoom in" on a particular center of influence. The center from one perspective is context from another. Thus, context is not inherently peripheral to some "core," but a function of the viewer's perspective. The image of a forest is useful because many of its components are living, indicating that change is part of the image. Contextual influences are not static but change through their mutual influences, and through the interpretations, negotiations and agency of participants. In fact, some "branches" radiating from the plant centers of influence can be viewed as meanings and interpretations that participants (whether individuals, groups or organizations) assume and transmit.

While no image represents all features of a concept, the forest alternative to the typical concentric circles is more consistent with current perspectives on contextual features in relation to cognition and learning.[8]

Future Directions for the Study of Context

This school-level view of context has shown that studying contextual influences on teachers' and students' learning can be useful for understanding how an educational innovation is used in everyday classrooms.[9] However, there is a need for much further research on contextual influences.

Other research could provide a more detailed, "micro" examination of processes of contextual features' interwoven influences on teachers' and students' learning. Sociolinguistic researchers, for example, could examine *how* teachers and students (individually and jointly) develop and negotiate their meanings of educational innovations in particular classrooms.

Work that examines "macro" processes also is sorely needed. This study, like many others drawing on the cultural-historical tradition, did not focus on larger cultural and institutional influences outside the school.

As Wells, Hirshberg, Lipton, and Oakes (1995) and McLaughlin and Talbert (1993) have argued, studies that include a wide range of micro and macro analyses would be especially useful.

There are many influences on teachers and students other than those discussed above. For example, teachers are influenced by their beliefs about how to teach different students, by their prior school experiences, by their professional cultures, and by their disciplines (McLaughlin & Talbert, 1993). They also are influenced by their gender, religious, and ethnic cultures.

Like teachers, students are influenced by their gender, religious, and ethnic cultures. They also are influenced by peer cultures, which are sometimes referred to as the "cultures of childhood."

Teachers and students are influenced by other nonschool contextual features. In addition to institutional constraints from the school district, state-mandated requirements such as accountability tests may foster particular instructional practices (Cobb, Wood, &

Yackel, 1993). The impact of such requirements on teachers' and students' learning needs further examination.

Power relationships and political processes at local, state, and national levels can have great impact on education. Teachers' and students' power (or lack of power) is an important contextual feature that needs to be included in future analyses of context and learning. The varying ideas and values about what schools are supposed to do are frequently represented in different political agendas. Although many studies have been done of the politics of education, few have carried their analyses to the classroom level (Wells, Hirshberg, Lipton, & Oakes, 1995). Nespor's (1997) work used such a perspective to understand disputes among administrators, teachers, and parents around a cluster of educational innovations used in a particular school. He described city and school system politics that provided the context for the school's use of the innovations; he looked at teachers' views of the innovations; he showed how parents developed the political will to challenge the innovations; and he examined the different perspectives teachers and parents used to examine school practices.

Expectations of the larger society may also influence teaching and learning. For example, the recent emphasis on school and teacher accountability seems to assume that teachers and the other adult practitioners have the responsibility to *make* students learn; lack of learning is the teacher's "fault." Other cultures (notably, Japanese) place the emphasis on students' responsibility to learn. These cultural differences in the assignment of responsibility for learning may very well have significant influences on how teachers teach and how students learn.

Studies of contextual influences should not stop at national borders. Nespor (1994) has argued convincingly that in our global society we need to look beyond the local because the local is part of larger nonlocal patterns.

> There are no disembodied heads about, but neither are there isolated social interactions or localized communities of practice. We live in a global world system and no analysis of knowledge and learning will suffice that cannot take this into account: that my activity writing this and yours in reading it cannot be explicated without understanding how we're linked to one another, to those around us, to world economies and global flows of culture that shape and provide resources for everyday practice (p.6).

Examining teachers' and students' agency in relation to contextual influences is a crucial focus for future research in order to understand more about the ways in which teachers and students negotiate the complex and sometimes competing influences on them.

Even though there is a strong need for more research, the cases studied here and other research discussed above indicate that contextual influences are important, pervasive and interwoven as teachers learn to use cooperative learning and as their students learn within cooperative learning. I think it is time for developers, researchers, instructors, and users of educational innovations such as cooperative learning to attend explicitly to the influences of context. In chapter 8 I discuss the implications of this view for cooperative learning; in chapter 9 I discuss the implications for educational innovations more generally.

Eight

Practicing Cooperative Learning in Context

Cooperative learning is a potentially powerful instructional innovation. However, these case studies and other research demonstrate that the effectiveness of cooperative learning in everyday classroom depends to a very considerable degree on contextual influences and on how people respond to those influences.

This chapter explores how instructors, administrators, and teachers might maximize the success of cooperative learning by attending to how contextual features influence the use and effectiveness of this innovation. However, prior to exploring specific implications for these educational practitioners, I discuss some general issues based on what I learned from the two case studies. Although my focus in this chapter is on cooperative learning, what I say can apply to other educational innovations.

Teachers' responses to contextual influences vary. Sometimes a teacher changes features of a cooperative learning method in response to contextual influences. Miss Grant, for example, modified the procedures for team awards and delayed announcing team awards to temper students' responses when their team "lost." Sometimes a teacher (or a group of teachers) changes contextual features external to cooperative learning. Even though Mr. Harris, the principal at Maplewood School, wanted all classes to be mixed-ability, fourth grade teachers changed the context for instruction by grouping students according to mathematics achievement.

Changes in features of cooperative learning or in the context in which it occurs might be positive, neutral, or negative in their influence on teaching and learning. In my view, changes are neither inherently good nor inherently bad. The processes and outcomes following from the changes are what matters. Some changes may help a teacher meet his or her goals; other changes may decrease the contributions an innovation can make to a teacher's goals.[1] Such changes should be made thoughtfully because they can have unintended consequences.

Attention to context means being aware of contextual features and how they might influence teachers or students. Also, it means identifying the influences of contextual features, making conscious choices about change, and monitoring the influences of any changes made. If Miss Grant had been aware of her students' definition of the practice sessions as competitive games and of the influence of their definition on their interactions, she might have made efforts to change their definition of the situation to one that supported their helping one another learn.

A contextual perspective can be useful whether or not one approaches cooperative learning from a fidelity perspective. Fidelity criteria are features of cooperative learning that developers say are necessary for successful outcomes. The criteria can be viewed as contextual features that are likely to facilitate students' learning. However, in everyday classrooms, even diligent efforts to follow fidelity criteria may not guarantee success. In everyday classrooms, features of cooperative learning comprise only a small part of the contextual forest of influences on students' interactions and learning.

A contextual perspective could help practitioners who stress adherence to fidelity criteria to understand why cooperative learning is used in particular ways in everyday classrooms. It also could help them understand how fidelity criteria interact with other contextual features to influence students' interactions and learning. With such understandings, practitioners could then take steps to improve the processes and outcomes of cooperative learning in everyday classrooms.

If a practitioner uses a method of cooperative learning that does not have fidelity criteria, or if a practitioner does not approach cooperative learning from a fidelity perspective, a contextual perspective provides ideas about what to look for to understand and improve the processes and outcomes of cooperative learning in everyday classrooms.

If one accepts the importance of attending to contextual features, the question remains of when to address them. A widespread idea is that teachers should develop considerable proficiency in an instructional method prior to adapting it to their local setting (Hall and Hord, 1987). This view seems to make intuitive sense because one ought to learn a method before attempting to adapt it. However, failing to attend to contextual influences at an early stage can be costly. If students are not learning, the school experience becomes wasteful and frustrating, not educational.

Instructors

Instructors of cooperative learning, whether staff developers or university professors, have an important role in attending to contextual influences on cooperative learning. In discussing some recent studies, McLaughlin (1990) concluded that:

> externally developed programs and external consultants can be extraordinarily effective in stimulating and supporting local efforts to improve practice. In these instances, the external agents enabled local efforts to respond to or modify external practices or advice to suit the local setting (p. 14).

Instructors could also aid teachers in changing contextual features to be more supportive of cooperative learning.

Considerable information is available in the literature about components of effective staff development (e.g., Joyce & Showers, 1988, 1995; Sparks & Loucks-Horsley, 1990). Many scholars see the training model as the most effective way to assure the success of cooperative learning or other educational innovations (Sparks & Loucks-Horsley, 1990; Roy, 1996). Ideally, instructors not only would teach about cooperative learning, but also would follow up with onsite support as teachers and administrators learn to use cooperative learning in their particular settings.

If instructors provide only training about cooperative learning, without onsite support, they need to present *substantial* information about possible contextual influences so that teachers will have the tools to monitor contextual influences while learning to use cooperative learning on their own. If workshops or classes are followed by onsite support, instructors should help teachers attend to contextual influences as they learn to use cooperative learning in their classes.

A contextual approach to teaching about cooperative learning should attend to the theories and goals of the method of cooperative learning being taught.[2] Teachers are more likely to employ a particular method of cooperative learning effectively if they understand the assumptions on which the method is founded.

Because most teachers using cooperative learning expect it to facilitate students' learning, teachers should understand cognitive perspectives on cooperative learning. Although cognitive theories have not been primary sources for the development of cooperative learning methods, they are very important for understanding the influence of cooperative learning on the processes and outcomes related to students' learning. Such a focus would draw attention to the importance of the tasks assigned and of peer interaction processes.

The staff development literature indicates that training for an innovation is most effective when the innovation is clearly linked to school or district goals (Sparks & Loucks-Horsley, 1990). This suggests that goal setting should precede any planning for a training program. Training about cooperative learning should include examining the relationships between the goals of the school district, local school(s) and teachers, and the goals of the cooperative learning method being taught.

When teaching about cooperative learning, instructors should identify the differences between learning about cooperative learning and learning to use it in everyday classrooms. This would provide a good bridge to discussing contextual influences on learning to use cooperative learning. Instructors should identify and discuss contextual features that are likely to influence teachers' use of cooperative learning, and should help teachers anticipate contextual features that might facilitate or inhibit the success of cooperative learning. (See Table 8.1 and discussion below about specific contextual features.)

Several common pedagogical strategies could be helpful in contextually-sensitive instruction about cooperative learning. Instructors could present "teaching cases" (Shulman, 1992; Wasserman, 1993) about how teachers used cooperative learning in specific contexts. Teachers could also develop sample lessons for particular classes, and, as part of developing those lessons, explore relevant contextual issues.

Demonstrations are an important component of effective staff development (Joyce & Showers, 1988; Sparks & Loucks-Horsley, 1990). In my experience, most demonstrations are presented in an acontextual, idealized format. To sensitize teachers to contextual issues, demonstrations could include a discussion of particular contexts and how a teacher adapted cooperative learning or changed the context.

Courses that extend for long periods of time, such as university courses, could combine training about cooperative learning with instruction on learning to use it in the classroom. Such courses might provide instruction on teacher research as a way for teachers to monitor their use of cooperative learning, or a course on cooperative learning could be paired with a teacher research course.

Inquiry models of staff development (see Sparks & Loucks-Horsley, 1990) would be a useful way to provide contextually-sensitive onsite support to teachers as they learn to use cooperative learning. When providing onsite support, instructors should help teachers monitor the processes of cooperative learning to see how well the teachers are achieving their goals. For example, if a teacher's goals include using peer interaction to facilitate students' learning, he or she might tape record cooperative learning groups and examine the tapes in terms of the frequency and kinds of help students offer one another. Some observational instruments are available in the literature for specific methods of cooperative learning. Cohen (1994) presented a questionnaire for evaluating group activities. The Johnsons (D. W. Johnson, R. T. Johnson, & Holubec, 1993b, 1994b) offered ideas and charts for monitoring group functioning. Ford (1991) presented an observational scheme for monitoring whether second language learners in cooperative learning groups display discourse features that theorists suggest should foster second language acquisition.

If teachers do not seem to be achieving their goals, instructors should help them to identify contextual features that may be influencing teaching and learning and to develop strategies for addressing the problems. (See Table 8.1 and discussion below about specific contextual features.)

Inquiry methods of staff development would be particularly beneficial when conducted with groups of teachers at the same school. As Gerow (1997) has shown, there are many benefits of teacher researchers working in collaborative teams, not the least of which is that they can challenge one another's assumptions and push one another beyond the status quo. There also are potential political benefits to working in teams. If teachers find that aspects of the local context conflict or interfere with their successful use of cooperative learning, a group of teachers probably would have more influence than a single teacher in requesting changes.

Mrs. Parker's experience highlights several important issues regarding onsite support. Her use of LT was not static. When Mrs. Parker found that LT helped her meet her goals, she tried new ways to use it. Subsequent success led to further changes in her goals and behavior. Each change produced new challenges and new issues. This suggests that onsite support ideally would continue for the 2–3 years staff developers indicate it takes to learn to use a complex teaching method like cooperative learning. Unfortunately, external onsite support for learning to use cooperative learning will probably be possible for only a limited amount of time (if at all). As an alternative to long-term onsite support, instructors could help local groups of practitioners organize to support one another's efforts in using cooperative learning.

Existing Approaches and Context

Some prominent developers and instructors of cooperative learning have written about their approaches to cooperative learning training, which draw on effective approaches to staff development. Some also have incorporated attention to selected aspects of context.

Calderón (1994b, 1996) has developed and implemented an approach to cooperative learning training that involves long-term, ongoing training. Particularly relevant to my discussion here is her inclusion of collegial support groups (Teacher Learning Communities) in which teachers collect information about their classes and use this information to refine their practice. Hertz-Lazarowitz and Calderón (1994) combined this approach to training with the Six Mirrors of the Classroom model. In this combined approach, teachers study their classroom, analyzing it on the six dimensions of the model (physical organization, learning tasks, teacher communication, teacher instruction, students' social skills, and students' academic skills). This model could be supplemented by considering other contextual features that might influence the effectiveness of cooperative learning.

The Johnsons (D. W. Johnson & R. T. Johnson, 1994; D. W. Johnson, R. T. Johnson, & Holubec, 1993a) have written about their preferred approach to cooperative learning training, which comprises three years focused on cooperative learning (formal cooperative learning, informal cooperative learning, and base groups) and on processes for academic conflict and peer mediation. The Johnsons organize teachers into school-based collegial support groups, which are expected to meet weekly to support teachers' use of cooperative learning. They see teachers using their approach to cooperative learning as "engineers" who must apply and adapt the general principles of cooperative learning to the idiosyncratic situations found in classrooms (D. W. Johnson, R. T. Johnson, & Holubec, 1993a).

The Johnsons encourage teachers to focus on continuous improvement in using cooperative learning. They state that, after using cooperative learning with their students, teachers need to assess how well the lessons went, reflect on what they did and how it can be improved, and then use it again in a modified and improved way.

As discussed in chapter 7, the Johnsons have explicitly discussed the importance of consistency between the norms and behavior patterns of the school context and those of cooperative learning (D. W. Johnson & R. T. Johnson, 1994). Attention to other contextual features could easily be integrated into this approach.

Slavin and the Johns Hopkins team (Center for Social Organization of Schools, 1996; Slavin & Madden, 1996; Slavin, Madden, Dolan, & Wasik, 1996) discussed their approach to disseminating Success for All, an elementary school restructuring program in which cooperative learning is a central feature. After initial training, ongoing support and coaching is provided primarily by a full-time onsite facilitator that each school is required to provide. The local facilitators also have responsibility for monitoring program implementation and insuring fidelity. External trainers focus on enhancing local facilitators' skills; they also monitor the quality of implementation. Schools are required to provide time for grade level team meetings at least every two weeks for support and problem-solving activities. In addition, schools must conduct assessments every eight weeks.

The Johns Hopkins team has addressed some of the contextual features that may influence Success for All by requiring schools that use Success for All to make certain commitments. Prior to implementation, interested schools must demonstrate a clear commitment from district administrators, the principal, and the teaching staff. Schools are also required to provide: one-to-one tutoring in reading by certified tutors, a family support team, a full day kindergarten and/or half-day pre-kindergarten, Reading Roots and Reading Wings curricula, heterogeneous groups for homeroom and the school day (except for reading, where schools may group students homogeneously), a building advisory committee, scheduling adjustment to accommodate 90-minute reading periods and tutoring slots, a commitment to reducing special education referrals, a commitment to student retention, and library books that address the needs of the reading curricula.[3]

Administrators

A contextual approach to cooperative learning acknowledges that district level and local administrators play important roles in fostering cooperative learning's success. Policies developed by district level administrators can increase the likelihood of cooperative learning's success if the goals of the policies are consistent with the teachers' goals for cooperative learning. As with teachers, local administrators have work to do both before and during the use of cooperative learning.

Before cooperative learning is introduced to a school, local administrators should understand the theories and goals of the cooperative learning method to be used. They should be clear about school goals, and they should inquire about the teachers' goals. Any differences should be explored and resolved. Administrators should also try to identify and to address potential conflicts between cooperative learning and the local school cultures or structures. In supporting the purchase or development of curriculum materials, administrators should ask whether the materials are consistent with the goals of cooperative learning, whether the materials support the curriculum that the teachers are required to teach, and whether the materials present appropriate kinds of tasks at appropriate levels of difficulty.

Administrators need to see that teachers' training and use of cooperative learning takes a more contextual stance. They need to understand the kinds of onsite support teachers need to use cooperative learning successfully. Administrators also should provide teachers with adequate time for planning, reflection, research, and collaboration. Once teachers begin using cooperative learning, administrators should create a climate that supports teacher research on cooperative learning and should invite feedback from teachers regarding how context may be influencing teachers' use of cooperative learning.

Traditional top-down leadership is unlikely to satisfy these needs (see Ferguson, Forte, Regan, Alter, & Treacy, 1995). Tharp's (1993) discussion of the "weight" of local and larger social institutions on cooperative learning bears quoting here:

> cooperative learning encounters the same massive inertia that meets all violations of the meaning of school. Our analysis here leads us to suggest that cooperative learning—so long as the management of schools continues to be in the authoritarian assign-and-assess activity settings—will be no more than a passing fad, rapidly digested and quickly expelled. We cannot expect any change in the classroom to be maintained without parallel and supporting activity-setting protocols that interweave the subjective goals, meanings, and values of the entire school. In this instance, we cannot

expect cooperatively learning students to persist unless there are cooperatively learning teachers, principals, and professors (p. 281).

Work on "the cooperative school" (D. W. Johnson & R. T. Johnson, 1994; D. W. Johnson, R. T. Johnson, & Holubec, 1994a; Slavin, 1987a) and school restructuring (e.g., Elmore & Associates, 1990; Lieberman, 1995) provides ideas for how to build a school climate conducive to a contextually-sensitive approach to cooperative learning.

Researchers have identified broad features of school culture that tend to reinforce and support effective staff development practices. Administrators have the power to influence these features. Sustained practice and long-term use of innovations is more likely to occur in schools under the following conditions: administrators support change and growth, and promote norms of collegiality; administrators and teachers share high expectations for students, have a coherent set of goals, and believe that learning about teaching is never completed; and teachers believe that learning is possible for even the most difficult students, experiment to increase student success, and actively interact with one another to aid each other in achieving their goals (Little, 1982; Sparks & Loucks-Horsley, 1990).

Teachers

Most teachers who begin using cooperative learning (or other educational innovations) do not receive extensive support from instructors, administrators, or colleagues. Usually, teachers learn *about* cooperative learning in workshops or as part of teaching methods classes. However, workshops and classes often "ignore individual teacher's needs, ignore the context and diversity of the classrooms, and offer minimal support to teachers" (Calderón, 1996, p. 8). Although ongoing support is important for effective training (Joyce & Showers, 1988; Sparks & Loucks-Horsley, 1990; Hertz-Lazarowitz & Calderón, 1994, about cooperative learning in particular), these "best practices" are not the norm in most schools. Most teachers who use cooperative learning probably learned to use it on their own after limited workshops or training sessions, as was the case with Miss Grant and Mrs. Parker.

By identifying contextual features that may influence their use of cooperative learning before they actually use it, teachers may be able to anticipate potential problems.[4] For example, if teachers identify school goals that conflict with their cooperative learning goals, they might be able to remedy the situation in advance of using a cooperative learning method and thus improve the chances of its success.

Learning about cooperative learning methods is only the starting point. As the two cases here demonstrate, teachers still need to *learn to use* cooperative learning in particular contexts. As teachers learn to use cooperative learning in their classes, they need to be aware of the wide range of contextual features that may help or hinder them in reaching their goals. The two teachers in this study, like most teachers I know, were aware of many aspects of their context, but tended to focus primarily on the students, especially on variability in students' moods and behavior. A broader awareness of context could have helped the teachers use cooperative learning more effectively. As discussed above, if Miss Grant had been aware of the implications of her students' definition of the practice sessions as competitive games, she could have taken steps to change their definition so they focused on helping one another learn mathematics for the tournaments and assessments. Then the students probably would have received more benefit from their cooperative learning experiences. If Mrs. Parker had been aware that her use of a separate answer sheet for each student reduced their cooperation, she might have made other choices, such as requiring a single answer sheet for each group, with copies filed in each student's notebook.

This study suggests that teachers should be reflective and take an action research stance to cooperative learning (see also D. M. Johnson, 1994). Teachers should consciously identify their goals for using cooperative learning, identify contextual features that might enhance or hinder achieving their goals, structure classroom tasks to support the desired goals, and monitor the processes and outcomes in their cooperative learning classes to see if they are achieving their goals. If teachers find that they are not achieving their goals, they need to explore possible contextual influences and try to remedy the problems.

Observations of cooperative learning groups can provide useful process data to teachers. As Miss Grant's and Mrs. Parker's classes demonstrated, students' definitions of the situation and their interactions are central contextual influences on their learning. The teacher research literature (e.g. Bullough & Gitlin, 1995; Hitchcock & Hughes, 1995; Hubbard & Power, 1993) offers detailed suggestions for teachers interested in monitoring the processes and outcomes of their instructional activities such as cooperative learning.

Although a teacher could conduct action research by himself or herself, the research probably would be more effective if done in collaboration with other teachers.[5] Cooperative learning trainers and local administrators might also be involved if there is an appropriate level of trust. Master teachers might serve as peer consultants. Even without a local expert, teachers might find it helpful to work with a group of peers.

If a group peer support system is not feasible, teachers might work in pairs to reflect together and support one another as they learn to use cooperative learning in their classrooms. The recent interest in team teaching and in second language teachers working collaboratively with grade-level teachers offers an important opportunity. With two teachers present in a classroom, one might focus on monitoring while the other directs a lesson.

Contextual Features

Table 8.1 presents the contextual features discussed below in the form of questions that teachers could ask about cooperative learning. They are stated here in a form most relevant for teachers who are already using cooperative learning, but they could easily be adapted for teachers who are just learning about it. It is important to remember that contextual features are not unilinear causes, but are interwoven in complex ways that mutually influence one another. Because contextual features are interwoven, it may be necessary to attend to more than one contextual feature in order to understand what is happening or to bring about change in the setting.

Teachers should be aware that cooperative learning is not a single method of instruction, and that the different forms of cooperative learning derive from different theories and have different goals (see discussion in chapter 2). Teachers need to learn not only methods of cooperative learning but also the developers' theory and goals underlying a particular method. Congruence between teacher and developer goals is an important issue. Another issue is teachers' understanding of the theory behind a cooperative learning method. Understanding the theory and goals that underlie a cooperative learning method can guide the teacher as he or she uses it. If a teacher shares the goals of the developer of a particular cooperative learning method, then understanding the developers' theoretical base and goals would put teachers on firmer ground in making modifications that might be needed in their local context (see Cohen, 1993, for a similar argument). If a teacher does not share the goals

Table 8.1
Questions Teachers Might Ask about Contextual Influences on Cooperative Learning

Context and Teachers' Learning

Task Structure and Knowledge Domain

- How does my training about cooperative learning influence how I use it in my classroom?
- How does my understanding of the theory underlying the cooperative learning method I am using influence my use of cooperative learning?

Psychological and Technical Tools

- What books and other "tools" are available to me? How do they influence my use of cooperative learning?
- What "scripts" are available to me from my prior experience? How do they influence my use of cooperative learning?
- How do existing curriculum materials contribute to how I use cooperative learning?

Interpersonal Context

- How do interactions with members of my local professional community influence my use of cooperative learning?
- How do others' (colleagues', parents', students') responses and behavior influence my use of cooperative learning?

Individual and Social Meanings

- What are my goals for using cooperative learning? What is the match between my goals for cooperative learning and other goals I have for my students?
- What is the match between my goals and the developer's goals?
- What is the match between my goals and those of the school or district administration?
- What does cooperative learning mean to me?
- What are my beliefs about cooperation and competition? How do they match those of the developer of the cooperative learning method I am using?
- What do I communicate to my students about the meaning of cooperative learning?

Local Cultures and Institutions

- How do the local meanings of the subject matter I am teaching influence my use of cooperative learning?
- What aspects of the school's cultural values influence how I use cooperative learning?
- What aspects of the school's organization and behavior patterns influence how I use cooperative learning?

Table 8.1 (Continued)

Larger Cultures and Institutions

• What aspects of district policy influence how I use cooperative learning?
• What aspects of the local community and parents influence how I use cooperative learning?
• What aspects of the larger society influence how I use cooperative learning?

Context and Students' Learning

Task Structure and Knowledge Domain

• How do the tasks I assign in cooperative learning align with my goals for my students' learning?
• Are the tasks I assign at an appropriate level of difficulty to maximize the quality of students' interactions?
• How is this method of cooperative learning expected to promote students' learning?

Psychological and Technical Tools

• How do the task-related books and other materials align with my goals for my students' learning?
• How does the number of resources available to groups influence their cooperation?

Interpersonal Context

• What kinds of student-student interactions occur during cooperative learning? How do they contribute to my students' learning and relationships with one another?
• How do the participant structures I set up influence students' interactions and learning?
• How do students' social skills (or lack of them) contribute to their interactions and learning in cooperative learning groups?

Individual and Social Meanings

• How do my explanations of cooperative learning and the tasks within it influence my students' definitions of cooperative learning?
• How do my students' definitions of cooperative learning influence their interactions and their learning?

Local Cultures and Institutions

• What aspects of the school's cultural values influence students' use of cooperative learning and their learning?
• What aspects of the school's organization and behavior patterns influence students' use of cooperative learning and their learning?

Table 8.1 (Continued)

Larger Cultures and Institutions

• How do cultures and institutions of the larger society directly or indirectly influence my students' use of cooperative learning and their learning?
• How do influences on my students from outside this particular class (e.g., gender, ethnic and peer cultures, or status differences) influence students' interactions and learning within cooperative learning groups?

of the developer of a particular method of cooperative learning, or has conflicting goals, then the task of successfully using that method of cooperative learning becomes more difficult.

The degree of match between the goals of teachers and administrators is another important contextual feature. Without a high degree of congruency there can be conflicting demands and expectations that can contribute to problems with cooperative learning.[6]

Related to teachers' goals for cooperative learning is the "meaning" that cooperative learning has for them. What cooperative learning means to the teachers and how they communicate that meaning to their students is a central influence on cooperative learning's processes and outcomes. Early in Mrs. Parker's use of cooperative learning, she understood cooperative learning primarily as a motivator; later in the focus year, she began to understand its possible role in facilitating more complex learning. Students in Mrs. Parker's class had very different experiences of cooperative learning as her understanding of it changed.

School-level contextual features, such as school cultures, time constraints, school schedules and their interruptions, can influence how teachers use cooperative learning. For example, Nicolopoulou and Cole (1993) found that success of the Fifth Dimension program at two different after-school sites was influenced by the strength of collaborative learning culture at each site.[7] Ferguson, Forte, Regan, Alter, and Treacy (1995) identified other relevant school-level contextual features. They argued that the success of cooperative learning is maximized when a usable and complete curriculum is available to teachers and when a school possesses a "critical mass" of local expertise. Although features such as time constraints are a continuing lament of teachers, labeling them as contextual features and examining how these features affect teachers' use of cooperative learning may suggest strategies to bring about needed changes.

Cultures and patterns of the larger educational community influence teachers' use of cooperative learning. Certainly, the pervasiveness of competitive and individualistic norms in the United States and its schools, as well as school district beliefs and policies around standardized testing, can influence what happens in cooperative learning groups. In Miss Grant's class, the pervasiveness of competition probably contributed to her students' definition of the practice sessions as competitive games.

The tasks teachers assign to students is a central contextual feature for students' learning, whether or not the teacher uses cooperative learning. Currently there is widespread interest in "teaching for understanding" (e.g., National Council of Teachers of Mathematics, 1989; Talbert, McLaughlin, & Rowan, 1993), and cooperative learning is widely seen as an instructional method useful for achieving this goal. But cooperative learning can contribute to teaching for understanding only if the tasks assigned cooperative learning groups require understanding. As seen in the fourth grade mathematics class, using cooperative learning is not an automatic guarantee that conceptual understanding will occur.

Features of the task are also related to students' interactions and learning. In Mrs. Parker's social studies class, for example, more complex interactions occurred among students when the task was divergent and was neither too easy nor too difficult. When tasks were too easy, students did not need to discuss the answer; when tasks were too difficult, students often stopped cooperating and worked alone.

The content and structure of worksheets, books, and other task-related "tools" influence students' learning. The number of tools available also can influence students' interactions and subsequent learning. For example, separate answer sheets in the sixth grade social studies class seemed to impair cooperation among the students.

Participant structures a teacher sets up influence students' interactions with one another. Analyses of Mrs. Parker's class showed that the three different participant structures she set up contributed to different kinds of learning opportunities for her students.

How teachers explain cooperative learning and the tasks within cooperative learning sessions can influence students' definitions of the situation. Mrs. Parker's class is an example of students' assuming the teacher's definition of the task, i.e., finishing the worksheets. In Miss Grant's class the students developed their own definitions of the task, i.e., winning games.

Students' social skills can influence their learning. By monitoring the processes of cooperative learning, teachers can identify specific social skills students need to improve the quality of their interactions. (See D. W. Johnson, R. T. Johnson, and Holubec, 1986, 1993a, for suggestions about teaching cooperative skills and group processing and Webb and Farivar, 1994, for a discussion of the importance of academic helping skills.) In Mrs. Parker's class, for example, students would have benefited by having alternative strategies for dealing with difficult questions. When cooperative learning is implemented on a schoolwide basis, teachers might coordinate a curriculum for social skills across the grades.

Within a contextually-sensitive approach, developers' fidelity criteria (e.g., individual accountability, group recognition, and equal opportunity for success in TGT) can be viewed as contextual features that are likely to positively influence students' interactions and learning. Thus, teachers might also examine contextual influences on their use of fidelity criteria, and the influences of their use of fidelity criteria on students' interactions and learning.

Cultural and institutional patterns within school and the larger society can also influence students' learning within cooperative learning groups. Interruptions and pullouts might contribute to breakdowns in cooperation within cooperative learning groups. If competition is pervasive in the local or larger culture, students may have difficulty learning to cooperate and may easily revert to competitive behaviors.

Gender, ethnic, and peer cultures may influence students' approach to cooperative learning. Status differences outside the classroom may influence students' expectations of one another in cooperative learning groups, and these expectations may contribute to unequal participation among students in groups (Cohen, 1993; 1994). If teachers notice variations in quantity or quality of participation among subgroups of students, contextual features such as these might be contributing.[8]

Discussion

As I hope is clear from the preceding discussion, my emphasis on attending to contextual influences on an innovation like cooperative learning is compatible with what is currently considered good staff development practice for externally developed educational innovations.

As discussed above, some developers and instructors of cooperative learning have pointed to the importance of context even though they may not have discussed it in terms of contextual influences. Both Slavin (1994) and the Johnsons (D. W. Johnson, R. T. Johnson & Holubec, 1993a) recognized that teachers may adapt cooperative learning methods to their local settings. Hertz-Lazarowitz and Calderón (1994) described features of a setting needed to institutionalize cooperative learning and indicated that a setting would need to be changed if these features did not already exist. In published reports some cooperative learning developers and instructors have discussed how they have sought ways to address in their training practices at least some contextual influences. I suggest that, in order to maximize the benefits of cooperative learning in everyday classrooms, instructors, administrators, and teachers need to pay explicit and sustained attention to contextual influences on cooperative learning, and that they need to broaden the range of contextual influences they examine beyond those contextual features that are considered part of a cooperative learning method.

A legitimate question is how we can expect teachers to attend consciously to contextual influences while they are learning a new and complex innovation like cooperative learning, especially since time is already at a premium for them. Although the task may be challenging, I think that attention to contextual features is crucial for cooperative learning to be successful in everyday classrooms. Ideally, school districts and local schools should make changes that provide teachers more time and support to learn to use cooperative learning and other educational innovations in such a way that they are maximally successful.[9] As discussed above, individual teachers or instructors might link learning to use cooperative learning with action research and reflective practice. Combining these two elements could improve the success of cooperative learning in everyday classrooms. Such an approach would be consistent with the current focus on teacher professionalism and empowerment.

Another concern is whether an individual teacher should even attempt to use cooperative learning without meaningful support or whether a school should adopt cooperative learning as an isolated innovation. McLaughlin's (1990) reanalysis of the Rand Change Agent study suggested that innovations like cooperative learning are unlikely to succeed fully when adopted as an isolated "special project" because special projects usually "ignore the systemic and interconnected conditions that influence classroom practice" (p. 15). A contextual approach should help increase the effectiveness of cooperative learning in such circumstances because it specifically directs attention to interwoven contextual features.[10]

The patterns found in this study and the recommendations in this chapter are relevant not only for cooperative learning but also for educational innovations generally. In the next chapter I explore ways that context might be taken into account in the development, research, dissemination and use of all educational innovations.

Nine

Toward Contextually-Sensitive Approaches to Educational Innovations

Preceding chapters have shown that contextual features were central to teachers' learning to use cooperative learning and to students' learning within cooperative learning in the two classes studied. These findings suggest the following regarding educational innovations in general:

- Contextual features are central to understanding how educational innovations are used;

- Contextual features influence both teachers and students as learners;

- Relevant contextual features include task structure and knowledge domain, psychological and technical tools, interpersonal context, individual and social meanings, local cultures and institutions, and larger cultures and institutions;

- Many contextual features influence an educational innovation;

- Contextual features are interwoven; they are not unilinear causes; and

- Using an educational innovation changes the context, thus an innovation and its context mutually influence one another.

Other research on educational innovations and on learning (see chapter 1) supports the centrality of context on teachers' and students' learning and the patterns outlined above. If, as I suspect, the patterns from the case studies at Maplewood Elementary School are typical of the role of context on how teachers and students use educational innovations in everyday classrooms, they raise significant questions for educators. Notwithstanding some attention to context in the reports on dissemination of innovations (see chapter 8 for examples from cooperative learning), most educational innovations have been developed, researched, taught and used without significant attention to context (see also Snyder, Bolin, & Zumwalt, 1992). If context will have a substantial influence on how an innovation is actually used in everyday classrooms, what strategies might developers, researchers, instructors, and users of educational innovations use to anticipate and address the influences of context? In other words, what might contextually-sensitive approaches to educational innovations look like?

Innovations and Context

An acontextual stance permeates the conventional approach to the development, dissemination, and use of instructional innovations in education. Typically, a scholar or team based at a university or research center develops a new instructional method or curriculum, drawing on theory, research, or suggestions from teachers. A cycle of research and development usually follows, typically in experimental settings. The developer's goal is to develop a method that will "work" in a wide variety of settings. If data from experimental settings (whether laboratory or field) show that the innovation succeeded, the developer uses the data to promote the innovation for general classroom use. Subsequent research often examines the features and processes that contribute to the outcomes originally documented in experimental settings.

Once an instructional method is developed, it is taught by instructors, professors or staff developers, who usually assume that their goal is to train practitioners to implement the innovation exactly as it was developed. Teachers are then expected to implement the method in the classrooms exactly as they were taught it. Some instructors may provide followup training and support to assure that practitioners will implement the method "correctly."

If conventional researchers examine how an innovation is implemented in everyday classrooms, they typically use the "fidelity approach" (Snyder, Bolin, & Zumwalt, 1992). The fidelity approach involves comparing the practice observed against a list of criteria that developers or researchers determined were important for the "successful" implementation of the innovation. The fidelity approach assumes that any changes made by teachers to an innovation will have a negative impact on the outcomes of an innovation (Snyder, Bolin, & Zumwalt, 1992). Developers, researchers, and instructors using the fidelity approach generally prefer to minimize or to eliminate any local level adaptation of the innovation.

The acontextual assumptions of the conventional approach and the top-down orientation it supports have permeated educational research, practice, and teacher training (Schön, 1983). The educational bureaucracy generally has supported the conventional approach (Tyack, 1974).

A fundamental problem with the conventional approach is that innovations developed, researched, and disseminated through it often have been unsuccessful in everyday classrooms. To cite a familiar example, despite many reform efforts, teacher-centered instruction (in contrast to student-centered instruction) continued to dominate K–12 classrooms in the United States between 1890 and 1980 (Cuban, 1984).

One reason for the widespread failure of educational innovations in everyday classrooms may be that developers, researchers, instructors, and users of educational innovations fail to appreciate fully that contextual features in everyday setting can dramatically influence the use and success of an innovation. Developers operating within the conventional approach produce an innovation without attention to the contexts in which it will be used. Researchers usually study an innovation in experimental settings, and even when they do study an innovation in everyday settings, they tend to focus exclusively on whether the practitioners using the innovation have met the "fidelity criteria" and to ignore contextual features not involving the fidelity criteria.

The use of the experimental method for research contributes to the problem not only because the studies are conducted in experimental settings but also because in experiments researchers try to control contextual features. It is difficult to study the influences of contextual features within the experimental method because they are consciously controlled.

Some researchers have used field experiments as a way to address problems inherent in laboratory settings, but field experiments do not solve the problems of studying contextual features within the experimental method. The settings used for field experiments usually are provided extra support and resources and are monitored carefully so that teachers implement the method "correctly," creating an entirely different context than those that would prevail if the support and monitoring were withdrawn. Talbert, McLaughlin, and Rowan (1993) have criticized "research carried out in 'boutique' or 'hothouse' schools with special resources or advantages" (p. 62) because such research tells little about what happens in everyday classrooms that do not receive such support.

Contextually-Sensitive Approaches

In contextually-sensitive approaches to the development of educational innovations, developers would recognize from the beginning that teachers will interpret their innovations in terms of teachers' own pedagogical needs, values, and goals and that the teachers will use the innovation within a web of complex, interwoven contextual features. They would try to foresee the contextual influences on their innovation and to help the practitioners who use their innovation to anticipate and address contextual influences.

The perspective in chapter 8 about implications for instructors, administrators, and teachers of cooperative learning can be extended to other educational innovations. Instructors would help practitioners using the innovation to reflect on their own goals and values and compare them to administrators' and developers' goals and values; to anticipate contextual features that will help or hinder the innovation's success; and to address the contextual features that actually do influence the use of an innovation.[1] Presentations about an instructional approach would take a contextual perspective and would be followed by ongoing onsite support, whether from specialists or peers.[2] As discussed in chapter 8, action research conducted by teachers could easily focus on exploring contextual issues in relation to the processes and outcomes of an innovation.[3]

Preservice and inservice education occurring in schools of education also needs to take a contextually-sensitive approach. Without coordination and consistency between schools of education and local school districts, there is little chance for real change (see Eisenhart, Borko, Underhill, Brown, Jones, & Agard, 1993).

Gitlin and Margonis (1995) and Wasley, Donmoyer, and Maxwell (1995) independently made the important point that teacher resistance to an educational innovation should not automatically be disregarded. Although not all resistance signifies "good sense," teacher resistance "can direct our attention beyond the limits of the school change discourse to the fundamental institutional relations and school structures that help define relationships, roles, and the nature of teachers' work" (Gitlin & Margonis, 1995, p. 393). In other words, teacher resistance can actually point to contextual features that need to be addressed to maximize the success of an educational innovation.

For contextually-sensitive approaches to educational innovation to be truly successful, parallel changes need to occur in school bureaucracies and local schools. Administrators would need to support and encourage teachers to take a contextually-sensitive approach to innovations, to provide teachers with the authority and time needed for such an approach, and to provide the infrastructure needed to maximize an innovation's success.[4]

Although I know of no conceptual model that offers a fully developed contextually-sensitive approach to the development, research, dissemination, and use of educational innovations in everyday classrooms, ideas and projects in the literature offer intriguing possibilities.

One approach comes from scholars within the cultural-historical tradition who developed a new design, termed "formative experiments" (Davydov, 1988; Griffin, Belyaeva, Soldatova & the Velikhov-Hamburg Collective, 1993; Newman, 1990), in which researchers collaborate with teachers to meet an educational goal. Rather than take the existing context as "given," they modify the materials or the local social organization to bring about the desired goal. This approach uses data from research methods such as observation and videotaping to identify problems, develop possible solutions, and provide feedback.

Following the formative experiment approach, Newman and his colleagues (Newman, 1990; Newman, Goldman, Brienne, Jackson, & Magzamen, 1989) developed local area network (LAN) software and a sixth-grade earth science curriculum to encourage collaborative activities (both intragroup and intergroup) in one elementary school. They intended to provide an environment that supported cooperative work groups, communication, and sharing of data, thus giving students the experience of a microcosm of science.

Contrary to the typical approach, these developers did not develop the innovation fully beforehand. Instead, they gave teachers basic tools and suggestions for using them. The developers then worked with the teachers to develop and use the innovation in their classes. To achieve their goals the developers were prepared to "modify the design of the technology, introduce new software, develop curriculum materials, and conduct staff development workshops as needed" (Newman, 1990, p. 11).

The project not only met its original goals, but the collaborative effort also led to a richer approach to scientific instruction. The project increased the frequency of small group investigations (in the target classes and beyond), and the results of these group investigations contributed to common databases that the teachers used in whole class discussions that synthesized the work of the class. These whole class discussions provided opportunities for the teachers to reinterpret (or, in cultural-historical terms, to "appropriate") individuals' and groups' contributions to the overall effort. The LAN technology contributed to a number of other unanticipated changes: teachers used the network to collaborate and to build on the science groups; students began to use the network for their own work beyond that assigned; and both teachers and students used the email that was part of the network for a variety of uses.

This work by Newman and his colleagues provides an interesting example of a contextually-sensitive approach; however, they worked in only one school. Many developers are interested in their innovations being used much more widely.

Situated evaluation, developed by Bertram Bruce and his colleagues (Bruce & Rubin, 1993; Bruce, Peyton, & Batson, 1993), offers a way to approach and study innovations in everyday classrooms. Bruce distinguishes between innovations as idealizations and realizations. Idealizations include the purposes and uses of the innovations conceived and intended by the developers. Realizations are what happens when an innovation is used in a real social setting. Realizations involve a "process in which innovations are incorporated into a social system in a complex fashions that may lead to changes in the innovations, the social system, both, or neither" (Bruce & Rubin, 1993, p. 198). A situated evaluation assumes that there will be multiple realizations of an innovation and focuses on understanding those realizations. Rather than seeking to control contextual variation, a situated evaluation seeks to understand why innovations are used the way they are in different settings. Questions become: "What practices emerge as the innovation is incorporated into different settings? . . . . How well do *they* work? How can *they* be improved?" (Bruce & Rubin, 1993, p. 203).

Although the process of situated evaluation cannot be outlined as a set of procedures, Bruce and Rubin (1993) do list three major aspects of the process. First, they look at the idealization of the innovation to understand what was intended by the developers. Second, they examine the settings in which the innovation is being used, gathering information on such characteristics as cultural backgrounds, institutional features, teachers' goals and practices, students' roles, and the nature of academic tasks. Third, they examine the innovation's realizations in different settings and generate ideas about how and why these realizations developed as they did.

Bruce and Rubin (1993) suggested that developers could use situated evaluations to "improve . . . [an] innovation in terms of its interaction with different contexts" (p. 204). By studying an innovation's realization in many different contexts, developers may be able to identify common patterns of realizations and contexts. Such information could be useful in providing support to teachers in re-creating innovations in their local contexts that successfully meet the teachers' goals.

Anders, Richardson, and their colleagues (Anders & Richardson, 1991; Hamilton & Richardson, 1995; Richardson, 1994; Richardson & Anders, 1990) conducted a project that sought to help teachers reflect on their underlying beliefs and values related to reading instruction and to experiment with new practices. Their approach is based on Fenstermacher's (1986) practical argument process. Rather than advocating particular instructional innovations, they developed a staff development process that involves conversations between teachers and university-based "trainers." Hamilton and Richardson (1995) reported that the process focused on helping teachers to reflect on the beliefs and the assumptions that underlie how they teach reading comprehension and to consider alternative conceptions and practices.

> We thought that when teachers inquired into their beliefs and considered alternatives, they might wish to experiment with alternative practices in the classroom and discuss the results in subsequent staff development sessions (p. 373).

Such reflection can occur outside formal staff development programs. Reflective writing through personal journals and other genres may be an effective way for teachers to identify their own beliefs, values, and goals, as well as the values and goals of educational innovations and their local schools.

Work by Cobb, Wood, and Yackel (Cobb, 1995; Cobb, Wood and Yackel, 1990, 1993; Wood, Cobb, and Yackel, 1990, 1991; Yackel, Cobb, and Wood, 1991) attended to contextual influences on a teacher's learning of an innovation as well as to contextual features influencing students' learning. These researchers conducted a multi-year research, development, and dissemination project to introduce a constructivist approach to mathematics into second-grade public school classrooms. The project model called for students to engage in mathematics activities that have multiple solutions. Students would work in pairs to develop their own solution strategies, and in subsequent whole class lessons, students would explain and justify their interpretations and solutions.

Cobb, Wood, and Yackel initially collaborated with one teacher, who was part of the project staff that met regularly. To evaluate her current textbook-based practice, the teacher compared videotaped interviews of her students conducted at the beginning of the year prior to her use of a constructivist approach to interviews she conducted with two of her best students at the end of the year. The teacher discovered that the two students had not changed their understanding of place value even though they were proficient users of the traditional algorithm. The teacher's realization that her students had *not* learned through her previous instructional methods was a major impetus for the teacher's subsequent use of a constructivist approach.

Cobb, Wood, and Yackel worked with the teacher to develop instructional materials for her class. They did not develop detailed guidelines for the teacher's use of the materials because they viewed teaching "as a problem-solving activity in which teachers draw on their professional wisdom and judgment" (Wood, Cobb, & Yackel, 1990, p. 501).

During the year, Cobb, Wood, and Yackel studied the teacher's use of constructivist mathematics, identifying ways contextual features influenced her learning and use of the innovation, and the subsequent learning by her students. They found that the teacher's learning and use of constructivist instruction were influenced by the different "cultures" and contexts of mathematics and reading, and by features in the local and broader contexts that inhibited change from conventional practice. In looking at students' opportunities for learning, the researchers identified the following contextual features as central: classroom organization, student-student relations and interactions in small group problem solving sessions, teacher-student interactions during whole class discussions, and mutually constructed classroom norms.

What the researchers learned from the first classroom influenced how they extended the use of inquiry mathematics to twenty-four classrooms. They conducted a weeklong summer institute, focusing on: (1) helping teachers begin to question whether their current text-based instructional practices helped students learn with understanding, (2) giving teachers firsthand experience solving mathematical problems in small groups, (3) demonstrating constructivist mathematics lessons, and (4) investigating individual students' mathematical interpretations and solutions. During the first year of the teachers' use of constructivist mathematics, the researchers continued to support the teachers by meeting with the teachers to address pragmatic concerns and to help the teachers become aware of and critique assumptions guiding their practice.

As a result of their work with teachers in everyday classrooms, Cobb, Wood, and Yackel (1990) moved away from a strict fidelity perspective to a view that recognizes variability in teachers' contexts:

> In the course of these interactions [with teachers], we radically revised our beliefs about how we could help teachers reorganize their practice. At the outset of the project, we took for granted the goal of attempting to transform the teachers into constructivists who thought just like we did. It was only when working with teachers that we became aware of the gross hypocrisy implicit in this goal. Clearly, our tolerance for a diversity of ideas did not extend to our epistemology. Our goal, as we now see it, is to help teachers develop forms of pedagogical practice that improve the quality of their students' mathematical education, not to spread a particular philosophical doctrine (p. 145).

These reflections provide a good bridge to discussing context and current educational reform. Although this book has not focused explicitly on the recent discussions and efforts directed toward school reform and restructuring, the book's focus on cooperative learning and contextual influences is relevant to that work.

Educational Reform and Context

Cooperative learning is often part of current reform discussions and programs. For example, it is a central feature of middle school education and part of systemic reform efforts such as Success for All (Slavin, Madden, Dolan, & Wasik, 1996). Cooperative learning is also frequently discussed as a component of constructivist approaches that are central to the standards of the National Council of Teachers of Mathematics (1989, 1991) and other approaches to "teaching for understanding."

But the relevance of this book to educational reform does not end with the specifics of cooperative learning. The contextual perspective I present here is applicable to the more basic characteristics of school reform and to ideas for the kind of practitioner education and staff development needed to support school reform. Sparks and Hirsh (1997) identified three ideas central to current school reform: results-driven education, systems thinking, and constructivism. The approach to addressing contextual influences discussed in this chapter and in chapter 8 focuses attention on whether teachers are getting the processes and outcomes they desire. The contextual perspective presented here *is* a systems perspective. Moreover, it links a systems perspective to teachers' and students' learning processes and outcomes. Discussions of constructivism (also called "teaching and learning for understanding") often emphasize the need for more situationally-specific educational practices. "[C]ontext matters fundamentally to conceptions of teaching that assume an active role for students and their teachers in the construction of knowledge" (Talbert, McLaughlin, & Rowan, 1993, p. 46).

Such broad and fundamental changes in education require changes in teacher education and professional development programs and policies (Darling-Hammond & McLaughlin, 1995; McLaughlin & Oberman, 1996; Sparks & Hirsh, 1997). Sparks and Hirsh (1977) summarized major shifts in staff development in response to educational reform. The contextual perspective presented here is consistent with the themes they identified in the new staff development:

- Attending to the learning of individual school employees combined with improving the organizational context;

- Integrating innovation efforts into a coherent, integrated plan, with all components of the system working toward the same goals;

- Helping schools meets their own goals;

- Basing staff development on students' needs and learning;

- Using multiple forms of on-the-job learning (see also Lieberman, 1996);

- Encouraging teacher inquiry into teachers' practice and students' learning as a central method of staff development (see also Darling-Hammond & McLaughlin, 1995);

- Linking instructional skills and content skills;

- Creating new staff development roles for teachers and administrators; and

- Viewing staff development as indispensable to successful reform.

The broader school-level changes proposed in the school restructuring literature (e.g., Elmore & Associates, 1990; Fullan, 1993a; Goodlad, 1992; Jurich, 1996; Little, 1993, 1996) complement the view offered here. Site-based decision making, collaborative work cultures, leveling of the power hierarchy, teacher leadership roles such as mentors and coaches, integration of multiple innovations, development of a shared mission and goals among all school participants, and preservice and inservice professional development that empowers teachers and helps them focus on student understanding could create the kinds of contexts needed to support contextually-sensitive approaches to innovations.

Although there is widespread recognition in the educational literature that contextual influences are important to the success of educational innovations and reform, the challenge is to put these ideas into widespread practice. This book and approaches discussed in this chapter and in chapter 8 provide steps toward contextually-sensitive approaches. I hope that educational reformers, developers, researchers, instructors, and practitioners will collaborate to develop and use coherent, contextually-sensitive approaches to educational innovations in everyday classrooms. I hope this book contributes to that effort.

Appendix
Methods And Context Of This Study

Kaplan (1964) contrasted the "reconstructed logics" of methodology that are presented in research methods textbooks with the "logics-in-use" actually followed by researchers. Soltis (1984) pointed out that, because textbooks present reconstructed logics, students generally are taught idealized versions of methods unless they have the opportunity to work closely with a researcher in an apprenticeship mode. As a professor who regularly teaches research methods, I have long been interested in accounts that present researchers' actual logic-in-use.

Within anthropology and sociology there is a long tradition of methodological appendices that present the researcher's logic-in-use (e.g., Holland & Eisenhart, 1990; Lareau, 1989; Lareau & Shultz, 1996; Whyte, 1981). Although these appendices have generally addressed the basic methodological issues of the studies, they each have had different foci. Whyte's (1981) classic, for example, focused on his relationship with Doc, his primary informant. Lareau (1989) presented a very useful account of her struggles to frame and organize her written report. Holland and Eisenhart (1990) focused more on the role of their preconceptions, theories and motives.

Given the nature of this study, it is appropriate that I present my logic-in-use with a focus on the contextual influences that affected my learning and behavior in conducting this study. (See chapter 1 for an overview of my conceptual framework and research methods.)

My Background

I am a cultural anthropologist with a primary interest in education. Since my earliest days in graduate school I have wanted to use anthropology to help improve the quality of education in the United States. I tend to look at issues in terms of culture, context, and cognition, and to consider the practical implications of research. Since the early 1970s I have drawn upon the cultural-historical tradition, which is compatible with my perspectives and interests.

Although I have never taught in K–12 public education, I have worked in a school of education for more than fifteen years—teaching, collaborating with public school teachers, and learning from them. I currently teach courses on research methods, courses on educational anthropology and its applications, and an interdisciplinary course called "Ways of Knowing." As an "outsider" to K–12 public education, I sometimes see things differently than "insiders," who may take much of public education for granted.

Prior to conducting this study, I took classes and workshops on various forms of cooperative learning, including sessions run by the developers of the approaches studied here, Learning Together and Student Team Learning. I use cooperative learning in my teaching at the university level, and I have given workshops on cooperative learning.

Although I criticize the acontextual stance of the conventional approach to educational innovations, I nevertheless empathize with developers. I gained firsthand experience with some of the challenges developers face when I recently developed an innovation known as the "Cultural Inquiry Process," which combines the methods of action research with principles from educational anthropology to help teachers improve the education of culturally diverse students (see Jacob, 1995). During 1993–94 and 1994–95 I worked with teams of teachers in a middle school to use The Cultural Inquiry Process in a way that was responsive to the local context (see Jacob, Johnson, Finley, Gurski, & Lavine, 1996). Although I know from experience that taking a contextually-sensitive approach when disseminating an innovation is not easy or straightforward, I also know that it is necessary.

Origins of the Study

In 1984 I became increasingly interested in cooperative learning because of its potential benefits for culturally diverse students, both native speakers of English and second language learners. A considerable body of experimental research indicated that cooperative learning improved academic achievement, students' self esteem and attitudes toward school, and peer relationships. Although a few scholars (e.g., Swing & Peterson, 1982; Webb, 1982, 1983) were beginning to do process-product interactional studies, little attention had been focused on understanding the processes that contributed to cooperative learning's success (see also Johnson & Johnson, 1985; Sharan, 1985). Moreover, very little research had been conducted in everyday classrooms. I wanted to address these needs.

My opportunity to begin research on this topic came through the Center for Applied Linguistics (CAL), which joined with other organizations in a proposal to the National Institute of Education (NIE) to establish the Center for Language Education and Research (CLEAR). Because the focus of NIE's Request for Proposals was second language learners, my part of CAL's effort addressed cooperative learning and second language acquisition.

With funding through CLEAR I conducted a survey of educational practitioners who used cooperative learning to support second language acquisition. Teachers reported considerable benefits from using cooperative learning with second language learners (Jacob & Mattson, 1987, 1990).

Building on this survey, I decided to conduct a detailed study at one school to understand how cooperative learning contributed to second language acquisition. As discussed earlier, because of cooperative learning's strong track record in the experimental literature, I assumed it would be successful in everyday classrooms. My goal was to identify the processes that contributed to its success.

I received a study leave from George Mason University (GMU) to conduct fieldwork at a school. GMU also provided research assistants to help with data preparation and analysis, and funded small grants to help defray out-of-pocket expenses. Virginia's Commonwealth Center for Teacher Education awarded me two grants to support analysis of how teachers used cooperative learning.

Locating a School

I located the site for this study with the assistance of a colleague, who put me in contact with Mr. Harris, the principal at Maplewood Elementary School. Mr. Harris saw cooperative learning as a goal for the school, and he thought that my study's goals were consistent with the school's. He also thought that the information provided by the study would be useful to him as he sought to expand the use of cooperative learning in the school.

The school seemed like an appropriate site. The principal was supportive of cooperative learning and the study, some teachers at the school were already using cooperative learning, and there were enough second language learners to justify having two English as a Second Language (ESL) teachers at the school. Mr. Harris and I agreed that I would conduct the study there during the 1988–89 academic year.

"Outsiders" to the public schools often have trouble getting approval to conduct research in the schools. However, in this case, Mr. Harris sent the research proposal forward, and we encountered no delays or problems in getting approval.

Pilot Study

I conducted a pilot study at Maplewood School in November-December 1987, and March-May 1988. In addition to making general observations in the school and playground, I conducted some focused observations in ESL, science, social studies, and mathematics classes. I also had informal discussions with teachers about their teaching, classes, and cooperative learning.

These preliminary observations provided me with a general sense of the school and its classrooms. The observations also allowed me to refine my data collection techniques and analytic strategies.

Study Design and Participants

The design of the study went through several changes. My discussion of these changes highlights the various aspects of the context that influenced these changes.

Mr. Harris and I initially agreed that the naturalistic component of the study would focus on ESL students in one or two cooperative learning groups from the ESL classes. I would observe these students in their ESL classes and in their grade level classes throughout the school year. Because no data existed on the effectiveness of cooperative learning at Maplewood, we decided to include a comparative component in the study, comparing students who experienced cooperative learning in their ESL classes to students who received conventional ESL instruction.

Mr. Harris identified appropriate teachers and invited them to participate in the study. I met with them to explain the study in more detail. I made it clear that I would not be interfering with their classrooms, and that they would decide how and when to use cooperative learning. Several teachers decided to participate after these initial meetings.

In March 1988, while I was conducting the pilot study, Mrs. Archer, the ESL teacher who had earlier agreed to be part of the study, decided that she did not want to use cooperative learning or to participate in the study the following year. She said that things were going well in her classes, and she did not want to risk losing the success she had. She said that she did not think cooperative learning would work for her classes without a lot of effort, and she felt that she did not have the time to make it be successful. Mrs. Archer indicated that she did not even have the planning period required by her contract, and she had to meet new ESL certification requirements by that fall, which meant that she needed to take more courses.

Mr. Harris and I then agreed that I would focus in the naturalistic component on individual ESL students in their grade level classrooms. If one teacher in each of the three homerooms in grades 4–6 used cooperative learning, Mr. Harris and I thought I could still compare students who experienced cooperative learning to those who did not because the homerooms were heterogeneous and students were assigned "randomly" to them. Mr. Harris was particularly interested in cooperative learning's influence on school climate. At his request I added measures of self-esteem, school climate, and peer relationships to the comparative component of the study.

Several developments near the beginning of the focus year required further changes to the research design. After the focus of the study had shifted from ESL classes, I intended to follow individual ESL students in classes conducted by three grade-level homeroom teachers: Miss Grant, Mrs. Parker, and Mrs. Sullivan. However, prior to the beginning of the focus year, Mr. Harris made a change in the teacher participants. He replaced Mrs. Sullivan with Mrs. David, who was recognized as the school's cooperative learning expert.

Mrs. David was a special education teacher who also taught a mathematics class comprising students from grades 4–6 who were performing below grade level in mathematics. I collected data in Mrs. David's mathematics class, in which she used a combination of individualized instruction and cooperative learning. However, I decided not to include an analysis of Mrs. David's mathematics class in this book because her method of cooperative learning resulted in very little peer interaction between students and because there were no classes that did not use cooperative learning that were otherwise comparable to Mrs. David's class.

I also found out that the school had fewer ESL students than in the previous year and that the focus classes included few students taking ESL classes. I also realized that the students were highly mobile, and that focusing in detail on just a few individual students would be a problem if one or more of these students left during the year.

Mr. Harris announced at the opening teachers' meeting for the focus year that cooperative learning would be a schoolwide goal that year, and he encouraged all teachers at least to try cooperative learning. I discussed with him that this meant that we probably would not have a "clean" comparison of students who experienced cooperative learning to those who did not. Mr. Harris acknowledged this conflict in his comments to the faculty about the project at the October faculty meeting. He said that it would be cleaner for the study if some people used cooperative learning all the time and some not at all, but he wanted to leave it open to the teachers. He had said to the teachers, "This is the year to try it out and see what works. Try it out." In a conflict between school needs and research needs, it is not surprising (or inappropriate) that the school needs take precedence. However, Mr. Harris' decision made the comparative component of the study more difficult to interpret.

As the focus school year began, I wondered whether I should continue at Maplewood Elementary School or look for a new site. I decided to continue the study there. Although the quantitative comparisons might not be as "clean" as I had hoped, I decided to continue with that component, thinking that quantitative measures might contribute to determining whether cooperative learning was successful in the classrooms I studied.

Because of the limited number of ESL students I decided to expand my focus. I opted to study second language acquisition of second language learners who had "graduated" from ESL classes as well as those still taking ESL classes, and I decided to examine the learning of the class content by all students in the focus classes. I also decided not to follow individual second language learners across all their classes because of the high rate of student mobility in the school and because teachers would be changing the composition of the cooperative learning groups over the year.

In order to understand the broader school setting of the focus classrooms, I wanted to conduct general observations in Maplewood School and interview other teachers. The principal arranged for me to speak at a faculty meeting early in the focus year to give me, as he said, "an official stamp of approval."

Miss Grant's varied uses of cooperative learning also influenced the study's design. As discussed in chapter 4, she began the focus school year using the Learning Together approach in one of her science classes. However, she soon stopped, and then began to use the Teams-Games-Tournament approach in her mathematics class. This added a further complication to the comparative component of the study because the fourth grade teachers had decided not to teach mathematics in heterogeneous classes but to organize their classes based on students' previous achievement in mathematics.

In January of the focus year, Miss Grant decided to extend her use of cooperative learning to her language arts class. Although I collected data in that class, I have not included them in the book because the videotape data of cooperative learning groups covered a relatively short period of time and because I did not have pretest data for language arts students.

Collaboration

As should be clear from the preceding section, Mr. Harris and I collaborated in the design of the study from the beginning. He also influenced the study's design indirectly through his decision to ask all teachers to try to use cooperative learning. Mr. Harris decided that the study would focus on the middle grades and selected the teachers whom he invited to participate. As discussed previously, I added measures of students' self-esteem, attitudes toward school (i.e., school climate), and peer relationships to the study at Mr. Harris's request.

Before the study began, I asked the participating teachers what they wanted to learn from the study. The teachers wanted feedback on how cooperative learning "worked" in their classes. One disappointment for me is that I was unable to provide my analyses to the teachers or Mr. Harris sooner.

Early in our meetings about the study, Mr. Harris, the teachers and I discussed whether they would prefer to co-author a report of the study or to remain anonymous. Although Mr. Harris expressed some initial interest in having the teachers and himself co-author a report, the teachers were interested in anonymity, and we soon agreed on anonymity. Neither Mr. Harris nor the teachers ever expressed interest in being directly involved with analyzing data from the study.

Even though the teachers were not collaborators in the analysis and writing, I wanted to get their feedback on my analyses of their learning and use of cooperative learning. I gave each teacher (Miss Grant and Mrs. Parker) a copy of a draft of my analyses of her use of cooperative learning and asked for comments. Each teacher said that the description was accurate and that my interpretations were consistent with her experience. However, both teachers expressed some concern about how their natural speech "sounded" in print. Mrs. Parker suggested some specific changes in her quotes, essentially changing them from spoken to written text. To honor her concerns about how she would appear in print, I summarized some of her comments rather than use direct quotes, and, when I did quote her, I used her suggested revisions, which did not change the content of what she had said.

A typical arrangement between a researcher and a school is for the researcher to give some reciprocity after the study is finished. When Mr. Harris and I discussed how I might repay the school in some way, he said that he wanted me to serve as a "consultant" to the school to help them use cooperative learning. Several grade-level teachers were already doing cooperative learning, but Mr. Harris thought that I might be able to help them and other teachers.

Actively intervening in the school's activities at the same time I was trying to do a naturalistic study seemed contradictory to me. I proposed that I give my "payback" *before* the study, acting as a free consultant to the school on cooperative learning issues before the official study began. Then during the official study year, I would assume my "researcher" role and no longer serve as a consultant. This became our agreement.

During March-May in the pilot phase, when I consulted informally with the focus teachers on cooperative learning, I wanted my interactions with them to reflect my commitment to reflective practice and teacher professionalism. Consequently, I did not initiate any conversations about how they were using cooperative learning. When the teachers asked me a question, I presented what I saw as options, but I stressed that they needed to decide what to do, based on their knowledge of their classroom and their responsibility for what happened there. Mrs. Parker and Mrs. David, who were already using cooperative learning, asked me questions from time to time. Miss Grant, who was new to cooperative learning, invited more extensive discussions. After Miss Grant attended a three-hour cooperative learning workshop in April and began to use cooperative learning in her science class, we discussed several options that she might try, including Numbered Heads (Kagan, 1985). These discussions were informal. I offered ideas in response to Miss Grant's questions, and Miss Grant decided what to do. At the focus teachers' request, I provided them with copies of Kagan's (1985) book on cooperative learning.

Prior to the focus year I collaborated with teachers at Maplewood Elementary School to design and provide two short inservice workshops on cooperative learning at the school. I also collaborated with Maplewood teachers and teachers from a nearby elementary school to offer a cooperative learning workshop for both schools during inservice days before classes began for the 1988–89 school year. Teachers took the lead in all these workshops; I assisted them.

I am glad I had provided some reciprocity *before* the study. Of the adults who were primary participants in the study, only Miss Grant remained at Maplewood School the following year. Mr. Harris announced in January of the focus year that he would be leaving the school to become principal of a new school. He took several Maplewood teachers with him, including Mrs. Parker; several other teachers transferred to other schools at the same time.

Data Collection and Preparation

The primary data collection occurred between late August 1988, and June 1989. I was in the school 3–4 days a week throughout the academic year. I tried to set aside one day a week for processing data and doing preliminary analyses.

I observed in the focus classrooms and throughout the school regularly, and I conducted semi-structured interviews with the teachers and students. I videotaped cooperative learning groups during the fall and spring. At the beginning and end of the school year, I collected measures of students' learning and attitudes, and of second language learners' English proficiency.

I completed most data collection by the end of May. My last visits to Maplewood Elementary School were in mid-June for a bridal shower for Miss Grant and a final visit to say goodbye and give small gifts to the teachers of the focus classrooms. It seemed natural to say goodbye as the end of the school year approached.

The following sections, which discuss the various kinds of data collected, convey a "smoother" picture of the process than actually occurred. The "official" school schedule was frequently changed, often at the last moment, creating a somewhat unpredictable setting for data collection. School closings because of snow often created scheduling havoc for days afterwards. Some changes came from or through the principal's office. For example, a mathematics class was rescheduled to accommodate the photographer taking class pictures; district-required testing meant that there was no room available for interviews; a mathematics class was cancelled because of visitors from another school; and a social studies class was rescheduled because students had inside recess due to bad weather. Teachers sometimes were absent or made last-minute decisions about changes in what they would do on a particular day. Student absences also created problems. Schools are not easy places in which to collect data.[1]

Observations

While at the school I was a participant observer. I would write quick notes to myself when I could do so unobtrusively.

I interacted informally with the teachers and other staff outside the classrooms. I ate lunch with teachers in the staff lounge and chatted informally with them about vacations, recipes, and activities in our personal lives. At Christmas time I brought gifts for the focus teachers and took cookies and candy to the staff lounge. In the spring I was invited to a surprise shower for Miss Grant, who was getting married in the summer.

The teachers and staff knew that I was a university professor. When asked, I offered advice on course-related concerns to several teachers enrolled at a local university. Miss Grant, for example, was taking courses for her Master's degree in education. I shared information on APA style, talked with her about her papers for her classes, and offered informal advising about how to handle problems she encountered at the university.

I collected many paper "artifacts" at Maplewood School. These included schoolwide letters to parents, announcements, copies of assignments for classes observed, and formal school reports. I numbered these sequentially as I obtained them, and then referred to them in the observation notes by description and number. That way I could index them by the appropriate topic and access them as needed.

I observed in the focus cooperative learning classrooms as well as in others. When observing in a classroom I usually sat in the back or on the side and took notes while I observed. These observations served not only to provide background information but also to check whether the videotaped data was "natural."

In the classrooms I was essentially a non-participant observer except for those few occasions when teachers asked me to assist. For example, I helped Mrs. David when her aide was absent, and watched Miss Grant's class when a substitute teacher for another class did not show up and she needed to cover that class.

I expanded and typed observation notes the same day I wrote them. I also wrote an overview of the day, recording what I did and how I felt.

I entered the expanded notes into The Ethnograph, a computer program for qualitative data analysis. One of the appeals of this program was that it allowed me to attach contextual information (e.g., date, time, type of data, source of data) to any segment of data.

Videotapes of Cooperative Learning Groups

I videotaped twelve cooperative groups in the sixth grade social studies class (six during November and December; six during March and April), and eleven cooperative groups in the fourth grade mathematics class (six during November and December; five during February, March, and April). For the sixth grade I had a total of 8 hours and 42 minutes of cooperative learning on videotape, for the fourth grade 5 hours and 21 minutes. I selected the groups in order to videotape all the second language learners and other culturally diverse students during each of the two videotaping periods.

I used a video cassette recorder, a color video camera, and a zoom lens on a tripod. The camera had an attached multidirectional microphone. After conducting pilot observations I realized that the on-camera microphone would not work to tape individual groups in a noisy cooperative learning classroom and, after some experimentation, found out that a PZM microphone placed on a desk of the focus cooperative learning group would solve the problem.

I tried having a graduate student present in the classroom to take observational notes while I operated the video camera, but that procedure created too much disruption, and the student did not have the background knowledge to interpret what she saw. Therefore, I decided to collect these data by myself. I discovered that I attracted the least attention when I was able to set up the camera before the students arrived in the classroom. After I started the camera I usually moved away from it and took observational notes. In these notes I would record the general flow of the class, including where students went and what they did when they left their cooperative learning group. These notes provided useful "off camera" context that was later incorporated into the videotape transcripts.

The teachers introduced me to the students as Mrs. Jacob and explained that I would be observing the class during the school year.

The students knew that I was neither a teacher nor an aide. I did not enforce class or school rules. At the beginning of the year and when I began videotaping, students sometimes seemed to be testing my reactions to their misbehavior. When they found that I did not "report" them and that there were no negative consequences to their behavior, they seemed to go about their activities as usual. At times students briefly "acted" for the benefit of the videotape or spoke directly to it. But these incidents were short and infrequent.

Mr. Harris monitored the impact of the study on school personnel and on instructional processes. In January he told me that he did not think my presence had influenced the instructional processes very much at all. In May the assistant principal said he marveled at how I had been able to see the classrooms in a natural, unobtrusive way. He used as an example the time he had monitored Mrs. Parker's class so she could attend a meeting and did not realize for a few minutes that I was present and videotaping the group with whom he was interacting. Mr. Harris and the assistant principal spontaneously commented to me several times throughout the year about how well the study seemed to be going, meaning that the study did not disrupt normal school processes.

Mr. Harris was also concerned about whether the teachers felt my data collection was an extra burden. At our January meeting he said that when teachers complained about being overloaded, they did not mention my activities as being a factor. Mrs. David cited the fact that she had not informed me of a change in schedule as an indicator of the degree to which I was unobtrusive. She said that forgetting to let me know about the change was an indication that she was so relaxed about me being there that she did not even think of me. However, I think that by late spring, as the school schedule got increasingly hectic and the teachers felt increasing pressure to complete the required curriculum, the focus teachers were ready for the videotaping, interviewing, and testing of their students to be completed.

Over the focus year, students came to see me as a part of their class. For example, when a student in Miss Grant's class left in February she gave me a hug and said she would miss me. Other students asked me to sign a going away card for her.

Research assistants produced draft transcriptions of the videotaped cooperative learning lessons, repeatedly refined and checked the transcriptions, and then typed them. I then checked the transcriptions myself by repeated viewing of the videotapes.

Most videotapes comprised one cooperative learning group. However, in the fourth grade data, three videotapes comprised two groups of two students. We transcribed each of these groups separately. On each of these transcripts we included all the focus students' comments and behavior as well as any comments or behavior by others directed to the focus students.

At the beginning of each transcript we recorded who transcribed it, the names of the focus group of students, and a general summary of their tasks. Because we planned to enter the transcriptions into The Ethnograph, we added contextual comments in the transcriptions every five minutes or when there was a significant change in activity, as from whole class instruction to cooperative learning. In each contextual comment we recorded the videotape number, the classroom taped, the date, and the time. We also recorded on the transcript the time as it changed in one-minute intervals between contextual comments. We entered the final transcriptions into The Ethnograph to produce text with each line numbered.

Interviews

I conducted semi-structured interviews with the teachers of the focus classes at the beginning and at the end of the focus year, discussing cooperative learning and their students. I interviewed other teachers toward the end of the school year about their uses of cooperative learning. I interviewed culturally diverse students (native English speakers and second language learners) in the focus classes in January and February.

Research assistants produced draft transcriptions of the interviews in word processing files. I then took the files, listened to the tape with the draft transcript on the computer screen, and checked their transcriptions. We then entered these files into The Ethnograph.

Quantitative Measures

I collected quantitative test score data to help understand the impact of cooperative learning. Such data have a privileged status within education and are widely used to make decisions about students' educational placement. However, I do not share the view of many that these data provide the only legitimate measure of an innovation's success. Instead, I see them as providing "snapshots," measures of students' performance at a particular time in a particular context.

Measures of Students' Attitudes

I administered several measures of students' attitudes to all students in the fourth and sixth grades early in fall and late in spring of the focus year. I administered the tests to an entire class of students in the students' regular classrooms with the teacher absent at times convenient to the teachers. Specific information on each test follows.

Classroom Climate Measure.   This is a 32–item questionnaire consisting of 16 pairs of positively and negatively worded statements to which students marked agree or disagree. (Pairs were not presented together but distributed throughout the questionnaire.) Statements included: "Learning math is a lot of fun" and "I do not have many friends in this class." A key was used to score the answers. Negatively worded questions were scored correct if the student answered "disagree;" positively worded questions were scored correct if the student answered "agree." High scores indicate positive climate on two factors: social relations and schoolwork. Zahn, Kagan, & Widaman (1986) reported the development of the instrument.

Coopersmith Self-Esteem Inventory.   This is a list of 58 statements that students marked as "like me" or "unlike me." Statements similar to ones included on the inventory include: "I am fun to be around," and "I am not making the kind of grades in school that I'd like to" (Borich & Madden, 1977). A scoring key was used. Negative items were scored correct if they had been answered "unlike me;" positive items were scored correct if they had been answered "like me." Thus, high scores correspond to high self-esteem. Several scores result: general self, social self—peers, home—parents, school—academic, total, and lie. Information on the validity and reliability of the test is available in Coopersmith (1987). Borich and Madden (1977) and the Ninth Mental Measurement Yearbook (1985) presented reviews.

Measures of Second Language Learners' English Proficiency

After consulting with colleagues in the area of second language acquisition, I selected the tests described below because they are good basic measures of English proficiency. However, as I proceeded with analysis of the data, I realized that, because of the paucity of beginning English learners and the level of proficiency of the second language learners, it was more appropriate to focus in the analysis of the videotaped data on their acquisition of academic language. The measures discussed below address aspects of both basic proficiency and academic language.

We administered measures of English proficiency to second language learners in grades four and six. We tested those students who were currently in ESL classes or who were from language minority backgrounds and performing below the mean on standardized tests.

An ESL specialist who had previously administered English proficiency tests and coordinated an ESL testing program, and who was my research assistant at the time, administered these measures.

Idea Oral Language Proficiency Test I (IPT I). The IPT I was designed to test four areas of English oral language proficiency: vocabulary, comprehension, syntax, and verbal expression (Ballard, Tighe, & Dalton, 1982). Although academic language is not a focus of the test, some aspects of the test relate to academic language. For example, the criteria for different levels of performance on the IPT I involve different levels of proficiency with conventional forms of stories. At Level C a student can "comprehend and remember major facts of a simple story," while at level F a student can "recall and retell the main facts of a story" (Ballard, Tighe, & Dalton, 1982, p. 14). Ballard, Tighe, and Dalton (1982) presented data on norms, validity, and reliability.

For the IPT I, the ESL specialist took students individually from class to an available room for testing, which took about fifteen minutes per student.

Language Assessment Scales Reading / Writing (LAS R / W). The LAS R/W measures "those English language skills in reading and writing necessary for functioning in a mainstream academic environment" (Duncan & DeAvila, 1988a, p. 2). It examines students' vocabulary, mechanics and usage, fluency, reading for information, finishing sentences, one-sentence descriptions, and short narratives (Duncan & DeAvila, 1988a). While the test does not explicitly measure the kind of academic language that I examined in the naturalistic data, it does examine familiarity with the conventions of English literacy and narrative forms. Duncan and DeAvila (1988b) presented data on validity and reliability.

The ESL specialist administered the LAS R/W test at the same time to all the students being tested from one class. She and I escorted the group to an available room (usually the lunch room). I remained to help during the testing process and escorted students back to their classroom as they finished the test.

Because scoring the writing portion of the LAS R/W involved subjective judgments, we developed procedures to maximize adherence to the guidelines in the scoring manual. Two ESL specialists scored the writing portion of the LAS R/W. For each of the three sections, they followed the manual's procedures for establishing reliability. They then independently scored students' responses for that section. Finally, they compared their scoring, discussed any differences, and reached agreement on final scores. I also reviewed the results of the original scoring process, independently scoring a sample of tests and comparing my scores to those of the ESL specialists. I found that the two scorers had followed the manual's guidelines in assigning the scores.

Data Analysis

I conducted several kinds of data analysis. I indexed all qualitative data using a broad range of categories. I also bracketed the cooperative learning transcripts into episodes and coded the episodes for topics related to students' content learning and acquisition of academic English. As discussed in chapter 1, I drew on the cultural-historical tradition for my conceptual framework in my analyses of the qualitative data. I analyzed the quantitative measures descriptively and inferentially.

Indexing the Qualitative Data

I conducted preliminary analyses of the observation data while still collecting data. After these data were entered into The Ethnograph, I indexed them using basic, descriptive categories such as: cooperative learning, the district, the school, Mr. Harris, Miss Grant, Mrs. Parker, ESL classes, Miss Grant's mathematics class, and Mrs. Parker's social studies class.Compilations of the data into folders for these categories provided a basic overview of the data for preliminary data analyses. I wrote analytic memos based on these preliminary analyses.

After data collection ended, I developed more focused categories for indexing the observation notes, interview transcripts, and videotape transcripts. Because my focus on context in understanding what happened in the classrooms developed from my preliminary analyses, the more focused categories and data influenced one another in the iterative process that often characterizes qualitative research.

To examine how the teachers learned to use cooperative learning and contextual influences on that learning, I compiled data on their training in cooperative learning, their understanding of cooperative learning, their goals, their daily class schedule, their views of benefits of cooperative learning, their views of problems with cooperative learning, their actual uses of cooperative learning, and various contextual influences. I subdivided the last category into relevant subject areas. By reading and rereading the data, I identified patterns within each category and then across categories. I also constructed time lines to "map" each teacher's use of cooperative learning over time.

To analyze the student interviews, I indexed them using categories such as their attitudes toward Maplewood Elementary School, their attitudes toward mathematics and social studies, their attitudes toward cooperative learning, their emotional responses in their cooperative learning group, and their friendships. For the second language learners I also indexed the data for categories such as their attitudes toward the United States, where they wanted to live as adults, the language(s) used at home, and why they came to the United States.

Analyzing the Videotapes for Students' Learning

Analyzing the videotape data involved several steps: bracketing the transcripts to identify episodes for analysis, developing categories for analysis, and applying them to the bracketed transcripts. Although previous research (e.g., Webb, 1989, 1991) and the cultural historical tradition provided general analytic tools, I developed specific categories through preliminary analysis of my data.

Because the videotapes usually included instruction other than cooperative learning, I needed to identify when cooperative learning began and ended. Since I was primarily interested in student interactions, I decided that cooperative learning began when the students first started doing tasks in cooperative learning (not when the teacher began to give instructions). I decided that cooperative learning ended when the focus students stopped doing tasks in cooperative learning. I used these guidelines to calculate the amount of time devoted to cooperative learning in particular classes.

Bracketing

Following the cultural-historical tradition, I wanted to find a "whole" unit of analysis that focused on actions rather than individuals. As discussed in chapter 1, Leont'ev's (1978, 1981) tri-level "activity" (activity, actions, and operations) provided a useful guide. "Actions" occurred at several levels—for example, doing a worksheet with many questions or answering an individual question on a worksheet. Individual questions (or their equivalent) seemed the most appropriate level to study. These are the basic units of my analyses; I refer to them as episodes or tasks in the book.

In the fourth grade class the episodes I examined involved students' efforts to answer questions during the practice sessions. An episode usually began as students exchanged papers. It usually ended when the students completed discussing the answer, which often typically occurred when the student with the answer sheet gave an evaluation of the other student's answer.

In the sixth grade most of the episodes involved the students' efforts to answer individual worksheet questions; I treated reading the text on a worksheet as one episode. Episodes in the sixth grade class frequently overlapped, especially when students were working on different questions at the same time.

Research assistants conducted preliminary bracketing of the cooperative learning videotape transcripts, identifying those sections of the transcript associated with students completing each academic task ("action"). After several rounds of discussions with me and clarifications of procedures, the research assistants finished the preliminary bracketing. I reviewed the bracketing carefully, correcting it as needed. To do the bracketing we read and reread the transcript and viewed the relevant videotape. We included all interaction and behavior within brackets that related to doing a particular task, including negotiations about how to do the task and what was involved in doing the task, and students' discussions about the task or how they were working together. The data also included talk that was a direct derivative of on-task talk. For example, if a student made a joke or side comment based on the task at hand, that was bracketed. However, subsequent talk that digressed further from the task was not bracketed.

We labeled each bracketed segment with a videotape number, a general task descriptor (usually a worksheet number), and a task number or acronym (usually a particular question on a worksheet). One task might comprise multiple bracketed segments if other talk or behavior by the teacher or students interrupted the students' work during a particular episode.

We did not enter the brackets into The Ethnograph as categories because we wanted the bracketed segments to remain in context and in sequence for analysis. However, we used the line numbers to help identify the location of specific segments.

We then examined the bracketed segments for students' content learning and second language acquisition.

Content Learning

The unit for the analyses related to content learning was a bracketed episode, comprising all of the students' interactions and behaviors related to addressing one task or "action." My goal was to describe the basic processes and "operations" involved in each task. To do this I read each episode multiple times, usually while also viewing the videotape.

To record my analyses I constructed summary sheets, putting the information for each videotape in a separate file. I created a table for each videotape, with a row for each episode and columns for information about the episode. Each row contained: identifying information (video, worksheet number or abbreviation of task, question or item number), starting line of episode, outcome (whether answer was correct, incorrect, unknown or not completed), and general processes involved (student doing task alone, student given help, student asking for help and not getting it, multiple students contribute to answer, etc.). Where appropriate, summary comments were recorded about what happened.

Because the fourth and sixth grade classes were organized differently, and because the sixth grade had many different participant structures, the other categories for the two classes differed somewhat. For the fourth grade I recorded the student working the problem, and person helping, and the kind of help received. For the sixth grade I recorded the participant structure set up by the teacher, the participant structure enacted by the students, the student requesting help or making a comment, the person giving help, and, where appropriate, notes about the social processes.

Sorting these files within different columns, I could review the data from different perspectives. For example, each file was sorted first by outcome, then by processes. This allowed me to compare episodes, to compute frequency counts, and to see similarities and differences among episodes with the same outcome and processes.

Second Language Acquisition

Many previous studies have compared cooperative learning to teacher-led classes in terms of the amount and complexity of communication (especially language functions) in the two situations. Because this study did not compare what happened in the groups to teacher-led classes, we did not focus on language functions.[2] Instead, we examined sequences of interaction that seemed to provide second language learners with explicit opportunities to acquire academic English—instances in which they exhibited problems with academic English or made links between academic and nonacademic language.

Because so little research exists on cooperative learning and second language acquisition in everyday classrooms, we developed our categories inductively. To identify categories, we reviewed the bracketed sections repeatedly (using both transcripts and videotapes) for evidence of behaviors that might contribute to acquisition of academic English. Given the frameworks guiding this study, our categories included some that were language-oriented and others that were culturally-oriented.

In both kinds of categories we looked for language that would not typically be heard outside the classroom, including lexical items and specialized syntactic structures more commonly found in academic prose. For the more language-oriented categories, we looked for problems with academic English, which occurred when a student's lack of understanding of a term, concept, or structure blocked the student's comprehension of the academic task.[3] Behaviors that indicated a student's lack of understanding included requesting assistance or clarification, pausing at an unfamiliar word when reading aloud, or receiving unsolicited assistance or correction from peers.

Using these procedures, we derived eight language-oriented categories: academic terms, difficult academic concepts, para-academic knowledge, conventions of written English, self-help, invitation to do more, missed opportunities, and negative input. The more culturally-oriented categories focused on links that students made between academic terms and nonacademic, everyday words. Familiar language can provide a bridge to academic language, and thus can contribute to second language acquisition (Britton et al., 1975, as cited in Jacobs, 1990). We derived two culturally-oriented categories: lexical and conceptual explorations, and homonyms.[4]

Analyzing the Quantitative Test Scores

We analyzed the scores on the measures of students' content learning, attitudes and English proficiency, and some descriptive information about the students, using SPSS (Statistical Package for the Social Sciences). As previously indicated, I conducted two kinds of comparisons using the subset of students who were present for both fall and spring testing. For the fourth grade students, I compared those in the focus (cooperative learning) mathematics class to those in two other "non-cooperative learning" mathematics classes. Similarly, for the sixth grade students, I compared those in the focus (cooperative learning) social studies class to those in two other "non-cooperative learning" social studies classes. In both the fourth grade and sixth grade, I also compared students who had the most and least cooperative learning across all their classes.

In the fourth grade, students with the most cooperative learning were in Miss Grant's mathematics class and in her homeroom, where she used cooperative learning about once a week. Students with the least cooperative learning were in a homeroom and mathematics classes in which cooperative learning was rarely or never used.

In the sixth grade, students with the most cooperative learning were in Mrs. Parker's homeroom. Students with the least cooperative learning were in a homeroom and mathematics classes where little or no cooperative learning was used.

I computed descriptive and inferential statistics for comparisons of tests given in the fall ("pretests") and spring ("posttests"), and gain scores. I examined the descriptive statistics for substantive differences between groups. For inferential statistics, I used ANOVA for all comparisons except those involving the IPT I, for which I used Kruskal-Wallis.

Reconceptualizing the Story

My basic theoretical orientation has remained the same throughout this study. Within a broad anthropological framework I used the cultural-historical tradition to examine context and learning. In other ways my conceptualization of this study changed over time.

As stated earlier, I expected initially to report a "success story." Although cooperative learning at Maplewood Elementary School had not previously been documented as successful, I expected cooperative learning to succeed there because the principal and focus teachers were interested in using cooperative learning and the district supported this goal. I expected that analysis of the quantitative "pretests" and "posttests" would show that cooperative learning methods led to better test scores than traditional instructional methods.

As I started analyzing students' interactions in the cooperative learning groups, I realized that there was both more and less going on than the literature had led me to expect. Webb (1985, 1989) had extolled the centrality of explanations in cooperative learning, yet I saw many positive kinds of interactions that did not include explanations. I also saw student interactions that were less than ideal.

I began to think about the significance of different kinds of cooperative learning. I also saw that the nature of the task was important, as were participant structures (both what the teachers set up and what the students actually did). The naturalistic data presented a complex picture.

The quantitative analyses made it clear that, by the quantitative measures I employed, the cooperative learning I had observed and recorded was not an unqualified "success." In fact, these data presented a fairly strong picture that cooperative learning had few quantitative effects.

These experiences presented me with a dilemma. Given my prior assumptions, the fact that the cooperative learning I observed was not a total "success" seemed to be a major obstacle. How was I to approach this project if I was not going to be documenting the processes by which cooperative learning is a success? I slowly began to realize that the "story" here was a more complex one. I sought to understand this complexity by examining the contextual influences on cooperative learning, and teachers' and students' responses to those influences.

As I came to view context as my focus, I realized that this formulation addressed my concerns about the conventional approach to educational innovations more broadly. Although I continued to draw on the cultural-historical tradition for many of my analyses, I conceptualized cooperative learning in everyday classrooms in a more complex way than I did initially. At the beginning of this study I used the cultural-historical tradition for its specific ideas about the interactional processes that might contribute to cooperative learning's success. While I still see this as a benefit of the cultural-historical tradition, I now see it as also offering a "way of looking" at context that can be used to focus particular attention on contextual influences on teachers' and students' learning.

Agar (1993) talked about those moments in fieldwork when the researcher's expectations are not met as "rich points" because they hold up a mirror to the researcher's own assumptions. Rich points are indications that the researcher needs to probe further to understand a reality different from his or her own. Based on my experience, researchers can have similar rich points while analyzing their data. When patterns do not meet a researcher's expectations, it is an opportunity to probe further, both into one's own assumptions and into what one is studying. It also presents a challenge to tell a more complex story that is closer to the experiences of the participants who have allowed the researcher into their lives. I hope this book meets this challenge.

Notes

1. STUDYING CONTEXTS OF COOPERATIVE LEARNING

1. I use the term "everyday" to indicate naturally occurring classrooms in which a researcher has not directly intervened in some way. Everyday classrooms contrast with both experimental settings and field experiments, where researchers explicitly seek to control or influence contextual features.

2. Some integrative treatises on educational change also address issues related to contextual influences, although they do not always approach contextual influences in the same way I discuss here. For example, Fullan and Stiegelbauer (1991) discussed the influences of what I term "contextual features"; their emphasis on the meaning of change is particularly relevant. Sarason's (1996) focus on the "culture of the school" can be read with an eye to identifying contextual influences that may be relevant in particular schools. However, he focused on what he terms the "modal" school and the "modal" teacher.

3. In a similar vein, Oakes (1987) examined the influence of context on the persistence of the widespread practice of educational tracking.

4. In doing this I do not intend to take a position in the debate in the educational literature about what is group work, cooperative learning, or collaborative learning.

5. Much of the recent research that draws on the cultural-historical tradition has focused on cognition. In contrast, this book emphasizes context.

6. See Sarason (1996) and Fullan and Stiegelbauer (1991) for other discussions of teachers as learners in the context of educational change.

7. See Eisenhart (1995) for a discussion of this in relation to cultural learning.

8. See Lave (1996) for a recent extension of this approach in which she reconceptualizes teaching from the perspective of learners learning.

9. This approach is drawn from Wertsch, Minick, and Arns (1984). "Doing mathematics" and "doing social studies" are particular forms of "doing school."

10. The concept of "context" is used here rather than the usual anthropological focus on "culture" because context allows for attention to influences and processes that are individual as well as those that are shared or cultural.

11. Gutierrez (1992, 1994) also used the cultural-historical approach to study contextual influences on an educational innovation—process writing.

12. Some studies examining contextual influences on education have taken broader perspectives, focusing on teaching in general or using a wider lens to examine contextual influences. For example, recent work by the Center for Research on the Context of Secondary School Teaching (e.g., McLaughlin, 1993; McLaughlin & Talbert, 1993) found that secondary school teachers identified students as the primary contextual influence on their teaching, that teachers' ideas about good teaching practice and their pedagogical responses to their students varied widely, and that teachers' professional communities (at the department, school, and district levels) were important influences on teachers' ideas of good teaching practice. Moreover, state policies were an important contextual influence that when combined with strong professional communities, enabled teachers to adapt their practice to their students' needs.

13. Minick (1989) pointed out that English-speaking scholars' focus on tools and social interaction as Vygotsky's primary foci is a result not so much of the predominance of these contextual features in Vygotsky's thinking but of the selective translation of his work from Russian into English.

14. Ecological psychologists (e.g., Barker, 1968; Barker & Wright, 1955; Schoggen, 1978) have approached context in this way.

15. See Nespor (1997) for a useful examination of extra-school influences on the use of whole language and, more broadly, of how schools can be viewed as "a knot in a web of practices that stretch into complex systems beginning and ending outside the school" (p. xiii).

2. COOPERATIVE LEARNING

1. This broad definition reflects the wide range of non-teacher-led classroom practices that have been called cooperative learning (e.g., Davidson, 1990; Kagan, 1992).

2. Kagan's (1992) book contains many teacher-developed methods. The *Cooperative Learning* magazine has articles by teachers, and newsletters of

regional associations (e.g., Great Lakes Association for Cooperation in Education and Mid-Atlantic Association for Cooperation in Education) regularly present methods and teaching tips from teachers.

3. The names of the school, principal, teachers, and students are pseudonyms.

4. Student Teams-Achievement Divisions (STAD) involves four similar components, with individual quizzes replacing tournaments as the means of assessment.

4. TEAMS-GAMES-TOURNAMENTS
IN FOURTH GRADE MATHEMATICS

1. Miss Grant managed some of the pressure she felt by writing required papers in her university course on cooperative learning.

2. The wall chart also said individuals were responsible for filling roles (checker, encourager, recorder, etc.), but Miss Grant told her students that they would not be using roles now.

3. This procedural approach to mathematics contrasts with the current emphasis on conceptual approaches to teaching mathematics (e.g., National Council of Teachers of Mathematics, 1989, 1991), which received increased emphasis in the local school district the year after this study ended. It also is important to note that the developers of TGT currently use cooperative learning as part of MathWings, which is based on the National Council of Teachers of Mathematics standards and as part of the Roots and Wings program for systemic reform (see Slavin, Madden, Dolan, & Wasik, 1996).

4. Miss Grant mentioned a similar concern in the spring about language arts. She was supposed to finish the language arts books, but the STL materials did not match the text completely.

5. Convergent thinking is defined as that which is "appropriate for closed-solution-type (one-answer) problems whereby the individual attempts to operate according to prescribed and tested forms of analysis, method, and judgment" (Good, 1973, p. 608). See also Guilford's (1956) work.

6. The exception involved two girls, one African American and the other African American and Hispanic American. Gender or ethnicity may have contributed to this variation, but a discussion of the influence of those contextual features in the data must wait for future analyses.

7. Students sometimes manifested team spirit at the end of tournament sessions. For example, some students added together the points earned by individual team members to determine how their team fared in the tournament. However, this was not the predominant focus. Most students compared how they did individually.

8. Miss Grant's brief use of challenging, a feature of the tournaments, in the practice sessions may have contributed to the students' using the tournaments as a model for how they approached the practice sessions.

9. As discussed above, this decision was influenced by her desire to temper the competitive aspect of TGT. Also, because the students came from all three homerooms, Miss Grant was not able to announce team awards later the same day.

10. Future work can examine the role of the students' peer culture(s) on their definition the TGT practice sessions as games.

11. The sixth grade teachers were similarly successful in grouping students for mathematics.

5. LEARNING TOGETHER
IN SIXTH GRADE SOCIAL STUDIES

1. I draw on two systems of classification here. I derived the convergent/divergent contrast from Guilford's (1956) work. Convergent tasks or questions involve those with one acceptable correct answer; divergent tasks or questions involve open-ended problems for which there is not one correct answer. I derived the comprehension/analysis/synthesis contrast from Bloom's (1956) taxonomy. Comprehension involves students "know[ing] what is being communicated and . . . be[ing] able to make some use of the material or ideas contained in it" (p. 89). Analysis "emphasizes the breakdown of the material into its constituent parts and detection of the relationships of the parts and of the way they are organized" (p. 144). Synthesis involves "putting together of elements and parts. . . . in such a way as to constitute a pattern or structure not clearly there before" (p. 162).

2. This was published by Milliken Publishing Co., copyright 1970.

3. This is from *Hands-on Geography*, NYSTROM (Division of Carnation Co.), copyright 1984.

4. Mrs. Parker varied in the instructions she gave for the helping participant structures. At times she told the students the they *may* help one another; at other times she said that they *must* work together. How students enacted the participant structure did not seem to be related to whether Mrs. Parker said that they *may* or *must* work together.

5. The influence of Mrs. Parker's goals on her use of cooperative learning can been seen explicitly in her earliest uses. She wanted students to be more consistent in turning in their homework, and she assigned points and gave group rewards, which she saw as features of cooperative learning, to meet that goal.

6. Another example occurred during the pilot phase of this study. Mrs. Parker stopped giving points to groups based on the grades group members attained on spelling tests because students were cheating: "I told them that's why I was stopping giving points in spelling. They grade their own papers [in each group] so they were working for the group. I tried collecting the papers and passing them around, that helped, but I soon stopped that also. I don't want them to think 'I have to make a hundred this time.'"

7. This draws from Parten's (1932) work on parallel, associative, and co-operative play.

8. There are also instances at the utterance level where students asked for help but did not get a response, but such instances are not the focus of analysis here.

9. Although the major emphasis from students was on finishing the tasks, they did make some comments and efforts directed at understanding.

10. Two students said that they would tell the teacher about the offensive behavior.

6. ACQUIRING ENGLISH IN CONTENT CLASSES

1. Theorists discuss the benefits of cooperative learning in terms of pre-modified input that focuses on meaning in low-anxiety contexts (Krashen, 1985; Wong Fillmore, 1991), interactionally modified input (Long, 1983, 1985; Pica, Young, & Doughty, 1994; Rivers, 1994), and comprehensible output (Swain, 1985; Swain & Lapkin, 1989). In recent discussions (e.g., Faltis, 1993) advocates of cooperative learning also argue that it provides a means for improving the academic achievement and social integration of second language learners.

2. Although recent research conducted in everyday classrooms by Duran and Szymanski (1995) and by Gumperz and Field (1995) is not explicitly focused on second language acquisition, some of their findings describe opportunities for second language acquisition in cooperative learning groups.

3. Dalton (1982) reported studies establishing norms, validity, and reliability for the IPT I.

4. Duncan and DeAvila (1988b) reported studies establishing the validity and reliability for the LAS R/W.

5. For a discussion of these students' opportunities for acquiring academic English in terms of input and output, see Jacob, Rottenberg, Patrick, and Wheeler (1996).

6. While the process of linking the unfamiliar to the familiar may help second language learners acquire unfamiliar concepts, it also carries a danger that students may apply the familiar to the unfamiliar inappropriately.

7. Cooperative learning can also be beneficial for second language learners in bilingual classrooms. See research reports (Calderón, 1994b; Calderón, Tinajero & Hertz-Lazarowitz, 1992; Ivory, 1994) about BCIRC (Bilingual Cooperative Integrated Reading and Composition), a form of Student Team Learning, and Cohen's (Cohen, 1994; Cohen, Lotan & Catanzarite, 1990) research on *Finding Out/Descubrimiento* combined with strategies of complex instruction. However, in both of these projects teachers received considerable support from staff developers to achieve the positive results. Cohen (1993) stated: "the dramatic gains that we have seen with Finding Out occur *only* when teachers and students receive adequate preparation for complex instruction that involves extensive training for cooperation, multiple roles for students at the learning stations, and delegation of authority by the teacher. The curriculum materials are marvelously engineered, but they are not magic" (pp. 154–155).

7. CONTEXT AND COOPERATIVE LEARNING

1. Gutierrez (1992, 1994) used another, but similar, set of categories drawn from the cultural-historical approach to conduct analyses of contextual influences on process writing. Her analyses "included consideration of all the components of the activity setting: (a) *who*—who was present in the learning activity, and who assisted students' performance? (b) *what*—what was the nature of the writing task? (c) *goals and values*—what were the teacher's instructional goals and values? (d) *how*—how was the instruction instantiated? and (e) *why*—why was a particular writing pedagogy used?" (Gutierrez, 1992, p. 249).

2. In addition, during the pilot phase of this study, I responded to the teachers' questions about cooperative learning.

3. See Stodolsky (1988, 1993) and Grossman and Stodolsky (1995) for discussions of the role of subject matter on instruction.

4. The fidelity criteria for TGT and LT could be discussed within this same framework. The LT requirement for teaching students small group skills is relevant to the interpersonal context. Many of the criteria for TGT and LT are motivational devices intended to influence students' meanings. Individual accountability, for example, is intended to motivate all students to learn the class material. Team recognition in TGT is designed to motivate students to succeed as a team.

5. As discussed earlier, recent work by the developers of TGT (Slavin, Madden, Dolan, & Wasik, 1996) uses cooperative learning in MathWings, a constructivist mathematics program based on the standards of the National Council of Teachers of Mathematics.

6. Although the Six Mirrors of the Classroom model points to relevant contextual features within classrooms, it is different from the approach

taken here because it is an idealized model. Each mirror (i.e., aspect of the classroom) has five levels of increasing complexity, with the ideal being for classrooms to function on similar levels of complexity in each on the mirrors (Hertz-Lazarowitz, 1992).

7. The work of Cobb, Wood, and Yackel (1993) and Florio-Ruane (1991) also show that the contextual features are interwoven in their influence on cognition and learning.

8. Although Nespor (1997) approached his study from a different perspective than I use in this book, his image of the school he studied as "an intersection in social space, a knot in a web of practices that stretch into complex systems beginning and ending outside the school" (p. xiii) offers an interesting complement to the notion of contextual forest I discuss here.

9. Research on other educational innovations (e.g., Cochran-Smith, Paris & Kahn, 1992; *Educational Evaluation and Policy Analysis,* 1990; Elmore & McLaughlin, 1988; Grant, Peterson, & Shojgreen-Downer, 1996; Hamilton & Richardson, 1995; Huberman & Miles, 1984; Little & McLaughlin, 1993; Michaels, 1990; Pace, 1992; Smith & Keith, 1971; Smith et al., 1988; Staessens, 1993; Sturtevant, 1996; Talbert, McLaughlin, & Rowan, 1993) supports the importance of contextual influences.

8. PRACTICING COOPERATIVE LEARNING IN CONTEXT

1. McLaughlin (1990) made a similar statement, focusing on projects begun through public policies. In discussing local responses to policy initiatives, McLaughlin (1990) stated that "[t]he term *replication* no longer [means] mechanistic reproduction, but rather adaptive implementation that remained true to the project's core philosophy and central strategies" (p. 14). From an outsider's perspective, which policy developers are, the projects' philosophy and strategies may be core. However, from an insider's perspective, which teachers are, the teacher's goals are central. (I discuss the importance of examining the relationship between a teacher's and developer's goals later in this chapter.)

2. See Joyce & Showers (1988) about the importance in general of teachers understanding the theory behind innovations they are learning.

3. The Johns Hopkins team (Slavin, Madden, Dolan, & Wasik, 1996) have reported considerable success in replicating the program and improving student learning. They conclude that their results indicate that "comprehensive, systemic school-by-school change can take place on a broad scale in a way that maintains the integrity and effectiveness of the model" (Slavin, Madden, Dolan, & Wasik, 1996, p. 215).

4. See Ferguson, Forte, Regan, Alter, and Treacy (1995) for a similar argument.

5. This view is consistent with recent work by the Center for Research on the Context of Secondary School Teaching (e.g., McLaughlin, 1993), which found that strong professional communities that had the capacity for reflection, feedback, and problem solving were essential for teachers to respond effectively to today's students.

6. Ferguson, Forte, Regan, Alter, and Treacy (1995) found that it also was important for local practitioners to be committed to cooperative learning in their attitudes and behavior, and to be interested in lifelong learning.

7. The Fifth Dimension Program was designed to provide basic computer literacy and to use computer software as a tool for the development of more general cognitive and social skills.

8. When an inequality is identified, teachers can take steps to equalize participation. Cohen (1994) designed the Complex Instruction method with the goal of equalizing the frequency of participation among students, thus reducing the effects of expectation states.

9. See Murphy (1997) for a discussion of how some schools have found time for faculty study groups to meet weekly.

10. Recent discussions in the cooperative learning literature of the "cooperative school" (D. W. Johnson & R. T. Johnson, 1994; D. W. Johnson, R. T. Johnson, & Holubec, 1993a, 1994a) situate use of cooperative learning in a larger context that is compatible with it and thus more likely to support its success. As discussed in chapter 9, cooperative learning has now become part of wider efforts at systemic reform, which is another way to address the concerns about the effectiveness of using cooperative learning as an isolated project.

9. TOWARD CONTEXTUALLY-SENSITIVE APPROACHES TO EDUCATIONAL INNOVATIONS

1. These foci are consistent with other research (Hamilton & Richardson, 1995) that identified the failure of conventional staff development programs as being linked to ignoring participants' knowledge, understandings, and beliefs as well as to ignoring school context and culture.

2. Onsite followup and peer coaching are widely recognized as "best practice" in staff development (Sparks & Loucks-Horsley, 1990).

3. The situated evaluation approach (Bruce & Rubin, 1993; Bruce, Peyton, & Batson, 1993) discussed below could be adapted to teacher research as a way to attend to local contextual influences.

4. Recent work by Fullan (1993a) and Sparks (1996), which applies Senge's (1990) concept of the learning organization to schools, provides some relevant ideas.

APPENDIX: METHODS AND CONTEXT OF THIS STUDY

1. See also Wong's (1995) discussion of challenges in conducting teacher research.

2 However, there is evidence from another analysis of the sixth grade data (i.e., Lara, 1993) that both native speakers and second language learners in the classroom were exposed to and participated in a wide range of language functions.

3. We did not include as "language problems" the grammatical problems or incorrect word usage more commonly associated with language difficulties. Instead, we focused on instances in which language became a focus of the academic discourse rather than simply a medium for transmitting ideas within it.

4. See Jacob, Rottenberg, Patrick, & Wheeler (1996) for definitions of the second language acquisition categories.

References

Agar, M. (1993, April). *Ethnography: An aerial view.* Paper presented at the Workshop on Rapid Assessment, Washington Association of Professional Anthropologists, American University, Washington, DC.

Anders, P. L., & Richardson, V. (1991). Research Directions: Staff Development that Empowers Teachers' Reflection and Enhances Instruction. *Language Arts, 68*(4), pp. 316–321.

Ballard, W., Tighe, P. L., & Dalton, E. F. (1982). *IPT I English—Examiner's manual: IDEA oral language proficiency test, Forms A and B.* Brea, CA: Ballard & Tighe.

Barker, R. (1968). *Ecological psychology: Concepts and methods for studying the environment of human behavior.* Stanford: Stanford University Press.

Barker, R. G., & Wright, H. F. (1955). *Midwest and its children.* New York: Harper & Row.

Bejarano, Y. (1987). A cooperative small-group methodology in the language classroom. *TESOL Quarterly, 21,* 483–504.

Bloom, B. S. (1956). *Taxonomy of educational objectives: The classification of educational goals.* New York: Longman.

Borich, G., & Madden, S. (1977). *Evaluating classroom instruction.* Reading, MA: Addison-Wesley.

Borko, H., Eisenhart, M., Brown, C. A., Underhill, R. G., Jones, D., & Agard, P. C. (1992). Learning to teach hard mathematics: Do novice teachers and their instructors give up too easily? *Journal for Research in Mathematics Education, 23*(3), 194–222.

Brown, J. S., Collins, A., & Duguid, P. (1989). Situated cognition and the culture of learning. *Educational Researcher, 18*(1), 32–42.

Bruce, B. C., Peyton, J. K., & Batson, T. (1993). *Network-based classrooms: Promises and realities.* New York: Cambridge University Press.

Bruce, B. C., and Rubin, A. (1993). *Electronic Quills: A situated evaluation of using computers for writing in classrooms.* Hillsdale, NJ: Lawrence Erlbaum.

Bullough, R. V., Jr., & Gitlin, A. (1995). *Becoming a student of teaching: Methodologies for exploring self and school context.* New York: Garland.

Calderón, M. (1994a, April). Cooperative learning is a powerful staff development tool for school renewal. American Educational Research Association, New Orleans.

Calderón, M. (1994b, April). Building bilingual teachers learning communities: The basis of a strong staff development model. American Educational Research Association, New Orleans.

Calderón, M. (1996, April). Educational change for language and discourse development of teachers and students in two-way bilingual programs. American Educational Research Association, New York.

Calderón, M., Tinajero, J. V., & Hertz-Lazarowitz, R. (1992). Adapting Cooperative Integrated Reading and Composition to meet the needs of bilingual students. *The Journal of Educational Issues of Language Minority Students, 10,* 79–106.

Castle, S., & Arends, R. I. (1992). *The Practice of Teaching: Cooperative Learning* [ERIC Document # ED350277] (34 pp).

Center for Social Organization of Schools. (1996). *Success for All / Roots and Wings: Considerations for Adoption.* Baltimore: Johns Hopkins University, Center for Social Organization of Schools.

Chaiklin, S., & Lave, J. (1993). *Understanding practice: Perspectives on activity and context.* Cambridge: Cambridge University Press.

Clark, C. M., & Peterson, P. L. (1986). Teachers' thought processes. In M. C. Wittrock (Ed.), *Handbook of research on teaching* (pp. 255–296). New York: Macmillan.

Cobb, P. (1995). Mathematical learning and small-group interaction: Four case studies. In P. Cobb & H. Bauersfeld (Eds.), *Emergence of mathematical meaning: Interaction in classroom cultures* (pp. 25–129). Hillsdale, NJ: Lawrence Erlbaum.

Cobb, P., Wood, T., & Yackel, E. (1990). Classrooms as learning environments for teachers and researchers. In R. B. Davis, C. A. Maher & N. Noddings (Eds.), *Constructivist views on the teaching and learning of mathematics* (pp. 125–146). Reston, VA: National Council of Teachers of Mathematics.

Cobb, P., Wood, T., & Yackel, E. (1993). Discourse, mathematical thinking, and classroom practice. In E. A. Forman, N. Minick, & C. A. Stone (Eds.), *Contexts for learning: Sociocultural dynamics in children's development* (pp. 91–119). New York: Oxford University Press.

Cochran-Smith, M., Paris, C., & Kahn, J. (1992). *Learning to write differently.* Norwood, NJ: Ablex.

Cohen, E. (1993). From theory to practice: The development of an applied research program. In J. Berger & M. Zelditch Jr. (Eds.), *Theoretical research programs: Studies in the growth of theory* (pp. 385–415). Stanford: Stanford University Press.

Cohen, E. (1994). *Designing groupwork: Strategies for the heterogeneous classroom.* New York: Teachers College Press.

Cohen, E. G., & Lotan, R. (1991). *Producing equal-status interaction in the heterogeneous classroom.* Unpublished manuscript, School of Education, Stanford University.

Cohen, E. G., with Lotan, R., & Catanzarite, L. (1988). Can expectation for competence be altered in the classroom? In M. Webster, Jr. & M. Foschi (Eds.), *Status generalization: New theory and research* (pp. 27–54). Stanford: Stanford University Press.

Cohen, E., Lotan, R., & Catanzarite, L. (1990). Treating status problems in the cooperative classrooms. In S. Sharan (Ed.), *Cooperative learning: Theory and research* (pp. 203–229). New York: Praeger.

Cole, M. (1996). *Cultural psychology: A once and future discipline.* Cambridge: The Belknap Press of Harvard University Press.

Cole, M., & Griffin, P. (1987). *Contextual factors in education.* Madison: Wisconsin Center for Education Research, University of Wisconsin-Madison.

Collier, V. P. (1987). Age and rate of acquisition of second language for academic purposes. *TESOL Quarterly, 21,* 617–641.

Collier, V. P. (1989). How long? A synthesis of research on academic achievement in a second language. *TESOL Quarterly, 23,* 509–531.

Collier, V. P. (1995). Second-language acquisition for school: Academic, cognitive, sociocultural and linguistic processes. In J. E. Alatis, C. A. Straehle, B. Gallenberger & M. Ronkin (Eds.). *Georgetown University Round Table on Languages and Linguistics 1995* (pp. 311–327). Washington, DC: Georgetown University Press.

Coopersmith, S. (1987). *SEI: Self-esteem inventories.* Palo Alto, CA: Consulting Psychologists Press.

Crandall, J. A. (1993). Content-centered learning in the United States. *Annual Review of Applied Linguistics, 13,* 111–126.

Cuban, L. (1984). *How teachers taught: Constancy and change in American classrooms, 1890–1980.* New York: Longman.

Cuban, L. (1993). *How teachers taught: Constancy and change in American schools, 1890–1990 (*2nd ed.). New York: Teachers College Press.

Cummins, J. (1981). Age on arrival and immigrant second language learning in Canada: A reassessment. *Applied Linguistics, 2,* 132–149.

Cummins, J. (1984). Language proficiency, bilingualism and academic achievement. In J. Cummins (Ed.), *Bilingualism and special education: Issues in assessment and pedagogy* (pp. 130–151). San Diego, CA: College-Hill Press.

Dalton, E. R. (1982). *IPT I: Technical manual, English.* Brea, CA: Ballard & Tighe.

Darling-Hammond, L., & McLaughlin, M. W. (1995). Policies that support professional development in an era of reform. *Phi Delta Kappan, 76*(8), 597–604.

Davidson, N. (Ed.). (1990). *Cooperative learning in mathematics: A handbook for teachers.* Menlo Park, CA: Addison-Wesley.

Davydov, V. V. (1988). Problems of developmental teaching: The experience of theoretical and experimental psychological research. Part 2. *Soviet Education, 30*(9), 3–83.

Deering, P. D. (1992). An ethnographic study of cooperative learning in a multiethnic working class middle school (Doctoral dissertation, University of Colorado, Boulder, 1992).

Doyle, W., & Carter, K. (1984). Academic tasks in classrooms. *Curriculum Inquiry, 14,* 129–149.

Duncan, S. E., & DeAvila, E. A. (1988a). *Examiner's manual: Language assessment scales reading / writing.* Monterey, CA: CTB/McGraw Hill.

Duncan, S. E., & DeAvila, E. A. (1988b). *Technical report, validity and reliability: Language assessment scales reading / writing.* Monterey, CA: CTB/McGraw Hill.

Duran, R. P., & Szymanski, M. H. (1995). Cooperative learning interaction and construction of activity. *Discourse Processes, 19,* 149–164.

Educational Evaluation and Policy Analysis (Vol. 12, no. 3). (1990).

Eisenhart, M. (1995). The fax, the jazz player, and the self-story teller: How *do* people organize culture? *Anthropology & Education Quarterly, 26,* 3–26.

Eisenhart, M., Borko, H., Underhill, R., Brown, C., Jones, D., & Agard, P. (1993). Conceptual knowledge falls through the cracks: Complexities of learning to teach mathematics for understanding. *Journal for Research in Mathematics Education, 24*(1), 8–40.

Elmore, R. F., & Associates. (1990). *Restructuring schools: The next generation of educational reform.* San Francisco: Josey-Bass.

Elmore, R. F., & McLaughlin, M. W. (1988). *Steady work: Policy, practice, and the reform of American education.* Santa Monica, CA: RAND Corporation.

Engestrom, Y. (1993). Developmental studies of work as a testbench of activity theory: The case of primary care medical practice. In S. Chaiklin & J. Lave (Eds.), *Understanding practice: Perspectives on activity and context* (pp. 64–103). New York: Cambridge University Press.

Erickson, F. (1982). Taught cognitive learning in its immediate environments: A neglected topic in the anthropology of education. *Anthropology & Education Quarterly, 13,* 149–180.

Erickson, R., & Shultz, J. (1981). When is a context? Some issues and methods in the analysis of social competence. In J. Green & C. Wallat (Eds.), *Ethnography and language in educational settings* (pp. 147–160). Norwood, NJ: Ablex.

Erickson, F., & Shultz, J. (1992). Students' experience of the curriculum. In P. Jackson (Ed.), *Handbook of research on curriculum* (pp. 465–485). New York: Macmillan.

Faltis, C. J. (1993). *Joinfostering: Adapting teaching strategies for the multilingual classroom.* New York: Macmillan.

Fenstermacher, G. D. (1986). A philosophy of research on teaching: Three aspects. In M. C. Wittrock (Ed.), *Handbook of research on teaching* (3rd ed.) (pp. 37–49). New York: Macmillan.

Ferguson, B. T., Forte, P., Regan, J., Alter, J., & Treacy, S. (1995). Maximizing cooperative learning success. *Journal of Instructional Psychology, 22*(3), 214–224.

Florio-Ruane, S. (1991). Instructional conversations in learning to write and learning to teach. In B. F. Jones & L. Idol (Eds.), *Educational values and cognitive instruction: Implications for reform, Vol. 2* (pp. 365–386). Hillsdale, NJ: Lawrence Erlbaum.

Ford, E. (1991). Criteria for developing an observation scheme for cooperative language learning. *Canadian Modern Language Review, 48,* 45–63.

Forman, E. A., & Cazden, C. (1985). Exploring Vygotskian perspectives in education: The cognitive value of peer interaction. In J. V. Wertsch (Ed.),

Culture, communication, and cognition: Vygotskian perspectives (pp. 323–347). Cambridge: Cambridge University Press.

Forman, E. A., Minick, N., & Stone, C. A. (1993). *Contexts for learning: Sociocultural dynamics in children's development.* Oxford: Oxford University Press.

Foster, G. (1969). *Applied anthropology.* Boston: Little, Brown and Company.

Fullan, M. (1993a). *Change forces: Probing the depth of educational reform.* London: Falmer Press.

Fullan, M. G., with Stiegelbauer, S. (1991). *The new meaning of educational change* (2nd ed.). New York: Teachers College Press.

Gardner, R., & Lambert, W. (1972). *Attitudes and motivation in second-language learning.* Rowley, MA: Newbury House.

Gerow, S. J. (1997). Teacher researchers in school-based collaborative teams: One approach to school reform. Unpublished doctoral dissertation, George Mason University, Fairfax, VA.

Gitlin, A., & Margonis, F. (1995). The political aspect of reform: Teacher resistance as good sense. *American Journal of Education, 103*(4), 377–405.

Goldman, S., & McDermott, R. P. (1987). The culture of competition in America. In G. Spindler (Ed.), *Education and cultural process* (pp. 282–299). Prospect Heights, IL: Waveland Press.

Good, C. (1973). *Dictionary of education.* New York: McGraw-Hill.

Goodlad, J. I. (1992). *Toward educative communities and tomorrow's teachers. Work in Progress Series, No. 1.* Seattle, WA: Institute for Educational Inquiry.

Goodwin, C., & Duranti, A. (1992). Rethinking context: An introduction. In A. Duranti & C. Goodwin (Eds.), *Rethinking context: Language as an interactive phenomenon* (pp. 1–42). Cambridge: Cambridge University Press.

Gould, S. J. (1995, March). Evolution by walking. *Natural History,* pp. 10–15.

Grant, S. G., Peterson, P. L., & Shojgreen-Downer, A. (1996). Learning to teach mathematics in the context of systemic reform. *American Educational Research Journal, 33*(2), 509–541.

Griffin, P., Belyaeva, A., Soldatova, G., & the Velikhov-Hamburg Collective. (1993). Creating and reconstituting contexts for educational interactions, including a computer program. In E. A. Forman, N. Minick, & C. A. Stone (Eds.), *Contexts for learning: Sociocultural dynamics in children's development* (pp. 120–152). New York: Oxford University Press.

Grossman, P. L., & Stodolsky, S. S. (1995). Content as context: The role of school subjects in secondary school teaching. *Educational Researcher,* 24(8), 5–11, 23.

Guilford, J. P. (1956). The structure of the intellect. *Psychological Bulletin,* 53(4), 267–293.

Gumperz, J. J., & Field, M. (1995). Children's discourse and inferential practices in cooperative learning. *Discourse Processes, 19,* 133–147.

Guskey, T. (1986). Staff development and the process of teacher change. *Educational Researcher, 15*(5), 5–15.

Gutierrez, K. D. (1992). A comparison of instructional contexts in writing process classrooms with Latino children. *Education and Urban Society, 24*(2), 244–262.

Gutierrez, K. D. (1994). How talk, context, and script shape contexts for learning: A cross-case comparison of journal sharing. *Linguistics and Education, 5,* 335–365.

Gutierrez, K. D., & Meyer, B. (1995). Creating communities of effective practice: Building literacy for language minority students. In J. Oakes & K. H. Quartz (Eds.), *Creating new educational communities: Ninety-fourth yearbook of the National Society for the Study of Education* (pp. 32–52). Chicago: National Society for the Study of Education. Distributed by the University of Chicago Press.

Hall, G. E., & Hord, S. M. (1987). *Change in schools: Facilitating the process.* Albany: State University of New York Press.

Hamilton, M. L., & Richardson, V. (1995). Effects of the culture in two schools on the process and outcomes of staff development. *Elementary School Journal, 95,* 367–385.

Hertz-Lazarowitz, R. (1992). Understanding interactive behaviors: Looking at six mirrors in the classroom. In R. Hertz-Lazarowitz & N. Miller (Eds.), *Interaction in cooperative groups: The theoretical anatomy of group learning* (pp. 71–101). Cambridge: Cambridge University Press.

Hertz-Lazarowitz, R., & Calderón, M. (1994). Facilitating teachers' power through collaboration: Implementing cooperative learning in elementary schools. In S. Sharan (Ed.), *Handbook of cooperative learning methods* (pp. 300–317), Westport, CT: Greenwood Press.

Hertz-Lazarowitz, R., & Davidson, J. B. (1990). *Six mirrors of the classroom: A pathway to cooperative learning* [Booklet]. Westlake Village, CA: Joan B. Davidson.

Hitchcock, G., & Hughes, D. (1995). *Research and the teacher: A qualitative introduction to school-based research. 2nd ed.* New York: Routledge.

Holland, D., & Eisenhart, M. (1990). *Educated in romance: Women, achievement, and college culture.* Chicago: University of Chicago Press.

Hubbard, R. S., & Power, B. M. (1993). *The art of classroom inquiry: A handbook for teacher-researchers.* Portsmouth, NH: Heinemann.

Huberman, A. M., & Miles, M. B. (1984). *Innovation up close: How school improvement works.* New York: Plenum.

Ivory, G. M. (1994, April). The Bilingual Cooperative Integrated Reading and Composition (BCIRC) Project in the Ysleta Independent School District: Standardized test outcomes. American Educational Research Association, New Orleans.

Jacob, E. (1995). Reflective practice and anthropology in culturally diverse classrooms. *Elementary School Journal, 95*(5), 451–463.

Jacob, E. (1997). Context and cognition: Implications for educational innovators and anthropologists. *Anthropology and Education Quarterly, 28*(1), 1–19.

Jacob, E., Johnson, B. K., Finley, J., Gurski, J. C., & Lavine, R. S. (1996). One student at a time: The cultural inquiry process. *Middle School Journal, 27*(4), 29–35.

Jacob, E., & Mattson, B. (1987). *Using cooperative learning with language minority students: A report from the field* (Center for Language Education and Research). Washington, DC: Office for Educational Research and Improvement.

Jacob, E., & Mattson, B. (1990). Cooperative learning: Instructing limited-English-proficient students in heterogeneous classes. In A. Padilla, H. Fairchild & C. Valadez (Eds.), *Bilingual education: Issues and answers* (pp. 219–229). Newbury Park, CA: Sage.

Jacob, E., Rottenberg, L., Patrick, S., & Wheeler, E. (1996). Cooperative learning: Context and opportunities for acquiring academic English. *TESOL Quarterly, 30*(2), 253–280.

Jacobs, S. (1990). Building hierarchy: Learning the language of the science domain, ages 10–13. In U. Connor & A. Johns (Eds.), *Coherence in writing: Research and pedagogical perspectives* (pp. 151–168). Alexandria, VA: TESOL.

Johnson, D. M. (1994). Grouping strategies for second language learners. In F. Genesee (Ed.), *Educating second language children: The whole child, the whole curriculum, the whole community* (pp. 183–211). Cambridge: Cambridge University Press.

Johnson, D. W., & Johnson, R. T. (1983). *Circles of learning* (videotape). (Available from Interaction Book Company, Edina, MN).

Johnson, D. W., & Johnson, R. T. (1985). The internal dynamics of cooperative learning groups. In R. Slavin, S. Sharan, S. Kagan, R. Hertz-Lazarowitz, C. Webb, & R. Schmuck (Eds.), *Learning to cooperate, Cooperating to learn* (pp. 103–124). New York: Plenum.

Johnson, D. W., & Johnson, R. T. (1989). *Cooperation and competition: Theory and research.* Edina, MN: Interaction Book Company.

Johnson, D. W., & Johnson, R. T. (1991a). *Teaching students to be peacemakers.* Edina, MN: Interaction Book Company.

Johnson, D. W., & Johnson, R. T. (1991b). *Teaching students to be peacemakers* (videotape). (Available from Interaction Book Company Edina, MN).

Johnson, D. W., & Johnson, R. T. (1992). *Creative controversy: Intellectual challenge in the classroom.* Edina, MN: Interaction Book Company.

Johnson, D. W., & Johnson, R. T. (1994). *Leading the cooperative school (2nd ed.).* Edina, MN: Interaction Book Company.

Johnson, D. W., Johnson, R. T., & Holubec, E. J. (1986). *Circles of learning: Cooperation in the classroom.* Edina, MN: Interaction Book Company.

Johnson, D. W., Johnson, R. T., & Holubec, E. J. (1992). *Advanced cooperative learning.* Edina, MN: Interaction Book Company.

Johnson, D. W., Johnson, R. T., & Holubec, E. J. (1993a). *Circles of learning: Cooperation in the classroom.* Edina, MN: Interaction Book Company.

Johnson, D. W., Johnson, R. T., & Holubec, E. J. (1993b). *Cooperation in the classroom* (6th ed.). Edina, MN: Interaction Book Company.

Johnson, D. W., Johnson, R. T., & Holubec, E. J. (1994a). *The new circles of learning: Cooperative in the classroom and school.* Alexandria, VA: Association for supervision and curriculum development.

Johnson, D. W., Johnson, R. T., & Holubec, E. J. (1994b). *The nuts and bolts of cooperative learning.* Edina, MN: Interaction Book Company.

Johnson, D. W., Johnson, R. T., & Smith, K. A. (1986). Academic conflict among students: Controversy and learning. In R. Feldman (Ed.), *The social psychology of education* (pp. 199–231). Cambridge: Cambridge University Press.

Johnson, D. W., Maruyama, G., Johnson, R., Nelson, D., & Skon, L. (1981). Effects of cooperative, competitive, and individualistic goal structures on achievement: A meta-analysis. *Psychological Bulletin, 89*(1), 47–62.

Joyce, B., & Showers, B. (1988). *Student achievement through staff development.* New York: Longman.

Joyce, B., & Showers, B. (1995). *Student achievement through staff development (2nd ed.).* New York: Longman.

Joyce, B., Weil, M., & Showers, B. (1992). *Models of teaching* (4th ed.). Boston: Allyn & Bacon.

Jurich, D. L. (1996, April). Restructuring schools, rethinking teacher learning: Complementary processes in school change efforts. American Educational Research Association. New York.

Kagan, S. (1985). *Cooperative learning: Resources for teachers* (1988 ed.). Laguna Niguel, CA: Resources for Teachers.

Kagan, S. (1992). *Cooperative learning.* San Juan Capistrano, CA: Kagan Cooperative Learning.

Kagan, S., Zahn, G. L., Widaman, K. F., Schwarzwald, J., & Tyrrell, G. (1985). Classroom structural bias: Impact of cooperative and competitive classroom structures on cooperative and competitive individuals and groups. In R. Slavin, S. Sharan, S. Kagan, R. Hertz-Lazarowitz, C. Webb, & R. Schmuck (Eds.), *Learning to cooperate, Cooperating to learn* (pp. 277–312). New York: Plenum.

Kaplan, A. (1964). *The conduct of inquiry: Methodology for behavioral sciences.* New York: Thomas Crowell.

Krashen, S. (1985). *The input hypothesis: Issues and implications.* London: Longman.

Lara, J. (1993). Status relationships in multi-ethnic cooperative learning groups. (Doctoral dissertation, George Mason University, 1993). *Dissertation Abstracts International-A, 54/02,* 420.

Lareau, A. (1989). *Home advantage: Social class and parental intervention in elementary education.* London and Philadelphia: Falmer.

Lareau, A., and Shultz, J. (Eds.). (1996). *Journeys through ethnography: Realistic accounts of fieldwork.* Boulder, CO: Westview Press.

Lave, J. (1988). *Cognition in practice: Mind, mathematics and culture in everyday life.* New York: Cambridge University Press.

Lave, J. (1996). Teaching, as learning, in practice. *Mind, Culture, and Activity: An International Journal, 3*(3), 149–164.

Lave, J., Murtaugh, M., & de la Rocha, O. (1984). The dialectic of arithmetic in grocery shopping. In B. Rogoff & J. Lave (Eds.), *Everyday cognition: Its development in social context* (pp. 67–94). Cambridge, MA: Harvard University Press.

Lave, J., & Wenger, E. (1991). *Situated learning: Legitimate peripheral participation.* New York: Cambridge University Press.

Leont'ev, A. N. (1978). *Activity, consciousness, and personality.* Englewood Cliffs, NJ: Prentice-Hall.

Leont'ev, A. N. (1981). *Problems in the development of mind.* Moscow: Progress Publishers.

Lieberman, A. (Ed.). (1995). *The work of restructuring schools: Building from the ground up.* New York: Teachers College Press.

Lieberman, A. (1996). Practices that support teacher development. In M. McLaughlin and I. Oberman (Eds.). *Teacher learning: New policies, new practices* (pp. 185–201). New York: Teachers College Press.

Little, J. W. (1982). Norms of collegiality and experimentation: Workplace conditions of school success. *American Educational Research Journal, 19*(3), 325–340.

Little, J. W. (1993). Teachers' professional development in a climate of educational reform. *Educational Evaluation and Policy Analysis, 15*(2), 129–151.

Little, J. W. (1996, May). Organizing schools for teacher learning. AERA Invitational Conference on Teacher Development and School Reform.

Little, J. W., & McLaughlin, M. W. (Eds.). (1993). *Teachers' work.* New York: Teachers College Press.

Long, M. (1983). Linguistic and conversational adjustments to nonnative speakers. *Studies in Second Language Acquisition, 5,* 177–193.

Long, M. (1985). Input and second language acquisition theory. In S. Gass & C. Madden (Eds.), *Input in second language acquisition* (pp. 377–393). Rowley, MA: Newbury House.

Long, M., Adams, L., McLean, M., & Castanos, F. (1976). Doing things with words—Verbal interaction in lockstep and small group classroom situations. In J. Fanselow & R. Crymes (Eds.), *On TESOL '76* (pp. 137–153). Washington, DC: TESOL.

Long, M., & Porter, P. (1985). Group work, interlanguage talk, and second language acquisition. *TESOL Quarterly, 19,* 206–228.

McLaughlin, M. W. (1990). The Rand Change Agent Study revisited: Macro perspectives and micro realities. *Educational Researcher, 19*(9), 11–16.

McLaughlin, M. W. (1993). What matters most in teachers' workplace context? In J. W. Little & M. W. McLaughlin (Eds.), *Teachers' work: Individuals, colleagues, and contexts* (pp. 79–103). New York: Teachers College Press.

McLaughlin, M. W., & Oberman, I. (Eds.). (1996). *Teacher learning: New policies, new practices.* New York: Teachers College Press.

McLaughlin, M. W., & Talbert, J. E. (1993). *Contexts that matter for teaching and learning: Strategic opportunities for meeting the nation's education goals.* Palo Alto, CA: Center for Research on the Context of Secondary School Teaching, Stanford University.

Mehan, H. (1979). *Learning lessons: Social organization in the classroom.* Cambridge: Harvard University Press.

Meloth, M., & Deering, P. (1994). Task talk and task awareness under different cooperative learning conditions. *American Educational Research Journal, 31,* 138–165.

Michaels, S. (1990). The computer as a dependent variable. *Theory into Practice, 29,* 246–255.

Minick, N. (1989). Mind and activity in Vygotsky's work: An expanded frame of reference. *Cultural Dynamics, 2,* 162–187.

Murphy, C. (1997). Finding time for faculties to study together. *Journal of Staff Development, 18*(3), 29–32.

National Council of Teachers of Mathematics. (1989). *Curriculum and evaluation standards for school mathematics.* Reston, VA: Author.

National Council of Teachers of Mathematics. (1991). *Professional standards for teaching mathematics.* Reston, VA: Author.

Nespor, J. (1994). *Knowledge in motion: Space, time and curriculum in undergraduate physics and management.* London: Falmer.

Nespor, J. (1997). *Tangled up in school: Politics, space, bodies, and signs in the educational process.* Malwah, NJ: Lawrence Erlbaum Associates.

Newman, D. (1990). Opportunities for research on the organizational impact of school computers. *Educational Researcher, 19*(3), 8–13.

Newman, D., Goldman, S., Brienne, D., Jackson, I., & Magzamen, S. (1989). Computer mediation of collaborative science investigations. *Journal of Educational Computing Research, 5*(2), 151–166.

Nicolopoulou, A., & Cole, M. (1993). Generation and transmission of shared knowledge in the culture of collaborative learning: The Fifth Dimension, its play-world, and its institutional contexts. In E. A. Forman, N. Minick, & C. A. Stone (Eds.), *Contexts for learning: Sociocultural dynamics in children's development* (pp. 283–314). New York: Oxford University Press.

Oakes, J. (1987). Tracking in secondary schools: A contextual perspective. *Educational Psychologist, 22*(2), 129–153.

Pace, G. (1992). Stories of teacher-initiated change from traditional to whole-language literacy instruction. *Elementary School Journal, 92,* 461–476.

Parten, M. B. (1932). Social participation among preschool children. *Journal of Abnormal and Social Psychology, 27,* 243–269.

Perrenet, J., & Terwel, J. (1997, March). Interaction patterns in cooperative groups: The effects of gender, ethnicity and ability. American Educational Research Association. Chicago.

Piaget, J. (1926). *The language and thought of the child.* New York: Harcourt Brace.

Pica, T., & Doughty, C. (1985). The role of group work in classroom second language acquisition. *Studies in Second Language Acquisition, 7,* 233–248.

Pica, T., Young, R., & Doughty, C. (1994). The impact of interaction on comprehension. In R. Barasch & C. James (Eds.), *Beyond the monitor model: Comments on current theory and practice in second language acquisition* (pp. 97–119). Boston, MA: Heinle & Heinle.

Richardson, V. (Ed.). (1994). *Teacher change and the staff development process: A case in reading instruction.* New York: Teachers College Press.

Richardson, V., & Anders, P. (1990). *Reading Instruction Study. Final Report. Part I: The Study* [ERIC Document #ED324655].

Rivers, W. (1994). Comprehension and production: The interactive duo. In R. Barasch & C. James (Eds.), *Beyond the monitor model: Comments on current theory and practice in second language acquisition* (pp. 71–95). Boston, MA: Heinle & Heinle.

Rogoff, B. (1984). Introduction: Thinking and learning in social context. In B. Rogoff & J. Lave (Eds.), *Everyday cognition: Its development in social context* (pp. 1–8). Cambridge: Harvard University Press.

Rogoff, B., & Lave, J. (Eds.). (1984). *Everyday cognition: Its Development in social context.* Cambridge, MA: Harvard University Press.

Roy, P. (1996). Staff development that makes a difference. *Cooperative Learning, 16*(2), 3–12.

Sarason, S. B. (1996). *Revisiting "The culture of school and the problem of change."* New York: Teachers College Press.

Schoggen, P. (1978). Ecological psychology and mental retardation. In G. Sackett (Ed.), *Observing behavior. Vol. I. Theory and applications in mental retardation* (pp. 33–62). Baltimore, MD: University Park Press.

Schön, D. A. (1983). *The reflective practitioner: How professionals think in action.* New York: Basic Books.

Scribner, S., & Cole, M. (1981). *The psychology of literacy.* Cambridge: Harvard University Press.

Senge, P. M. (1990). *The fifth discipline: The art and practice of the learning organization.* New York: Doubleday.

Sharan, S. (1980). Cooperative learning in small groups: Recent methods and effects on achievement, attitudes, and ethnic relations. *Review of Educational Research, 50*(2), 241–271.

Sharan, S. (1985). Cooperative learning and the multiethnic classroom. In R. Slavin, S. Sharan, S. Kagan, R. Hertz-Lazarowitz, C. Webb, & R. Schmuck (Eds.), *Learning to cooperate, Cooperating to learn* (pp. 255–262). New York: Plenum.

Sharan, S., Bejarano, Y., Kussell, P., & Peleg, R. (1984). Achievement in English language and in literature. In S. Sharan, P. Kussell, R. Hertz-Lazarowitz, Y. Bejarano, S. Raviv, & Y. Sharan (Eds.), *Cooperative learning in the classroom: Research in desegregated schools* (pp. 46–72). Hillsdale, NJ: Lawrence Erlbaum.

Sharan, S., Kussell, P., Sharan, Y., & Bejarano, Y. (1984). Cooperative learning: Background and implementation of this study. In S. Sharan, P. Kussell, R. Hertz-Lazarowitz, Y. Bejarano, S. Raviv, & Y. Sharan (Eds.), *Cooperative learning in the classroom: Research in desegregated schools* (pp. 1–45). Hillsdale, NJ: Lawrence Erlbaum.

Sharan, S., & Shachar, H. (1994). Cooperative learning and school organization: A theoretical and practical perspective. In S. Sharan (Ed.), *Handbook of cooperative learning methods* (pp. 318–335), Westport, CT: Greenwood Press.

Short, D. (1994). Expanding middle school horizons: Integrating language, culture, and social studies. *TESOL Quarterly, 28*(3), 581–608.

Shulman, J. H. (1992). *Case methods in teacher education.* New York: Teachers College Press.

Shulman, L. S. (1986). Paradigms and research programs in the study of teaching: A contemporary perspective. In M. C. Wittrock (Ed.), *Handbook of research on teaching* (3rd ed.) (pp. 3–36). New York: Macmillan.

Shultz, J. J., Florio, S., & Erickson, F. (1982). Where's the floor? Aspects of the cultural organization of social relationships in communication at home and in school. In P. Gilmore & A. A. Glatthorn (Eds.), *Children in and out of school: Ethnography and education* (pp. 88–123). Washington, DC: Center for Applied Linguistics.

Simpson, J. A., & Weiner, E. S. (Eds.). (1989). *Oxford English Dictionary* (2nd). Oxford: Clarendon Press.

Slavin, R. E. (1980). Cooperative learning. *Review of Educational Research, 50*, 315–342.

Slavin, R. E. (1983). *Cooperative learning.* New York: Longman.

Slavin, R. E. (1986). *Using student team learning: The Johns Hopkins team learning project.* Baltimore, MD: Johns Hopkins Team Learning Project.

Slavin, R. E. (1987a). Cooperative learning and the cooperative school. *Educational Leadership, 45*(3), 7–13.

Slavin, R. E. (1987b). Developmental and motivational perspectives on cooperative learning: A reconciliation. *Child Development, 58,* 1161–1167.

Slavin, R. E. (1990). *Cooperative learning: Theory, research, and practice.* Englewood Cliffs, NJ: Prentice Hall.

Slavin, R. (1994). *Using student team learning.* 4th ed. Baltimore, MD: Center for Social Organization of Schools, The Johns Hopkins University.

Slavin, R. E. (1996). Research on cooperative learning and achievement: What we now, what we need to know. *Contemporary Educational Psychology, 21*(1), 43–69.

Slavin, R. E., Madden, N. A., Dolan, L. J., & Wasik, B. A. (1996). *Every child, every school: Success for all.* Thousand Oaks, CA: Corwin Press.

Slavin, R. E., & Oickle, E. (1981). Effects of cooperative learning teams on students achievement and race relations: Treatment by race interactions. *Sociology of Education, 54,* 174–180.

Smith, L. M., & Keith, P. M. (1971). *Anatomy of an educational innovation: An organizational analysis of an elementary school.* New York: Wiley.

Smith, L. M., et al. (1988). *Innovation and change in schooling: History, politics and agency.* New York: Falmer.

Snyder, J., Bolin, F., & Zumwalt, K. (1992). Curriculum implementation. In P. Jackson (Ed.), *Handbook of research on curriculum* (pp. 402–435). New York: Macmillan.

Soltis, J. F. (1984). On the nature of educational research. *Educational Researcher, 13*(10), 5–10.

Spanos, G. (1989). On the integration of language and content instruction. *Annual Review of Applied Linguistics, 10,* 227–240.

Sparks, D. (1996). A new form of staff development is essential to high school reform. *The Educational Forum, 60,* 260–266.

Sparks, D., & Hirsh, S. (1997). *A new vision for staff development.* Alexandria, VA: Association for Supervision and Curriculum Development.

Sparks, D., & Loucks-Horsley, S. (1990). Models of staff development. In W. R. Houston (Ed.), *Handbook of Research on Teacher Education* (pp. 234–250). New York: Macmillan.

Staessens, K. (1993). Identification and description of professional culture in innovating schools. *International Journal of Qualitative Studies in Education, 6*(2), 111–128.

Stein, J. (1967). *The Random House dictionary of the English language.* Unabridged ed. New York: Random House.

Stodolsky, S. S. (1988). *The subject matters: Classroom activity in math and social studies.* Chicago: University of Chicago Press.

Stodolsky, S. S. (1993). A framework for subject matter comparisons in high schools. *Teaching and Teacher Education, 9*(4), 333–346.

Sturtevant, E. G. (1996). Beyond the content literacy course: Influences on beginning mathematics teachers' uses of literacy in student teaching. In D. J. Leu, C. K. Kinzer, & K. A. Hinchman (Eds.), *Literacies for the 21st Century: Research and practice. Forty-fifth yearbook of the National Reading Conference* (pp. 146–158). Chicago: National Reading Conference.

Swain, M. (1985). Communicative competence: Some roles of comprehensible input and comprehensible output in its development. In S. Gass & C. Madden (Eds.), *Input in second language acquisition* (pp. 235–253). Rowley, MA: Newbury House.

Swain, M., & Lapkin, S. (1989). Canadian immersion and adult second language teaching: What is the connection? *Modern Language Journal, 73,* 150–159.

Swing, S. R., & Peterson, P. L. (1982). The relationship of student ability and small-group interactions to student achievement. *American Educational Research Journal, 19*(2), 259–274.

Talbert, J. E., McLaughlin, M. W., & Rowan, B. (1993). Understanding context effects on secondary school teaching. *Teachers College Record, 95*(1), 45–68.

Tharp, R. (1993). Institutional and social context of educational practice and reform. In E. A. Forman, N. Minick, & C. A. Stone (Eds.), *Contexts for learning: Sociocultural dynamics in children's development* (pp. 269–282). New York: Oxford University Press.

Tobin, J. J., Wu, D. Y. H, & Davidson, D. H. (1989). *Preschool in three cultures: Japan, China, and the United States.* New Haven: Yale University Press.

Tyack, D. (1974). *The one best system: A history of American urban education.* Cambridge, MA: Harvard University Press.

Van Maanen, J. (1988). *Tales of the field: On writing ethnography.* Chicago: University of Chicago Press.

Vygotsky, L. S. (1978). *Mind in society: The development of higher psychological processes* (M. Cole, V. John-Steiner, S. Scribner, & E. Souberman, Eds.). Cambridge, MA: Harvard University Press.

Vygotsky, L. S. (1981). The genesis of higher mental function. In J. V. Wertsch (Ed.), *The concept of activity in Soviet psychology* (pp. 144–188). Armonk, NY: Sharpe.

Wasley, P. A., Donmoyer, R., & Maxwell, L. (1995). Navigating change in high school science and mathematics: Lessons teachers taught us. *Theory into Practice, 34*(1), 51–59.

Wasserman, S. (1993). *Getting down to cases: Learning to teach with case studies.* New York: Teachers College Press.

Webb, N. M. (1982). Peer interaction and learning in cooperative small groups. *Journal of Educational Psychology, 74*(5), 642–655.

Webb, N. M. (1983). Predicting learning from student interaction: Defining the interaction variables. *Educational Psychologist, 18*(1), 33–41.

Webb, N. M. (1985). Student interaction and learning in small groups: A research summary. In R. Slavin, S. Sharan, S. Kagan, R. Hertz-Lazarowitz, C. Webb, & R. Schmuck (Eds.), *Learning to cooperate, Cooperating to learn* (pp. 147–172). New York: Plenum.

Webb, N. M. (1989). Peer interaction and learning in small groups. *International Journal of Educational Research, 13,* 21–39.

Webb, N. M. (1991). Task-related verbal interaction and mathematics learning in small groups. *Journal for Research in Mathematics Education, 22,* 366–389.

Webb, N. M., & Farivar, S. (1994). Promoting helping behavior in cooperative small groups in middle school mathematics. *American Educational Research Journal, 31*(2), 369–395.

Wells, A. S., Hirshberg, D., Lipton, M., & Oakes, J. (1995). Bounding the case within its context: A constructivist approach to studying detracking reform. *Educational Researcher, 24*(5), 18–24.

Wertsch, J. V., Minick, N., & Arns, F. (1984). The creation of context in joint problem-solving. In B. Rogoff & J. Lave (Eds.), *Everyday cognition: Its development in social context* (pp. 151–171). Cambridge, MA: Harvard University Press.

Whyte, W. F. (1981). *Street corner society* (3rd ed). Chicago: University of Chicago Press.

Wong, E. D. (1995). Challenges confronting the researcher/teacher: Conflicts of purpose and conduct. *Educational Researcher, 24*(3), 22–28.

Wong Fillmore, L. (1991). Second language learning in children: A model of language learning in social context. In E. Bialystok (Ed.), *Language processing in bilingual children* (pp. 49–69). Cambridge: Cambridge University Press.

Wood, T., Cobb, P., & Yackel, E. (1990). The contextual nature of teaching: Mathematics and the reading instruction in one second-grade classroom. *Elementary School Journal, 90*(5), pp. 497–513.

Wood, T., Cobb, P., & Yackel, E. (1991). Change in teacher mathematics: A case study. *American Educational Research Journal, 28*(3), 587–616.

Yackel, E., Cobb, P., & Wood, T. (1991). Small-group interactions as a source of learning opportunities in second-grade mathematics. *Journal for Research in Mathematics Education, 22*(5), 390–408.

Zahn, G. L., Kagan, S., & Widaman, K. F. (1986). Cooperative learning and classroom climate. *Journal of School Psychology, 24,* 351–362.

Index

Accountability: group, 20, 33, 38; individual, 18, 19, 20, 33, 38, 62, 68, 103, 104–105, 204*n4;* school, 144; teacher, 144; tests, 143

Action, 6, 126, 127, 193, 195

Activity, 6, 193, 194; classroom, 105; cognitive, 7; context and, 140; goals of, 7; practical, 126; settings, 204*n1;* social meanings, 7; team-building, 30, 31, 71, 76

Administration, 24–25; contextual influences and, 153–155; standardized tests and, 39; support from, 137; views on cooperative learning, 31

Assistance: academic achievement and, 42; amount of, 44, 45; associative, 80, 85; as continuum, 42; effects of, 14; effects of competition on, 49–53; eliciting, 104; frequency of, 1, 58; giving answers, 42, 43, 45, 82, 87; guesses, 42; hints, 42; lack of, 46–47; language-related, 117, 119–120; minimal, 102; missed opportunities for, 1, 58, 60, 117, 118, 120, 133; negative input, 118; provision of, 19, 41; responsibilities for, 68; second language requests, 109–110, 113; student-student, 138; task-related, 46; from teachers, 85

Base groups, 18, 152

Bellwork, 25, 66, 67

California Achievement Test, 24

Case studies; comparative component, 10; larger setting of, 23–28; Learning Together method, 65–106; naturalistic components, 4–10; Teams-Games-Tournaments method, 29–63

Cheating, 53, 66

CIRC. *See* Cooperative Integrated Reading and Composition program

Circles of Learning, 19, 28, 67, 104

Classroom: activities, 105; contextual influences in, 137, 204*n6;* interruptions, 25, 26, 75, 76, 95–96, 102, 130, 134; norms, 172; organizational structure, 3, 105, 137, 172; rules in, 68; tasks, 136; tracking, 27, 28, 199*n3*

Classroom Climate Measure, 190

Cognition, 5, 199*n5;* context and, 141; everyday, 126; growth in, 6

Collaboration, benefits of, 14

Community: demographics, 123, 135; of practice, 5, 58, 100, 200*n12;* professional, 200*n12,* 206*n5*

Competition: attempts to minimize, 38, 128, 139; community, 90, 102; cooperative learning and, 47–48, 139; in larger community, 54, 102; peer support and, 51; pervasiveness of, 59, 128, 135, 139, 161; reservations about, 34, 128, 139; school, 30, 54, 90, 102, 139; student reaction to, 36; in Teams-Games-Tournaments method, 33, 49–53; value on, 61

227